Pleasure
in the NEWS

THE NEW BLACK STUDIES SERIES

Edited by Darlene Clark Hine and Dwight A. McBride

A list of books in the series appears at the end of this book.

Pleasure
in the NEWS

AFRICAN AMERICAN
READERSHIP AND SEXUALITY
IN THE BLACK PRESS

KIM GALLON

UNIVERSITY OF
ILLINOIS PRESS
Urbana, Chicago, and Springfield

Library of Congress Cataloging-in-Publication Data
Names: Gallon, Kim T., author.
Title: Pleasure in the news: African American readership and
    sexuality in the Black press / Kim Gallon.
Description: Urbana : University of Illinois Press, [2020]
    | Series: The New Black studies series | Includes
    bibliographical references and index. |
Identifiers: LCCN 2019054548 (print) | LCCN 2019054549
    (ebook) | ISBN 9780252043222 (cloth) | ISBN
    9780252085093 (paperback) | ISBN 9780252052101 (ebook)
Subjects: LCSH: African American newspapers—History—
    20th century. | Sex—Press coverage—United States—
    History—20th century. | Sex role—Press coverage—
    United States—History—20th century. | Press and
    politics—United States—History—20th century.
Classification: LCC PN4882.5 .G35 2020 (print) | LCC PN4882.5
    (ebook) | DDC 071.308996073—dc23
LC record available at https://lccn.loc.gov/2019054548
LC ebook record available at https://lccn.loc.gov/2019054549

For
Ciara, Kai, Khephren, and Emory

CONTENTS

ACKNOWLEDGMENTS

To publicly acknowledge or express gratitude in a first book is a joyous occasion as it signifies a successful end of many years of work. Acknowledgments also reveal the significance of relationships that were instrumental to the research and writing process. In this regard, I would like to thank a number of people who played a key role in the publication of this book.

First, I would like to thank Dawn Durante and the University of Illinois Press for their assistance in helping me bring this book to fruition. I am honored that my book sits alongside incredible scholarship in the New Black Studies Series.

I would also like to thank Margaret Puskar-Pasewicz for her commitment and time spent in getting me to a place where I found confidence in myself and the project. Your coaching and support from the beginning to the end of the process played an integral part in the development of the book.

Thank you to Kathy Peiss and Barbara Savage. You were unfailing in your belief in me. I owe you a tremendous debt for your embodiment of what I could achieve with hard work and commitment.

I also owe a great deal of gratitude to Jane Rhodes who has been and continues to be one of my biggest supporters. Your advice and counsel has helped me time and again to avoid making costly professional mistakes. When I look at you, I see someone I hope to become in the years to come.

Thank you to Susan Curtis. You were an incredible cheerleader as I struggled to negotiate the various minefields in the publication process. I am so grateful for your careful examination of the manuscript and assistance in preparing it for an external review.

Thank you to Rebecca Klein-Pejšová and Fritz Davis. Both of you provided helpful advice and personal stories about similar challenges in writing your own books. Your words bolstered me and enabled me to depersonalize the process and see the bigger picture.

A particularly special thank you to Marlo David and Jennifer Marshall. You offered me support and care though some of the more difficult times in the publication process. Both of you offered me a shoulder to cry on as well as strategic ideas on how to move forward when I believed I had hit a wall. I am eternally grateful that you allowed me to be vulnerable without fear of judgment.

A big thank you goes to Cornelius Bynum who is a constant friend and mentor. You talked me down from the metaphorical ledge that I attempted to jump off numerous times while writing this book. Since I have known you, you have always been there for me. I deeply, deeply appreciate your friendship and support.

Thank you to Denise Perry. You have been a true friend to me since high school. You always ask about my work no matter what you might be going through. I love you for always accepting me unconditionally . . . despite my "weird" ways.

A similar thank you to Terza Lima-Neves. You have taught me how to have grace under fire and accept people for who they are. I will always fondly remember our time together in you know where.

To my parents, Icilda Johnson and Jerome Gallon . . . thank you for your love and the gift of intellectual curiosity and critical thought that inspires me to study and write about black people. Daddy, growing up watching you read several daily newspapers from cover to cover demonstrated the value of knowledge. Mommy, your love of reading and the regular trips to the library with Desiree, Ava, and April taught me the beauty and power of words. I am deeply indebted to the foundation and sense of the world you both imparted to me.

Finally, to my beautiful masterpieces, Ciara, Kai, Khephren, and Emory, thank you for your patience and unremitting love.

A NOTE ON TERMINOLOGY

The language in the book is neutral when it is not clear how individuals would have defined their gender and sexual identities. *Gender-nonconforming expression* is used to reference biological men or women dressing in clothing that was not traditionally worn by members of their sex. The terms *pansy* or *fairy* are used only in quotations and are indicative of language that Black Press reporters used to discuss homosexual life and gender-nonconforming expression. The terms *homosexual* and *lesbian* are used only when referring to same-sex desire or same-sex sexual encounters between men and women, respectively. The term *female impersonator* is used to refer to an individual who was born a man and chose to dress in women's clothing for pleasure, to work in the entertainment and sex industry, or for other undisclosed reasons. By the same token, *male impersonator* in this study refers to women who dress in men's apparel for pleasure, work in the entertainment industry, or other undisclosed reasons. This language is more historically accurate than the terms *drag queen* or *drag king* as the communities this book examines used the words *female impersonator* and *male impersonator* in an expansive fashion.

INTRODUCTION

On April 18, 1925, Chandler Owen, writer and founder of the literary journal, *The Messenger*, published a front-page article, "Why the Press Prints Crime and Scandal News," in the *Chicago Defender*.[1] According to Owen, the article was long overdue. Readers regularly complained about the *Defender* and other early-twentieth-century black papers' coverage of unsavory news about African American communities that did not fit the uplift and advocacy mission the Black Press had long espoused. As one reader, Edward G. Martin, put it, black newspapers could hardly afford to report "dirt."[2] Other concerned African American readers warned reporters that news of this sort besmirched a race already under regular attack by whites for perceived criminal and hypersexual behavior.

Owen responded to this criticism by arguing that he and other journalists believed that readers demanded sensational coverage. Only a "negligible number of people crave news of the good," reported Owen. Most readers, according to Owen, desired coverage that revealed how "Mary Smith was caught in a compromising position with a man and John Smith has divorced her" over news that a new African American national bank was flush with business.[3] Despite his claims to know what type of news readers wanted, Owen provided little evidence. Existing sources, other than relatively small numbers of letters to the editor, fail to reveal whether black readers really preferred "soft news" about sex and crime over "hard news" topics such as protests against racism and racially uplifting stories.

Indeed, *Pittsburgh Courier* writer and special features editor, Floyd Calvin, took issue with "Owen's Theory" that the Black Press was beholden to announcing news about "Mary Jane, an obscure roomer" who was "caught with another woman's husband" in red headlines on the front pages of black papers.[4] Like Owen, Calvin's example of objectionable news coverage focused on sexual behavior. Both men's references suggested that this type of coverage was more scintillating than crime. However, to Calvin, the issue was less that readers desired news about sexual scandals than that some editors unnecessarily chose to play up the sensational elements of stories. Despite their differences, both Owen and Calvin believed that black papers chose, out of a self-imposed responsibility, to "print crimes, scandal and human foibles."[5] In making the case that editors and reporters made strategic decisions to report on personal sexual matters, Owen and Calvin established the power of the Black Press in creating a variety of black sexual public spheres in early-twentieth century African American newspapers.

Like all newspapers, the Black Press defined news as topics they imagined were important to readers. If the content in black newspapers was any indication, sex, in part, was on the minds of many of its readers in the 1920s and 1930s. Sexual topics in news, images, and popular features received a significant amount of coverage in African American newspapers. *Pleasure in the News: African American Readership and Sexuality in the Black Press* examines the textual and visual representations of sexuality in the Black Press that include editorials, fictional stories, news reports, cartoons, photographs, and letters to the editor between 1925 and 1940, otherwise known as the interwar period in the United States. In making sexuality a significant topic of news to appease readers, I argue that news editors and reporters created a set of overlapping black sexual public spheres or mediated spaces where black readers could view, discuss, and share information about sexuality. The construction of black sexual public spheres relied on two sets of actors: (1) news editors and reporters who constructed spaces and curated sexual content for readers, and (2) readers who chose to view and, at times, comment on this content.[6] Despite debates about the relationship between the public good and the coverage of sexuality, editors' and reporters' belief that sexual content was a source of pleasure for readers helped to expose the inequities produced by race, class, gender, and sexual identity in everyday black life.

Widely cited and referenced, the public sphere is a contested concept. Defining exactly what the public sphere is and where it shows up in society has been the source of much debate among scholars.[7] This book draws on a basic understanding of Jürgen Habermas's theory in his 1962 book, *The Structural Transformation of the Public Sphere*. In the broadest sense, Habermas seeks to explain the evolution of a bourgeois public sphere that critiqued and analyzed the state apparatus. Spaces in which private people came together to participate in politically driven public discursive practices included coffee shops and salons of eighteenth-century Europe. Habermas's lack of attention to race and gender, however, has inspired scholars to develop alternative theories of discursive spaces. Nancy Fraser's conceptualization of subaltern counterpublics as parallel spaces where members of marginalized identities "invent and circulate counterdiscourses, which in turn permit them to formulate oppositional interpretation of their identities, interests and needs" is often cited as one of the most prominent challenges to Habermas's theories about the relationship between democracy and public discourse.[8]

It is tempting to think about the black sexual public spheres discussed in this work as subaltern counterpublics to a racist construction of sexuality of African American respectability politics. In general, the Black Press certainly functioned as a traditional subaltern counterpublic sphere to the white, mainstream press. It, according to Michael Huspek, produced a "transgressive rhetoric" that created occasions for African Americans to challenge racist institutions and practices when and where they lacked electoral rights to advocate for civil and social rights.[9] Much of the scholarship that takes up the Black Press as a subaltern counterpublic, however, fails to consider social inequalities operating within the discursive space. Markers such as class, gender, and sexuality not only shaped and influenced discourse within the Black Press but they also muted and excluded certain voices relative to others.[10]

Thus, describing black sexual public spheres as counterpublics is far too reductive and obscures the complexity of how sexual coverage worked in the Black Press. Instead, black sexual public spheres and the overall counterpublic sphere of the Black Press existed as concentric spheres that shared race as a common midpoint. To be clear, black sexual public spheres on their own did not generate discourse that was designed to engage in mass action or make demands on the State. Nor were black sexual public spheres constructed to "stand in a contestatory relationship" to dominant black publics.[11] However, coverage of sexuality in the Black Press reflected the perceived interests and desires of socially marginalized communities among African Americans and included sexual topics as sources of debate and pleasure.

Largely motivated by commercial interests and the desire to attract readers, black editors and reporters sexualized coverage in African American newspapers by reporting on profane topics such as sexual scandals, women's physical bodies, interracial relationships, and homosexuality. In so doing, the Black Press created spaces for sexual coverage that filled the interstices between antiblack sexual stereotypes and respectability politics. This coverage coexisted, and at times overlapped, with news that exemplified the uplift and racial advocacy mission of the Black Press. To this end, black sexual public spheres acted as echo chambers about what was respectable as well as exposed the class, gender, and sexual divisions between different groups of African Americans. Therefore, black sexual public spheres challenge a conception of the Black Press as wholly fostering racial solidarity within African American life relative to a dominant white public sphere. They, instead, highlighted the rich diversity of black thought and sexual expression in the early twentieth century.

Concentric and overlapping black public spheres are not unusual nor are they unique to a specific time and place in African American history. Catherine R. Squires argues that multiple black public spheres connected by their concerns to racial identity have long operated within African American communities.[12] Squires and other scholars who have examined how these spheres operated in relationship to each other tend to focus on the competing visions of approaches to racial progress. Broken down into categories such as "culturalist discourse" versus "conversionist discourse," "accommodationist versus assimilationist," and "nonviolence versus violence," scholars have paid a great deal of attention to the various ways that discourse in black public spheres collectively, albeit differently, called on the state to respond to black people's call for civil rights.[13] In these instances, black newspapers and civil rights organizations spoke out against racism and projected "a militant oppositional discourse into wider publics."[14] Black sexual public spheres, in contrast, functioned differently than counterpublics constructed on a shared black sensibility. While discourse about competing ideas on racial progress and its relationship to sexuality occurred within black sexual public spheres, particularly in discussions about interracial sexual relationships, the notion of desire and pleasure also underscored their existence within the broader space of the Black Press.

In addition to the Black Press, the Black Church and black educational institutions were important sites for dialogues about racial inequality and social progress. Black sexual public spheres existed within these larger institutional spaces. Preachers' sermons regularly condemned sexual behavior and attitudes that conflicted with biblical scripture and teaching. Since ministers railed against premarital sex and homosexuality and regularly rebuked parishioners for adulterous acts, few occasions existed where churchgoers could respond to church leaders or participate in public exchanges about sexuality. Tying racial uplift to Victorian morals that framed progress around sexual self-restraint and social decorum, black churches largely produced conservative discourses on the topic of sexuality.[15]

Black educational institutions on the other hand provided opportunities for students to reveal their private sexual selves. LaKisha Michelle Simmons notes that life history assignments at Howard University offer a window into young black men and women's views about sexuality in the early twentieth century.[16] Exploring the dynamics of student protests at Howard and Fisk universities in 1926, Martin Summers indicates that Fisk students used their college newspaper to discuss sexuality. Editorials featured critiques of Fisk administrators for making dancing impermissible between young men and women.[17] Although churches and educational institutions fostered discussions and representations of sexuality that coexisted with racial advancement, black newspapers presented a much wider range of occasions and spaces for African Americans to discuss sexual topics.

The expansive nature of sexuality in the Black Press reflected editors' and reporters' conceptualization of a diverse readership. Editors and reporters in the 1920s and 1930s spent a great deal of their time discussing the desires of their readers. As I discuss in Chapter 1, black papers understood that their existence relied on mass consumption. Despite whatever impulse black male editors might have had to solely publish news that tilted the path of racial uplift in a direction that strengthened their status as elite and middle-class men, they understood that the power of the Black Press rested in the hands of the masses and their consumption of their papers. Unable to rely on advertisements for revenue due to many white companies' racist disregard for an emerging black consumer base, African American newspaper publishers depended on individual newspaper sales and subscriptions to keep their businesses up and running. To this end, black editors and publishers realized that their papers would remain solvent only if they engaged a wide variety of readers.[18] One *Courier* columnist noted, "Whereas most daily [white] newspapers address themselves to certain social classes in a community, the Negro newspaper must address itself to all of the Negroes."[19] In this sense, a diverse readership contributed a level of complexity to black papers and meant that the imagined desires of everyday African Americans heavily influenced what the Black Press covered.

THE IMAGINATION OF A MASS BLACK READERSHIP

This book draws on the term *imagined* as conceptualized in Benedict Anderson's work *Imagined Communities*. Imagining is a process, according to Anderson, for bringing a specific community into existence, in his case a nation, that shares values and a sense of identity. The relationship between the Black Press and its readers demonstrates Anderson's idea that a collective body is forged through readers' "simultaneous consumption ('imagining')" of a world created by newspapers.[20] Imagination not only demonstrated the power of the Black Press, but it also created conditions that revealed the ways African Americans negotiated intraracial class, gender, and sexual systems of power. Julia Guarneri argues that early-twentieth-century newspapers "facilitated an imaginative relationship to city and region, conjuring the experiences, qualities, and commitments that supposedly bound readers to their metropolitan neighbors."[21] In a similar way, the Black Press constructed an imagined relationship between their readers through its coverage of sexuality. Black sexual public spheres, then, brought into sharper relief the real positionality of various African Americans to each other. Thus, the Black Press' imagination of readers' desires was not simply about creating community but also about working out where specific groups of people fit within the black community.

At first glance, black sexual public spheres are invisible to historians and scholars of the Black Press. They appear to be conventional newspaper sections such as local/community news, editorials, entertainment/celebrity gossip, comics, and letters to the editor and advice columnists. In truth, they were sites of sexual discourse that reflected class, gender, and sexual politics. Throughout the book, I describe how readers used black newspapers to construct their views on specific sexual topics and their relationships to symbolic and material concerns in everyday life. Readers' letters to the editor in different newspapers, for example, demonstrate that many African Americans recognized that sexual content gave them opportunities to speak and think about sex. In turn, black news editors staged and fostered debates through letters to the editor in newspapers to inculcate a sense of democratic deliberation and reader empowerment. Thus, black sexual public spheres provided space for representations and discussions about a variety of contested sexual matters, including respectability, interracial marriage, divorce, the sexualization of women's bodies, and homosexuality within early-twentieth-century black communities.

Even as coverage of sexuality in the Black Press created black sexual public spheres, it also offered African Americans legitimate cultural and social spaces to be sexual. Whereas public leisure sites such as dance halls, nightclubs, and speakeasies served as literal sexual zones, associations with illicit behavior dominated public perceptions of these places.[22] Black newspapers, on the other hand, were inherently respectable, allowing readers to partake of erotic narratives bundled in hard and soft news coverage. While they operated within the broader scope of the Black Press as a subaltern counterpublic that challenged racist discourse and policies, I argue that black sexual public spheres functioned as synchronous iterations and refutations of specific black dominant discourses that attempted to institute normative and conventional gender and sexual behavior among African Americans. In short, discourses and representations of sexuality in the Black Press simultaneously constructed and rejected sexuality as a site of pleasure that fostered dynamic black sexual expressions.

Disclosing black sexual selfhood that is immersed in pleasure has not been an easy task for African American historians. Since Michele Mitchell's call for historians to break "lingering silences" on African American sexuality, scholars have located black sexual pleasure in a variety of physical spaces such as the cabaret, poolroom, and dance hall.[23] In these instances, scholars have defined pleasure through the public and private acts that everyday African Americans engaged in to resist white and black reformers' efforts to channel physical expression into appropriate forms of behavior and labor. Tera Hunter argues that dancing provided black working-class women in Atlanta with a means to experience pleasure and deny employers exclusive access to their bodies. In a similar vein, Davarian Baldwin demonstrates that African Americans who attended buffet flats and rent parties enjoyed taboo sex and consumed alcohol outside the purview of white authority figures and black middle-class condemnation. Moreover, African American attendance at storefront churches in Detroit, according to Victoria Wolcott, allowed migrants to participate in more expressive forms of worship in which they found pleasure over the "sanctified ritual" of black mainline churches, which sanctioned more restrained services.[24]

This book builds on these conceptions of African American sexual pleasure but takes another view that articulates an understanding of sensual pleasure that is imbricated in the act of reading and viewing. *Pleasure in the News* explores how editors and reporters correlated readers' joy with consuming sexual material within the Black Press. Coverage of specific sexual topics and the spaces it provided for readers to engage with this material and each other empowered African Americans to craft what Kimberly Springer defines as a "sexual subjectivity": the ability to "speak on their own terms about who they are as sexual beings, which sexual acts they enjoy (doing and having done), how they relate to their bodies, and myriad expressions that fall within the bounds of sexuality."[25] While readers did not control how their views on sexuality would be expressed, or which ones would be included for that matter, the very act of reading and viewing sexual content provided African Americans with sexual agency even if it was not always articulated. Just as importantly, Black Press editors' and reporters' imagination of readers' desire for sexual content validated an African American sexual selfhood that was ignored and repressed in other contexts.

Readers of black newspapers experienced reading as both a "spectator and participant activity."[26] Recent works on African American print culture observe that historical black reading practices shaped African American identities. Elizabeth McHenry argues that the vast majority of nineteenth-century black Americans did not possess the wealth to purchase bound books. Instead, newspapers served as literary reading for elite and middle-class African American communities. They developed literary associations, according to McHenry, to resist racism that excluded elite and middle-class blacks from upper-echelon groups in U.S. society. Nineteenth-century and early-twentieth-century black readers of newspapers also found other ways to actively read. Ellen Gruber Garvey indicates that readers created scrapbooks out of much of the material about African Americans that they found in the white press. Reading with scissors, argues Garvey, gave readers opportunities to reframe white narratives of black life into ones that were endemic to their interests. Nazera Sadiq Wright's work also focuses on the creation of scrapbooks by nineteenth-century African American women and suggests that the Black Press of that era imagined an idealized middle-class black readership that used newspapers to perform "models of public citizenship" to engage in racial uplift.[27] Similarly, Frances Smith Foster suggests that nineteenth-century Black Press writing was less about the reality of black lives and more about what writers desired and hoped African Americans life could be.[28]

CLASS AND AFRICAN AMERICAN SEXUALITY

Editors and reporters of the 1920s and 1930s conjured up an idealized readership, but it was one that possessed a "news hunger" for sexual material that was coterminous with the distinct qualities of the interwar period.[29] Between World War I and World War II, U.S. society experienced a shift in values where liberalism supplanted traditional and Victorian mores that had emphasized sexual restraint and passionlessness, especially for the middle class. The sexual revolution, the jazz age, and the economic downturn produced by the Great Depression served as different backdrops for the coverage of sexuality in the Black Press. Moreover, significant events such as the New Negro movement and the Harlem Renaissance meant that African Americans paid a great deal of attention to cultural expressions and how African Americans were represented in everyday life. African Americans "turned inward to the exciting black world" and debated the meanings of racial stereotypes.[30] Figures such as Langston Hughes, W. E. B. Du Bois, Alain Locke, and George Schuyler deliberated over art and its role in challenging racism.[31] The rise of black photography and African American visual art further complicated these discussions as more options for how the bodies of black people might be displayed emerged.

Black sexual public spheres within African American newspapers arose among these dialogues and developments. They expanded and affirmed the Black Press's function as a democratic institution that filled the void left by African Americans' inability to formally engage the state on matters of policy. Readers' ability to publicly participate in oppositional performances about sexual topics promoted greater awareness about sexuality and encouraged African Americans to critically debate issues related to sex, class, and race.

Mass migration and urbanization significantly influenced the interwar period and functioned as a metalanguage for the rise of black sexual public spheres in the Black Press. Both developments contributed to the unprecedented popularity of black newspapers and their high circulation numbers. The expansion of literacy and participation in industrial economies also helped to shoulder the rise of a black consumer marketplace. Black Press editors believed that covering sexual issues such as adultery and trysts would satisfy the desires of working-class African Americans, migrants and nonmigrants, for entertainment.[32]

Because many stereotypes revolved around the idea that blacks were inherently sexually immoral, weekly headlines and stories playing up sex made it difficult for many elite and middle-class African Americans to dissociate themselves from white labels of inferiority. Tensions between what might be better described as a black professional class and a working class, then, arose as an outgrowth of the Great Migration.[33] Comportment was a quality that many believed defined the middle and professional class from working-class African Americans. In this regard, early-twentieth-century black periodicals and social reformers' writings were arbiters and conveyors of temperance, sexual restraint, and thrift.[34]

When it came to coverage of sexuality, black newspapers walked an ambiguous line between "acceptable" representations and ones that appeared to uphold—if not reinforce—negative images of African American life. For early-twentieth-century African Americans, sexuality was almost always circumscribed by race, making it difficult to achieve the sexual autonomy of their white counterparts. Kevin Mumford and Chad Heap document white city residents' ability to cross urban racial borders to experience sex and express their sexuality.[35] Racism made it largely impossible for blacks to transcend their own racial group when it came to matters of sex. This did not, however, dampen the satisfaction that sex brought to their lives. African Americans found greater freedom to consume intraracial sexual images and participate in discussions because they could be expressed within the relatively safe space of the Black Press.

Nonetheless, the intersection between race, class, and gender charged representations of sexuality with a special significance. Made hyper-visible by racial homogeneity within black communities, class and gender marked sexual representations and ensuing discussions. Thus, different black sexual public spheres, in the guise of everyday coverage, created space for readers' debates, for example, on whether female nudity was appropriate for the stage. Yet, class also shaped these conversations. Far more anxiety surrounded the sexuality of women of lower socioeconomic means than middle- and upper-class black women. Even more, discourse about black women's sexuality existed with and traversed quests for African American civil rights and social justice. Black sexual public spheres, then, developed within a discourse on an early-twentieth-century African American morality that was perpetually tied to racial progress.

Emerging sociological and social reform discourses about the black family and black women represented one of the most visible backdrops for sexual coverage in the Black Press. In many ways, sociology is ground zero for understanding black sexuality. Roderick Ferguson writes, "Sociology has predominated as the epistemology from which we obtain sexual knowledge about African Americans."[36] Black social reformers and social scientists deployed ethnographic methods and tools to identify and solve the "negro problem" and provide evidence that social and moral deficiencies did not define African Americans. Sociological studies such as E. Franklin Frazier's *The Negro Family in the United States* and *Black Metropolis* by St. Clair Drake and Horace R. Cayton, with their extensive field notes and participant observations of poor African American communities, proved that racism produced environmental factors that explained immorality.[37] Nonetheless, their work also reified and strengthened the association between sexual immorality and poverty.

Fictional stories in the Black Press about the dangers that the city posed to sexually innocent girls from the countryside related similar accounts to the ones published in sociological studies. In so doing, weekly short stories mirrored the case studies black sociologists presented as evidence to counter the argument that African Americans suffered from a lascivious nature. Similarly, moralizing editorials and columns that purported to advise migrants on proper decorum in their new urban homes found common ground with social reformers who also worked overtime to instruct them on how to properly behave.

Yet, even as the Black Press shared in sociological conceptions of black sexuality, it also challenged social science discourse and social reform work that placed the burden of dissolute behavior on the shoulders of working-class and poor African Americans, particularly black women. Many news columns contradicted these images with depictions of the sexual peccadilloes of the black middle class. Front-page articles examining the sexual lives of middle- and upper-class community leaders such as ministers countered the judgmental gaze of black social reformers and sociologists. Readers' letters to the editor rebutted dehumanizing portrayals and treatment of gay and gender-nonconforming men who dressed in women's clothing. Other readers refuted the image of black women as fundamentally morally corrupt in their sexual behavior. Cartoons and photographs overhauled black women's sexuality into images that blended sexual autonomy and respectability. In necessarily visualizing their readers as the masses, the Black Press anticipated their desires and generated multiple black sexual public spheres that contradicted the social science party line that made poverty and gender synonymous with immorality. The Black Press and its readers engaged in discursive and visual practices that offered them opportunities to merge respectability with sexuality within the pages of newspapers.

Yet, in as much as black sexual public spheres gave voice to diverse perspectives on sexual matters, as well as produced more flexible meanings around sexuality, they did not evolve into a purely democratic space where all voices could be heard. Black male newspaper editors limited and regulated the process by which individuals could publicly respond or react to newspapers' sexual representations. Editors selectively published readers' letters and responses based on undisclosed criteria. In this sense, the Black Press shaped readers' ability to express opinions as well as managed and organized the presentation of their attitudes on sexuality. While black newspapers did not solely define public questions and dialogue on a variety of sexual issues (other black institutions and academic disciplines such as the Black Church, universities, and sociology departments contributed and shaped public dialogue on sex), they helped to limit and regulate the process of open discussion. Thus, readers' letters, no matter their perspective on sexual topics, demonstrated that the Black Press served as a forum for African Americans to talk back to the Black Press about sexuality. Accordingly, the Black Press, in covering different aspects of sexuality, created black sexual public spheres for individuals who desired opportunities and a place they could express their opinions and beliefs about sexuality.

The expression of sexual values within the Black Press helped to modify dominant notions of what it meant to be "race" men and women. I argue that one part of this redefinition process included the infusion of sexuality into early-twentieth-century conceptions of blackness. As Todd Vogel has observed, coverage in black papers signified a performance of one's class, race, and gender. However, black newspapers also acted out various scenes of sexual behaviors and attitudes in the context of race, class, and gender. Readers often viewed these cultural performances and struggled to negotiate them with rapidly changing ideas of blackness. Following Melani McAlister's line of argument, if we think of newspapers as cultural texts, they function not as simple mirror reflections of society but as "active producers of meaning."[38] In this sense, black newspapers created sexual meanings through their construction of black sexual public spheres.

THE BLACK PRESS

Traditionally, grouped under the broad category "Black Press," diverse black newspapers served as what Catherine Squires has identified as both a counter-public and an "enclave," a protected, safe space which allowed African Americans to develop "hidden scripts" to resist white oppression.[39] Mirroring the diversity of early-twentieth-century black communities, the Black Press reflected an assortment of racial, gender, and class ideologies; editorial philosophies; and cultural and regional differences. Thus, similar to the arguments that Barbara Dianne Savage has made about the term *Black Church*, the *Black Press* is a historical and ideological construction which often obscures a set of heterogeneous newspapers with common objectives but different methods and ideologies for accomplishing the social, political advancement and entertainment of African Americans.[40] Coverage of sexuality further illuminated this diversity. Some newspapers imagined a readership who desired salacious material; hence, they played up and constructed news that emphasized sex. Other papers maintained a more conservative approach since they believed their readership, or their own editorial philosophies, would not tolerate copious coverage of sexuality.

Some of the most compelling representations of sexuality occurred in five different newspapers, which serve as a microcosm of the larger Black Press in this book. The three most significant national black newspapers of the early twentieth century, the *Baltimore Afro-American, Chicago Defender*, and *Pittsburgh Courier*, and two local papers, the *New York Amsterdam News* and the *Philadelphia Tribune*, all, to varying degrees, featured sexual coverage that spoke to a conception of readers that desired this information. These five newspapers demonstrate how the Black Press created black sexual public spheres within the coverage on the variegations of African American life between 1925 and 1940. Each of these five newspapers emerged in tandem with key demographic shifts among African Americans at the dawn of the twentieth century. Together, they continued to press for social and political progress for the masses of African Americans increasingly spread across the United States. Collective in their mission but singular in their approaches, the papers' founders and editors recognized that black newspapers were no longer the exclusive property of a black elite. Instead, black newspapers imagined that their power and success lay within their ability to meet the demands and needs of a diverse and mass readership that they believed desired sexual images and narratives.

Regardless of the power of the Black Press in the early twentieth century, it remained a supplemental paper for the majority of African Americans who continued to consume daily white newspapers over their weekly black newspapers. White papers provided national and international news coverage, employment opportunities, and advertisements on a scale that was impossible for black newspapers to match.[41] Nonetheless, the auxiliary nature of the Black Press veritably underscores the importance of the Black Press and how readers depended on it to construct and create community, not simply provide news. Receiving their weekly black newspaper on Friday or Saturday, readers spent the two-day weekend, increasingly a period of time dedicated to leisure and time off from work as a cost-saving measure during the Great Depression, reading and viewing sexual representations among other content in the paper. Thus, the private but collective act of reading, viewing, and responding to sexuality demonstrates the central role the Black Press played in shaping the African American culture of sexuality.

The chapters that follow document the formation of black sexual public spheres in the Black Press. Although the book highlights editors and reporters' beliefs that sexual coverage was important to readers, I do not examine the impact it had on its readers. In addition, except in cases where readers' letters provide evidence, I do not speculate about reader reception. What and how large numbers of readers thought about sexual representations remains outside the scope of the book. Despite the important role the Black Press has played in African American life in both the nineteenth and twentieth centuries, reader reception is illusive. Nonetheless, the examination in *Pleasure in the News* of sexual representations in news, images, and popular features underscores the ways the Black Press fostered a sexual culture among its readers that mirrored and opposed broader early-twentieth-century African American values.

Unlike conventional historical narratives, this book is independent of a strict chronological order. Simply put, I do not tell a story about sexuality that is organized on a neat timeline that plots events to measure changes in how early-twentieth-century African Americans experienced sexuality. Instead this study is a critical curation, a studied and selective gathering, of discussions and representations of sexuality in the Black Press. Its structure is premised on the idea that critical curation is "embroiled in time, but not bound by it; entangled with periodizing urges, but not enslaved to them; committed to space, but of many kinds."[42] Even as the book is an exhibition and excavation of sexuality in the Black Press, it is no less driven by the argument that the Black Press was a forum for sexual discourse and representations.

In the broadest sense, *Pleasure in the News* recovers representations and discourses on sexuality that call for new understandings of the Black Press in a manner nuanced by class, gender, and sexuality. The Black Press created black sexual public spheres through its coverage and treatment of sexual topics. An unrecognized power of the Black Press lay in textual and visual representations of sexuality. Black sexual public spheres centered readers' desires, assumed and real. As African Americans jockeyed for a place in American society, black newspapers envisioned a mass black readership that sought spaces in which they could experience pleasure through viewing, responding to, and debating sexual topics. I argue that reading sensational news stories about sex scandals and divorce, "sexy" fictional stories, and cartoons as well as gazing at photographs of bathing beauty pageants and homosexual representations were all the more powerful because they were done within the broader space of the Black Press, a medium that was dedicated to the struggle for racial progress. Overall, editors' imagination of a mass African American readership's desire for news with sexual content uncovered pleasure in the news.

Chapter 1

THE BLACK PRESS
AND A MASS BLACK READERSHIP

On Saturday, August 12, 1933, readers of the *Pittsburgh Courier* unfolded their weekly issue and read the front-page headline declaring "Mad Lover Kills Wife" and an accompanying article, which revealed that Ramas Baker killed his wife because "she ran around with other men." The same front page announced that the *Courier* had assumed responsibility for collecting funds for the defense of the "Scottsboro Boys," a group of nine young African American men from Alabama charged with raping a young white woman. The top left of the front page also featured an attractive young woman and informed readers that she was recently awarded a $1,000 scholarship to attend college. In addition, the *Courier's* front page reminded its readers to register to vote in the upcoming primary but warned readers against voting for "Republican bosses who have failed to do anything for the Negro community" for the past twenty-five years.[1]

On first glance, the combination of a sexually scandalous murder case with the visual imagery of a young woman's educational accomplishment and the coverage of the Scottsboro case along with the questioning of African Americans' allegiance to the Republican Party in an upcoming election appear to be a chaotic and nonsensical form of news reporting. Quite to the contrary, the *Courier's* front page captured how sexual coverage and racial uplift news coexisted in most black newspapers in the first third of the twentieth century. To a large degree, the *Courier's* page was remarkable. Many American newspapers' front pages contained a wide variety of news stories. However, the *Courier's* front page also exemplified a mass black readership who, in tandem with editors and reporters, accepted and fostered a symbiotic relationship between melodrama and African American progress. The movement of southern blacks into the urban North and Midwest between 1915 and 1940 helped to transform black newspapers from "hard news" publications for elite African Americans into lively modern news and entertainment sources for the black masses across the nation. Between World War I and World War II, weekly black newspapers, such as the *New York Amsterdam News (Amsterdam News), Baltimore Afro-American (Afro-American), Chicago Defender (Defender), Philadelphia Tribune (Tribune),* and *Pittsburgh Courier (Courier)* spearheaded and contributed to this transformation by centering their coverage in what they imagined working-class audiences desired.

This chapter focuses on the rise of what has been defined as the "golden age" of black journalism between 1920 and 1945 and its relationship to a conception of a mass black readership. While it is commonly accepted that the power of the Black Press in the first half of the twentieth century rested in its capacity to speak truth to the white establishment, Black Press editors always believed that their ability to operate as business leaders and race men lay in the hands of everyday African Americans. Unlike their nineteenth-century predecessors, interwar black newspapermen could not afford to solely publish what they viewed to be best for black communities. Instead, Black Press editors of the golden age saw their task as speaking to multiple audiences and interests at once. In so doing, the Black Press became a reflection of not simply a collective effort to challenge racist depictions and oppression of black life but a manifestation of the imagined interests of a growing mass black readership.

HISTORY OF THE EARLY BLACK PRESS

Black newspapers have a rich history and tradition rooted in uplift and protest against racial injustice. Presbyterian minister and prominent abolitionists Samuel E. Cornish and John B. Russwurm created the first black newspaper, *Freedom's Journal* (1827–1829) on March 16, 1827. The first issue of the paper expressed the sentiments of its founders: "We wish to plead our own cause. Too long have others spoken for us. Too long has the public been deceived by misrepresentations in things which concern us dearly."[2] Many of the twenty or so antebellum black newspapers circulating at any given time in the years after the *Freedom's Journal* inception also devoted significant portions of their coverage to discussing the evils of slavery and racial discrimination and published writing that focused on the improvement of the black race in general.[3] However, to a significant degree, early Black Press editors, faced with few resources and one or two people to run the newspaper, relied on material reprinted from white papers. Syndicated news content apprised readers of news of national and widespread interest. It also allowed early Black Press news editors to sprinkle generally held aphorisms and didactic pieces throughout papers that might motivate readers to rise above their status.[4]

Since a major objective of the early Black Press centered around its perceived ability to guide and shape behavior, antebellum newspaper editors directed most of their coverage to free blacks living in the North. Enslaved populations in the South naturally had little to no access to the Black Press. Therefore, early black newspapers documented the humanity and accomplishment of elite and aspiring classes of northern free black communities, hoping at once to counter racist, white-constructed stereotypes and to inspire other African Americans to reach beyond their social conditions.[5] Black newspapers, then, stressed a class-inflected social responsibility in conformity with white conceptions of humanity that prefigured the "politics of respectability" used by middle-class blacks at the turn of the twentieth century to regulate the behavior of working-class blacks.[6] Newspaper editors and publishers believed it was their responsibility to set the stage for racial progress by publishing articles that promoted thrift and moral and religious virtue among northern black populations.[7] Viewing freedom as a process that demanded a set of moral values, early Black Press editors saw themselves as responsible for the inculcation of these principles so that free African Americans might lead the way to full black liberation.[8]

It is with these ideas in mind that black newspapers embarked on a "universal improvement" program that promised to unify, educate, and guide free blacks. Nazera Wright indicates that early black newspapers "served as conduct manuals" for African Americans who trusted that industriousness and moral behavior could alter the racist views of white Americans and would prepare free African Americans to participate as full members of the nation.[9] In this regard, early Black Press editors were subject to a form of republicanism that called on Americans to commit themselves and families to civic virtue.

Early black newspaper editors would have to wait over thirty-five years from the founding of the Black Press to witness African Americans' emancipation and the beginnings of civil rights. Yet, as blacks moved into the era of Reconstruction, a new set of problems presented both southern and northern blacks with challenges that black newspapers began to tackle. The realization that millions of former enslaved people would need to be educated in all ways, including socially and politically, inspired the publication of over 100 new northern and southern black newspapers.[10] Many of these papers emerged in southern states where it had been illegal for black publications to exist before the Civil War. Before 1865, black newspapers were almost exclusively published in the North. Southern newspapers that developed during Reconstruction mostly dedicated themselves to helping former enslaved people integrate into free black society.[11]

While African Americans witnessed dramatic developments in their status in the years following the Civil War, they still remained outside the realm of full citizenship. Illiteracy, high rates of unemployment, disenfranchisement, and pervasive discrimination persisted throughout black America. The evolution of racial subordination in the aftermath of slavery into the informal and formal systems of Jim Crow reinforced racist policies that limited employment, educational, and political opportunities for African Americans. Black newspapers, however, continued to foster programs that symbolically and literally helped African Americans overcome racial injustice. Accordingly, nineteenth-century newspaper coverage documented black accomplishment and protested racist laws and policies while ushering African Americans into the twentieth century.[12]

THE BIG FIVE: GOLDEN AGE BLACK NEWSPAPERS

The dawn of the early twentieth century saw black newspapers address a cross-section of African Americans across the nation. The shift in coverage reflected a transformation in black leadership and the development of a black entrepreneurial class in the early twentieth century. Both groups recognized that southern African Americans who moved to the North functioned as a critical base of economic and political support. Although in the years leading up to World War II most African Americans continued to reside in rural areas in the South, a large number of blacks moved into cities. In 1910, 72.7 percent of African Americans lived in areas identified as rural. By 1930, that number had dropped to 56.3 percent, so that nearly half lived in northern and southern cities. Yet, approximately 88 percent of the urban African American population lived in the North, mainly in New York, Chicago, Philadelphia, and Baltimore.[13] Expanding populations of middle- and working-class African Americans in the urban North provided business people, physicians, politicians, publishers, and other professionals with a new clientele able and willing to patronize black establishments. Newspaper editors along with other black professionals recognized the economic benefits of a larger and more diverse black populace. Racial advancement in this context was synonymous with African American commercial development. Uplifting the race could be both financially and morally profitable.[14]

If there was ever a set of newspaper businesses that could merge the objectives of racial progress and economic viability, it was the *Baltimore Afro-American, Chicago Defender, Pittsburgh Courier, Philadelphia Tribune,* and *New York Amsterdam News.* As some of the most influential black newspapers, they tapped into growing local and national modern black consumer markets. Popular newspaper critic and journalist Eugene Gordon consistently ranked all five papers as the best black newspaper outlets in the United States. Although he acknowledged that the papers "greatly resemble their more yellow daily contemporaries," white papers that utilized sensationalism, they were better than the 197 "Aframerican weeklies" that were "little more than waste paper."[15] Unlike small papers, the *Afro-American, Defender, Courier, Tribune,* and *Amsterdam News* were sizable corporations with independently owned newspaper plants that included more modern printing presses. Despite the need to use cheaper newsprint, these newspaper businesses could produce higher quality copies.[16] Publishers blanketed rural and urban areas across the United States with editions of each paper. While these papers were connected by their mutual engagement with national and local black communities over matters of racial uplift and protest, the five papers were distinctly different in their approaches. Each paper reflected a particular perspective based on its evolving readership and editorial predilection.

The *Defender,* known as "The World's Greatest Weekly," a play on the *Chicago Tribune*'s slogan, "The World's Greatest Newspaper," was, in some ways, the first modern black newspaper. Founded in 1905, it was an early adopter of prevailing twentieth-century features such as a full sports page, women's page, and regular cartoons.[17] The *Defender* was also the first to run weekly national and local editions. Abbott was also one of the first black editors to utilize sensationalism to report news.[18] Other black newspaper editors initially refused to do so, believing that they were compromising the mission of racial uplift. Although also socially conservative, Abbott allowed Smiley to use sensationalism to draw readers' attention to racial injustice and violent acts against African Americans. The *Defender* featured graphic, sensational headlines announcing regular occurrences of southern lynchings with language that described violence against African Americans in lurid detail. In fact, Gordon argued that the key to the *Defender*'s success lay in Abbott's willingness to copy methods like sensationalism and other features from white papers.[19] The belief that the Black Press' staying power could be found in the techniques they borrowed from the white press was common. Maxwell Brooks, an Ohio State University sociologist, writing in 1937, pointed out that "Negro newspaper men have aped these dailies in whatever feature appeared to contribute their journalistic success."[20] However, simply imitating other papers would not be enough. Abbott, as well as other editors, knew that readers were newspapers' lifelines.

Prior to the early twentieth century, a poor market existed for the black newspaper industry in Chicago. The city simply did not host enough African Americans to support a thriving Black Press. Nonetheless, when Abbott founded the *Defender* with 300 copies of the first issue, he began to meet the informational needs of a surging population of black Chicagoans that would grow by 113.7 percent between 1920 and 1930.[21] Many of the 233,903 blacks who lived in the city settled an area known as the South Side, which would also come to be known as Bronzeville. Chicago's early-twentieth-century black community, like Harlem's, gained national recognition for the large numbers of African Americans dominating the city's cultural life. Notable African American sociologists such as E. Franklin Frazier, St. Clair Drake, Horace Cayton, and Charles S. Johnson extensively researched and wrote about the social conditions of Chicago's diverse black communities.[22] This literature cast experiences of black Chicagoans as symbols of the larger "Negro Problem," which included racial discrimination and disproportionate rates of poverty.

Immediately before World War I, Abbott developed the paper into a national voice for African Americans in its "Great Northern Drive" to encourage black southerners to leave their homes for Chicago and other northern cities. Capitalizing on the labor shortages stemming from a smaller number of European immigrants, Abbott promoted Chicago as a place of vast economic opportunity and refuge from white violence for southern blacks.[23] The paper often found its way to numerous southern homes through the efforts of black railroad men. Pullman porters regularly acquired issues of the *Defender*, which they would distribute to friends and family members along southern routes.[24] By 1920, the *Defender* was selling two-thirds of its weekly copies outside of Chicago.[25] The paper was the most circulated out-of-town black newspaper in the South, according to Fisk University professor of economics Paul K. Edwards.[26]

As a result of Abbott and his staff's efforts, the *Defender* played a critical role in the migration of blacks from the South. Scanning the papers for jobs or housing, African Americans saw the *Defender* as a clearinghouse that could help to facilitate a successful transition to urban life. The *Defender* received thousands of letters from individuals responding to the paper's call for a great "northern drive." The *Defender* encouraged its southern readers to view the North as synonymous with personal and collective advancement for African Americans.[27] In an effort to help migrants prepare for the exigencies of progress, the paper published "Don'ts" on its editorial page that would help migrants to "conduct themselves as to reflect credit upon themselves" and to "disarm those who are endeavoring to discredit our Race."[28] Ironically, editorial tactics such as this reflected the paper's recognition of a new readership they believed required assistance in the transition from the rural to the urban life.

As other editors and publishers witnessed the *Defender's* booming circulation numbers, they decided to follow the paper's use of sensationalism and direct engagement with readers on matters of racial inequality. For example, the *Defender's* strongest local black newspaper competition, the *Chicago Whip* (1919–1939) and the *Chicago Bee* (1926–1940s?), hired reporters to cover stories that resonated with readers in Chicago.[29] Smaller Chicago papers that could not afford sufficient staff to cover news relied on the Associated Negro Press (ANP) for weekly news releases to fill their papers and keep readers informed of events outside of Chicago. Created by Claude Barnett in Chicago in 1919, the ANP played a major role in supplying black newspapers across the United States with news to satisfy the needs and interests of millions of black readers.

The *Defender's* sensationalism, however, would pale in comparison to other papers by the beginning of World War II.[30] While the *Defender* covered its fair share of sex scandals, murders, and other sensational topics, in large measure, it did not feature as many of the popular features that helped both the *Courier* and the *Afro-American* to successfully compete for readers. Initially a pioneer in journalism, the *Defender* was unable to completely move beyond Abbott's conservatism and his desire to operate the paper "in the interest of the black bourgeoisie."[31] The *Defender's* circulation dropped from its peak of approximately 200,000 weekly copies sold in 1925 (40,000 sold in Chicago and 160,000 nationally) to averaging 100,000 copies per week in the 1930s.[32]

Like all black papers, the *Defender* depended almost exclusively on circulation to remain in business. The sharp dip in circulation numbers devastated the financial standing of the paper. The Depression as well as Abbott's poor financial management and inability to keep abreast of modern trends in journalism utilized by the *Afro-American* and *Courier* were the most significant factors in the *Defender's* decline.[33] When Abbott died on the eve of the United States' official entrance into World War II in 1941, the paper still commanded the attention of loyal readers and maintained its claim that it was "The World's Greatest Weekly." Nonetheless, it would be the *Pittsburgh Courier* that would take the lead in guiding and entertaining African Americans through the challenges of modern America in the 1930s.[34]

The *Courier*, founded in 1907, was initially a simple two-page literary publication that contained the personal writings of Edwin Nathaniel Harleston, a guard at a local packing plant in Pittsburgh. Two years later, Harleston contacted

Robert Lee Vann, a well-known black attorney in the Pittsburgh area, and others for financial assistance to transform the paper into a larger publication. Vann was unable to offer monetary support, but he agreed to serve as counsel for the *Courier*. Vann's decision to be involved with the paper would prove transformative. Shortly after he agreed to be the *Courier's* lawyer, the paper's backers incorporated and asked Vann to work as editor of the paper. From 1912 to his death in 1940, Vann developed the paper into what he called "America's Best Weekly" and one of the most popular national black newspapers of the twentieth century.[35]

The *Courier's* circulation overwhelmingly reflected a national audience. At its apex, fourteen editions flowed through small towns and cities. *Courier* staff reported that only 20,000 copies, out of the approximately weekly circulation of 50,000–75,000 papers, consistently sold in the Pittsburgh area in the 1920s and 1930s.[36] Some of the *Courier's* wide circulation stemmed from Vann's decision to send acerbic columnist George Schuyler on a nine-month tour of the South in 1925 to describe the region's culture and social conditions. Schuyler's promotion of the *Courier* in southern locales—its subsequent series of articles—increased the circulation of the paper by at least 10,000 copies. One *Courier* letter writer declared in reference to the paper, "I read it with care and then send it between 200 and 300 miles for others to read."[37] Because Pittsburgh's relatively transitory black migrant population might have made it difficult for *Courier* editors to envision local readers whom they could court to generate sales, a national audience was integral to its success.

In 1910, before the migration of blacks from the South, the African American population of Pittsburgh represented a mere 4.8 percent. By 1930, this number had just about doubled so that African Americans comprised 8.2 percent of the total population of Pittsburgh. The city's new black community was relatively young in the 1920s and 1930s: 52 percent of migrants moving to Pittsburgh in 1916 were under the age of thirty, while another 27 percent were in their thirties. Unlike other cities with large numbers of migrants, Pittsburgh was often a temporary destination. Steel plants and manufacturing industries often complained bitterly about high turnover rates.[38] As a result, the *Courier's* national and local editions varied little in their coverage; the paper did not seem to believe it was necessary to specifically gear front-page articles and columns toward a Pittsburgh audience.

The *Courier* was based on the same principles as most black papers. Vann and his staff's primary goals were to participate in the racial uplift of blacks and to fight racism. The *Courier* demonstrated the ability to attract more readers in the 1930s through the end of World War II than any other black paper of the time period. During this period, the *Courier* spearheaded many public campaigns, which included the protest against *Amos 'n Andy*, a popular radio show that stereotyped blacks; the call for African Americans to leave the Republican Party in the presidential election of 1932; and the anticommunist stance on the Scottsboro case. In addition, the *Courier's* coverage of boxing champion Joe Louis's defeat of Max Schmeling of Germany in 1938 and ongoing discussions of the Italian invasion of Ethiopia helped to make the *Courier* the most widely circulated black newspaper of the 1930s and 1940s.[39]

The *Courier* staff tried to steer clear of more salacious stories but ultimately attempted to find a middle ground between sensationalism and straightforward coverage. Vann abhorred sensationalism, believing that it had no place in a paper that was committed to "uplifting the race." Yet, as much as Vann believed that it cheapened his paper, he could not deny the larger circulation numbers when the *Courier* used sensationalism to promote a 1922 murder case. Vann happened to be the defending attorney of the case in which a young black man, Joe Thomas, had been accused of killing a white woman. Vann lost the case and the defendant was sentenced to death by electrocution. The *Courier* front page recounted every grim detail of the electrocution. The paper sold out on every newsstand that carried issues of the *Courier* that week.[40]

While the *Courier* might have initially chosen to be more discriminating about sensationalism, this did not preclude publishing photographs of young, sexually attractive women as a regular feature on its front pages. Young women from groups such as Delta Gamma Theta sorority, bathing-beauty pageant winners, and homecoming queens from black colleges regularly appeared in the *Courier*. More often than not, these women represented the very best of black middle-class communities across the United States. Although similar representations appeared in other black papers, the *Courier* tended to have more of them, which certainly helped the paper to reach the milestone of a quarter-million circulation in 1937.[41] Upon his death in 1940, Vann left the *Courier* as the most widely read black weekly in the United States.

While the *Courier* drew large numbers of national readers, the *Baltimore Afro-American* carved out its own niche in the black newspaper market. Founded in 1892, the *Afro-American* emerged out of the union of three small church newspapers. Initially edited by Reverend William Alexander, pastor of the Sharon Baptist Church, the paper served as a public forum for protest against race discrimination in Baltimore. Alexander named the paper *Afro-American* to reflect his dislike for the term *Negro*, which he found offensive when it was used to refer to African Americans.[42] Like many black newspapers, the *Afro-American* faced financial difficulty in the beginning. Alexander sold his share of the paper to John H. Murphy Sr., an ex-slave and former Union Army sergeant, in 1897. When Murphy died in 1922, he left the paper to be guided by his son, Carl J. Murphy. Under Carl Murphy's guidance, the *Afro-American* became one of the most widely read black weeklies in the years leading up to World War II.[43]

The *Afro-American*'s popularity among African Americans corresponded to the migration of blacks to Baltimore at the beginning of the twentieth century. Although Baltimore is located below the Mason-Dixon Line, the cultural and regional boundary separating the North from the South in the United States, Baltimore's black residents did not necessarily see themselves as "southern." Added to this perception was the fact that Baltimore's economic and labor patterns reflected patterns found in northern industrial centers more than they did the South, which was primarily agriculturally based even as late as the early twentieth century. The *Afro-American* capitalized on the increasingly urbanized ethos of black Baltimoreans and their neighbors in Washington, DC.[44]

Baltimore's black population grew by 31.2 percent between 1920 and 1930 so that 142,106 African Americans called Baltimore home by 1930. By 1940, Baltimore's black population had increased by 50 percent, a number that included 33,102 families. Only 17 percent of these families owned their own homes, while the remaining 83 percent lived in rented housing. Large numbers of these families made West Baltimore their home. West Baltimore replaced the East Baltimore area near Fells Point as the heart of the city's black community. The cramped section of the neighborhood surrounded by Pennsylvania and Druid Hill Avenues and Biddle and Preston Streets was so unhealthy that it would come to be known as "Lung Block" during the tuberculosis epidemic following World War I.[45] Nonetheless, black Baltimoreans possessed substantial buying power, to the tune of $45 million per year in 1929. Much of this money was spent on services or goods offered by black businesses. The *Afro-American*, serving as one of the few businesses that employed more than six African Americans and one of the city's leading black businesses, managed to capture some of the new black dollars circulating in West Baltimore and outside the city.[46] On average, the paper circulated close to 60,000 copies per week throughout the 1930s.[47]

News coverage of African Americans' feats and accomplishments dominated large sections of the *Afro-American*. The paper also launched campaigns against racial injustices on its editorial pages, which included the fight to integrate the Baltimore police force and a campaign to give white and black teachers equal pay. Added to this, the *Afro-American*'s call for the moral transformation of the masses of African Americans mirrored much of early-twentieth-century black elite's uplift ideology.[48] Despite the *Afro-American*'s religious roots and focus on respectability politics, headlines featuring crimes, sex, and similar topics appeared on the front pages of the *Afro-American* beginning in 1917. "Sexy" stories also appeared in the weekly features section of the newspaper. Much more provocative than what other local and national black papers would allow, these stories suggestively beckoned readers to an alternative world outside the political and educational commentaries that appeared in other areas of the paper. And while both editors of the *Defender* and *Courier* grudgingly used sensationalism, Murphy possessed a higher tolerance for it and seemed more inclined to transgress ideals of respectability. The *Afro-American* editors believed that sensationalism merged with the paper's race-advocacy function. The publication of crime and scandal, argued *Afro-American* editors, brought it to the attention of the authorities who could then deal with issues that affected the black community.[49]

Murphy and his staff's conception of Baltimore and the surrounding area's demographics also appeared to impact the paper's sensational bent. Relative to other rapidly urbanizing areas, Baltimore sustained a greater proportion of working-class African Americans to middle-class and elite blacks. Furthermore, the black literacy rate of 83 percent, while clearly higher than any other southern city, was lower than those of Chicago, Pittsburgh, Philadelphia, and Harlem. Added to this, the close proximity of residents in Washington, DC, surely shaped the *Afro-American's* coverage. The *Afro-American's* Baltimore and Washington, DC, editions were generally more sensational than national editions in their tone and featured a larger percentage of crime and sexually related news and topics. The national editions, which editors distributed in the South and other areas of the country, while still featuring sensational coverage, consistently exhibited less sexually provocative material. The difference in editions suggests that *Afro-American* editors believed that local urban African Americans communities were more likely to purchase papers that contained sensationalism and featured sexually explicit coverage. Murphy's emphasis on crime and scandal contributed to the success of the *Afro-American* throughout the Depression and World War II. In this respect, the *Afro-American* surpassed the pioneer of black newspaper sensationalism, the *Defender*.[50]

While the *Defender, Courier, and Afro-American* addressed both national and local African Americans, local papers, such as the *Tribune* and *Amsterdam News*, captured the greater attention of a wide swath of local black communities based in Philadelphia and New York City. South Carolina native James Henry Anderson started the *Amsterdam News* in 1909 with "six sheets of blank paper, a lead pencil and dress-maker's table."[51] Anderson initially chose to ignore national news and concentrate solely on news of the Amsterdam neighborhood and the surrounding community, earning the paper the name the "people's paper" and later, "Harlem's Largest Weekly Newspaper." According to writer Aubrey Bowser, the paper's focus on "intensely personal news" helped Anderson sell papers like "hot waffles at a skating rink." The "Rubberneck Column," which recounted local events and situations without identifying the figures involved, served as the most popular feature in early issues of the *Amsterdam News*.[52] This sort of coverage simulated the community networks of information many readers were familiar with in southern towns and small cities. Migrant readers relished reading tidbits of information about suspected neighbors, friends, and relatives that appeared in the column.

New York was home to the most visible urban African American communities of the early twentieth century. It was one of the greatest points of destination for black southerners seeking better lives in the North. From 1890 to 1920, New York City's black population increased from 36,000 to 152,000. In particular, residential segregation made Harlem home for blacks that spanned different classes. An emerging group of Caribbean immigrants also added diversity to Harlem neighborhoods.[53] The black population in Harlem reached 185,000 by 1930. Harlem's growth continued throughout the 1930s and 1940s as blacks, responding to developments in African American art and culture and labor opportunities prompted by the outbreak of World War II, moved to Harlem to participate in the culture and economy.

Black elites and members of the black intelligentsia in and around Harlem regularly snubbed the *Amsterdam News* for the staid coverage found in the "ultra-conservative" *New York Age* (1887–1960), which received wide support from Booker T. Washington in the early twentieth century.[54] "America's great pictorial weekly," the *Interstate Tattler* (1925–) and the black tabloid, *New York News* (?–1935), two of the *Amsterdam News* major newspaper competitors, attracted their own audiences. *Negro World* (1918–1933), the publication organ of the Universal Negro Improvement Association, founded by Marcus Garvey, also captured a segment of the black newspaper reading market in New York City. The *Amsterdam News*, however, managed to outlive its rivals by appealing to a broader audience of readers. Incorporating modern approaches to journalism, the *Amsterdam News* balanced sensationalism with traditional racial advocacy and uplift. Gordon called it the "best local Negro newspaper in the country" for its professionally educated and trained staff.[55] Education and training allowed *Amsterdam News* editors and reporters to capture the nuance of their local market and apply modern approaches to journalism.

The *Amsterdam News* was the ideal combination of instruction and entertainment. The *Amsterdam News*'s protests such as the "Don't Buy Where You Can't Work" campaign and a 1929 protest against Sears-Roebuck and Company for discriminating against blacks wishing to purchase houses from the company attracted aspirational readers who desired greater access to employment and equitable housing opportunities. The paper's masthead regularly advised readers: "Wherever possible trade with stores in Harlem that do not practice discrimination in the selection of their employees."[56] Furthermore, the *Amsterdam News* actively published editorials decrying police brutality in Harlem and won accolades for being the only paper to publish the New York Mayor's commission report of the 1935 Harlem riot sparked by the rumored beating of a black teenager.

The *Amsterdam News* continued to fight against racial oppression through the 1930s despite a change in ownership that occurred in December 1935. Two prominent West Indian Harlem physicians and owners of the Powell-Savory Corporation, Dr. Clelan Bethan Powell and Dr. Phillip M. H. Savory, purchased the paper.[57] The Powell-Savory acquisition pumped new life into the *Amsterdam News*. Edited by Harvard graduate Earl Brown, sales of the paper jumped 290 percent while advertising increased 360 percent in the late 1930s. Powell and Savory attributed the success to the paper's continuing coverage and exposure of "conditions affecting [the black public's] health, educational housing, and economic conditions."[58] Harlem Renaissance poet and writer Claude McKay saw the increase in reader interest in the *Amsterdam News* from a different perspective. The paper's "sensational dressing up" of crimes with accompanying photographs, speculated McKay, made the paper "sharper and snappier" than it had been under the ownership of Warren.[59] Whether the *Amsterdam News's* newfound success in the 1930s was due to its reports of social issues affecting African Americans or its melodramatic appeals, the paper's ability to meet readers where they were provided it with the means to serve as the voice for Harlem's communities for the twentieth century.

Like the *Amsterdam News*, the *Tribune* privileged its local readership. However, it was much more conservative in its approach. Established as a weekly paper in 1884 by Chris J. Perry, a former writer for several black and white publications, he spent the next thirty-seven years of his life developing the paper into African Americans' primary mode of expression and representation in Philadelphia.[60] After Perry's death in 1921, his son-in-law Eugene Washington Rhodes led the *Tribune*. Rhodes, a lawyer with degrees from a variety of institutions, including Temple University law school, was a member of Philadelphia's black middle class and a staunch Republican. The *Tribune* reflected the deeply middle-class political and moral philosophies of both Rhodes and his wife, Bertha Perry Rhodes, during the 1920s and 1930s.[61]

A long-standing image of black Philadelphians as one of the first free black communities in the United States also played a role in the *Tribune's* conservative approach. According to Sadie Tanner Mossell, Philadelphia had been home to sizable numbers of African Americans, who were "[n]egroes of culture, education, and some financial means" throughout the nineteenth and early twentieth centuries. Philadelphia and New York City were the only cities in 1910 that sustained over 50,000 African Americans residing within their boundaries.[62] The long presence of elite and conservative African Americans in Philadelphia shaped the *Tribune's* coverage, despite the influx of working-class blacks into the city throughout the first half of the twentieth century.

Like other northern cities, Philadelphia saw a large number of African Americans make their way to the city to take advantage of labor opportunities beginning in 1916. Railroad and industrial plants offered many southern blacks the chance to greatly improve their standard of living. This growth continued throughout the 1920s and 1930s. In 1920, 134,229 African Americans lived in Philadelphia. This number increased to 219,599 in 1930, representing a 63.6 percent increase in the black population and 11.3 percent of the total population.[63] Nonetheless, Philadelphia was not host to the dramatic numbers of African American migrants that Chicago and New York accommodated in the first half of the twentieth century. As a result, Philadelphia's African American culture continued to be largely shaped by long-standing black residents who often took umbrage with their southern brothers and sisters' country ways. The *Tribune*, then, responded to the increase in Philadelphia's black population by advocating for civil rights, but reporters also attempted to prescribe proper behavior for their readers. With its relatively conservative mix in coverage, the *Tribune* managed to maintain a relatively substantial circulation for the first two decades of the twentieth century.

Rhodes's column and other areas of the paper represented a middle-class ethos for the first half of the twentieth century. Social prescriptions, which purported to help African Americans acquire bourgeois values, stood alongside articles denouncing racist and discriminatory practices against Philadelphia blacks. The *Tribune* maintained a distinctively conservative perspective on news and culture for African Americans in the period between World War I and II. Many black newspaper critics commented on its conservative approach, often lauding the *Tribune* for its ability to refrain from resorting to some of the sensationalistic techniques employed by other black papers. The *Tribune* lacked many of the lurid images that were found in other papers. There were few sexually provocative short stories, and it did not contain as many sensational headlines as the *Afro-American*, for example. The *Tribune* simply used less sensationalism and a more straightforward reporting style. The *Tribune* looked much more conservative next to many of its counterparts.[64] Despite the influx of diverse African American populations, the paper continued to court their core audience, an African American old guard, and to reflect Rhodes's more conventional approach to journalism.

Rhodes's decision to minimize sensationalism left the door open for other publishers to satisfy Philadelphia readers who desired sensational news stories and tabloid journalism. Nightclub owner Forest White Woodard billed his paper, the *Philadelphia Independent* (1931–1971) as the "World's Greatest Negro Tabloid." Founded in 1931, the paper competed for the *Tribune's* readers for forty years and surpassed it in circulation for a period of time.[65] Unlike Rhodes, Woodard deliberately created his paper for the masses and tilted its political sensibility toward the Democratic party. Kathryn (Kitty) Fambro Woodard, publisher of the *Independent* after her husband's death in 1958, described the paper as a publication "for the masses. The Tribune had always been the paper for the upper class. We were militant. We weren't afraid to take on issues like they were."[66] Although, the *Independent* enjoyed a great deal of popularity, the *Tribune* managed to outlive it and is one of the oldest currently published black papers in the United States.

At the height of the interwar America, the Black Press captured an emerging urban and divorced black populace produced by the Great Migration. Together, the *Defender, Courier, Afro-American, Amsterdam News,* and *Tribune* created news and included features they believed reflected this mass black readership. This readership, in the minds of black publishers and editors, was the life source of the black newspaper industry, and speaking to its interests meant imagining who these readers were.

A MASS BLACK READERSHIP

The lure of fewer racial restrictions and greater economic opportunities in the urban North motivated over a half-million African Americans to leave the South between 1915 and 1920. The *Defender* received thousands of letters from individuals responding to the paper's call for a great "northern drive." Letters to the *Defender* spoke to the hope and promise that the North, but perhaps any location other than the South, held for southern blacks.[67] These letters also reflected southern blacks' desire for greater personal freedom and economic opportunity.

Both the letters and the wide circulation of newspapers indicate the increase in literacy among African Americans in both the North and the South.[68] Prior to the twentieth century, Black Press editors found that an "underprivileged class" of readers that could barely read made up a sizable majority of African

Americans. Many everyday black southerners' reading material consisted of the "family bible."[69] Yet, census records indicate that 89.5 percent of blacks in the North and 66.7 percent in the South could read and write by 1910. Only 16.3 percent of the black population remained illiterate in 1930. The disproportionate rate of black illiteracy remained in the South. Still, the letters countered popular ideas that many of the early southern migrants were uneducated county bumpkins.

Letter writers often testified to reading the *Defender* on a weekly basis. One woman from Atlanta wrote in 1917, "I am a reader of you [*sic*] paper and we are all crazy about it and take it every Saturday and we raise a great howl when we don't get it." Others wrote in response to advertisements or articles featuring employment opportunities. Some readers even noted that their first encounter with the *Defender* prompted them to write letters asking for help establishing themselves in the North.[70]

Many readers revealed highly personal information and alluded to southern racism that put their lives in jeopardy. The more profound letters recounted the racial violence that "pushed" many African Americans to the North. An anonymous letter writer from Thomasville, North Carolina, wrote the *Courier* and described the lynching of two men who were "carried just over the county line and roasted like an opossum . . . while thousands stood by with about five hundred automobiles and witnessed the fact." The writer noted that violence such as this was largely the reason that African Americans sought refuge in the North.[71]

The letters that poured into the *Defender's* office demonstrate the growing importance of black newspapers for early-twentieth-century readers. Readers trusted Abbott and the *Defender*. In turn, these letters show that black newspapers acquired a new group of readers who left agricultural occupations and moved into domestic and personal service work in urban settings. By 1930, 28.6 percent of African Americans performed domestic and personal service, while 36.1 percent still remained tied to farm labor. More blacks in domestic service and personal service in cities translated into greater access to newspapers. The *Courier* noted that migrants offered value beyond their ability to provide service for white northerners. "Our brothers from the South are bringing more than bags and baggage. If we look about us we will see undertakers, barbers, carpenters, doctors and lawyers and tradesmen."[72] A shortened workday and an increase in wages compared to the southern labor system allowed migrants to indulge in a limited set of leisure and recreational activities. One of these activities included purchasing and reading both black and white newspapers.

As migrants slowly integrated themselves into the texture of urban life and eked out a place among more established African Americans, newspapers sought to maintain a growing and diverse audience of readers.[73] The *Defender*'s campaigns to attract southerners to the North fostered a deep and abiding respect for black newspapers that many migrants maintained once they established themselves in their new homes. Prior to the movement of migrants into urban areas, black editors struggled to acquire readers. Old settler residents in many cities, African Americans who lived in the urban North before the Great Migration looked at newspapers published by African Americans with great disdain. Many elite and middle-class African Americans believed that black newspapers fell below the standard of respectability and sophistication. Working and aspiring classes of African Americans, on the other hand, helped to transform the Black Press into a powerful black institution.[74] A 1938 *Defender* editorial noted the change in black newspaper readership. According to the editorial, "There was a time when newspapers published by black people carried little prestige, less power and no influence." The writer remarked, however, "A decided change has taken place in the last twenty years." Black newspapers were now "devoured and religiously read" by African Americans.[75] Melissa Mae Elliot wrote in 1931, "in one of the leading Negro colleges, after two days' use every Negro weekly has been so completely thumbed and handled that a fresh issue must be preserved for the rack."[76] Newspapers critics explained the revolution in black newspaper consumption by the growth of black urban communities in the North. They also attributed it to better distribution and higher quality newspapers that mirrored the techniques used by white papers.

Black papers also competed with white newspapers for readers. According to Floyd Calvin, special features editor for the *Courier*, the *New York Daily* (*Daily News*), the city's most popular tabloid, sold over 60,000 copies of their papers to black Harlemites each morning. Savvy enough to cover African Americans positively relative to other white papers, tabloid newspapers such as the *Daily News* and *Evening Graphic* cut into Black Press circulation and created a "cutthroat" competitive atmosphere among black papers.[77] Paul Edwards's 1932 study of southern black consumers reported that a large majority of African American families in Birmingham, Alabama, and Richmond, Virginia, indicated that they purchased a white daily newspaper. Conversely, much smaller percentages of southern African American communities subscribed to or purchased black newspapers.[78] This was certainly due to the difficulty that African Americans had procuring and reading black newspapers in the Jim Crow South. An editorial in the *Norfolk Journal and Guide* made this point clear:

The fact that our Negro newspapers which have the largest circulation are not published in the South is due in part to the fact that northern newspapers are published in the large metropolitan centers, where freedom of the press is one thing, while in the South, freedom of the press is quite something else.[79]

Black Press editors in some cases, however, believed that some African Americans continued to see black papers as inferior despite the large numbers of black readers. In 1940, *Defender* editor Lucius C. Harper declared, "There are Negroes today, mostly college bred, who [do] not admit openly that they are readers of color newspapers."[80] Although Harper cited anecdotal evidence of African Americans stating their preference for white papers, their motivation for consuming them was unclear. Some papers such as the *New York World* employed black journalists. Lester A. Walton, black feature writer for the paper between 1922 and 1931, noted that his impartial coverage of both whites and African Americans allowed him the unusual experience of working alongside white newspaper men.[81] Walton's even reporting made it easier for black readers, accustomed to hostile coverage of African American communities, to read the *New York World*. Claude McKay remarked, "The Negro weeklies are published in the large cities and must compete somehow with the white dailies which Negroes read more than they do their own newspapers."[82] In light of the competition for readers, the *Afro-American* took the extraordinary measure of changing the format of the paper to a tabloid format in April 1929 to provide their readers with the "information in fewer words with less effort." Less than a month later, the paper had resumed its regular layout in response to readers' rejection of its new tabloid arrangement.[83]

Even as Black Press editors recognized white papers as stiff competitors, they knew that white papers lacked the positive representations of black life that readers desperately sought. Harper remarked, "Our people get thrills when their likenesses are produced on the front page: they gloat and 'rare back' when editorials are written praising their efforts."[84] Thus, black newspapers featured commentaries that evoked race pride not only to uplift but to induce African Americans to read and support the Black Press. In this sense, the Great Migration marked not only a shift in physical location of the masses but also concerted attempts to challenge the demeaning and unsophisticated images of black life that were the seeds of American popular culture.[85]

Accordingly, Alain Locke—philosopher and father of the Harlem Renaissance—and others believed that the void left by the swift departure of these representations would birth black authored realities and depictions of African American humanity to act as soldiers in the continued fight for the black struggle for civil and social rights. Black print culture, particularly black newspapers, served as the testing ground for these new images. Nannie Burroughs, African American educator and founder of the National Training School for Women and Girls, in an article syndicated by the ANP and published in the *Tribune* in 1930, stated, "The Negro newspaper should have the unstinted support of the race because it publishes all of the good news and the constructive race ideals that will help us forward."[86] Readers often echoed Burroughs, encouraging other community members to support black papers

Despite black newspapers' push for larger numbers of readers, editors and publishers understood that a more consistent revenue lay in advertising. Yet advertising failed to bring in the much-needed funds that would allow black papers to possess a stronger financial base. Advertising found in black papers between 1900 and 1920 often represented local companies; however, at a penny per word, local advertising failed to generate enough funds to finance the operation of the papers. Real estate agencies, small grocery stores, and other local businesses used black papers to market their products and services. Still, a 1926 survey by the ANP revealed that only a small percent of black businesses actually utilized black papers to advertise their services. Madam C. J. Walker, the first United States woman millionaire and pioneer of black hair products, was a significant exception. The Walker Company was one of the largest advertisers in black newspapers during the 1920s.[87]

When black businesses did advertise in papers, they typically sent in a simple copy of a business card, avoiding a costlier and larger advertisement with graphics. As a result, white companies hawking products such as skin lighteners, hair straighteners, and quack or patent medicines were the chief advertisers in black newspapers.[88] These sorts of advertisements continued to dominate advertising in black papers throughout the first half of the twentieth century. Race record advertisements that promoted blues musicians such as Victoria Spivey and Mamie Smith, which often featured racial caricatures and sexual imagery, also made their appearance in the mid-1920s as record companies capitalized on blacks' musical tastes and increased buying power. Many of the ads attempted to reflect blues lyrics with visual images of the singing artists or scenes that mirrored the subject of the songs.

White record companies created most of the advertisements and often depicted working-class black life and romance as disorganized, dysfunctional, and violent.[89] Black commentators on black newspapers maintained a long-standing critique of these sorts of advertisements, most arguing that they conflicted with "race pride" and the uplift mission of the papers. "The TRIBUNE believes that advertisements of the 'Good Luck' type should not be carried by first-class newspapers," remarked one editorial writer. Readers also attacked papers for publishing this sort of advertising, believing that it conflicted with racial uplift. A *Defender* reader sardonically wrote, "While the race was busy having a National Negro Congress in Chicago, it seems the 'World's Greatest Weekly' was busy advertising 'Face Bleach.'" The reader ended his letter to the *Defender* with the remark, "Here's to fewer bleaching ads. (Use this space for worthwhile articles of benefit to the entire race. And a few pictures of beautiful colored girls of all complexions.)" Other readers voiced opposing views. As one reader stated, "White newspapers advertise them [hair straighteners and skin whiteners], why can't we?"[90] Debates such as this reflected a diverse mass black readership who could debate and dialogue with each other.

While white newspapers may have advertised these products, they could also depend on more "reputable" national companies to advertise in their papers. National advertising, which offered the largest revenue, was initially elusive for black newspapers. Many national companies believed that their advertising dollars were better spent in white publications. The few national advertisements featured in black papers were the result of the William B. Ziff Company. The Ziff Company's chief responsibility was to obtain national advertising accounts for the *Courier*, *Defender*, and *Afro-American*. Ziff, a white man, charged exorbitant commissions to the papers for bringing them advertisers. However, he guaranteed payment to newspapers, making it less likely that papers would take a loss from companies refusing to pay after their ads ran.

Despite the high commissions paid to Ziff, black papers gleaned additional income from advertising products manufactured by national companies such as Colgate-Palmolive-Peet and Pillsbury Mills.[91] Ziff was not only responsible for bringing in new advertising, but he also distributed the illustrated feature magazine that the *Courier*, *Defender*, *Afro-American*, and others published in their papers. Filled with serialized stories, advice columns, and entertainment news, the illustrated feature magazine made black papers accessible to modern readers who desired a blend of political and moralizing topics. The inclusion of these features was not without contention. *Courier* editor Vann and other editors came to dislike the illustrated feature magazine. Vann was convinced that the magazine tainted the otherwise good character of the paper with indecent stories and provocative images of women.[92]

Although the 1930s saw increased numbers of national companies and manufacturers broach the "Negro market," local businesses continued to make up the bulk of advertising found in black newspapers in the decades before World War II. Economic downturns, such as the Great Depression, however, greatly reduced the advertising all newspapers could obtain. During this period, black newspapers pulled in less than 30 percent of their income from advertising. The low advertising revenue, however, had some benefits. It meant that Black Press editors and publishers ultimately controlled what appeared in newspapers and were not influenced by business interests. Myrdal noted, "It is often pointed out by Negro newspapermen, that the paucity of advertising at least has one good effect, that the Negro press becomes freer from any outside control."[93] It was clear that by "outside control" Myrdal referred to white institutions and commercial enterprises.

Nevertheless, the harsh reality of little national advertising dollars and slightly more local "reputable" advertising forced many black papers to maintain a delicate balance between their need for advertising and their objective of uplifting the race and drawing in more readers. Lewis H. Fenderson, a *Courier* correspondent and poet, remarked in his PhD thesis, "Development of the Negro Press: 1827–1948": "Publishers learned that the costs of propaganda, regardless of its social value, required the outlay of actual cash, which for most of them, had to be partly realized from the sale of space."[94] The problem with Fenderson's statement was not that it was untrue. Rather, as discussed above, the sheer lack of advertising revenue, relative to their white counterparts led black editors to rely heavily on sales and subscriptions to their papers for financial support between 1925 and 1940.[95]

The key to this stream of revenue, argued black news editors, also meant paying greater attention to an audience that spanned different class, gender, and regional categories as well as sexual orientations.[96] A diverse readership, in the minds of black editors, added a level of complexity to black papers that was lacking in their white counterparts. A *Courier* column noted, "Whereas most daily [white] newspapers address themselves to certain social classes in a community, the Negro newspaper must address itself to all of the Negroes." Moreover, the column stressed, "Aside from being a teacher, informer, and moulder [sic] of public opinion, however the newspaper is also a business."[97] Being a commercial enterprise meant that the early-twentieth-century Black Press was perpetually concerned with the bottom line of selling newspapers to different segments of readers. National Association for the Advancement of Colored People (NAACP) leader W. E. B. Du Bois recognized the significance of Black Press editors' knowledge of their audience, describing them as, "very careful and often trained observers. They know what kinds of news Negroes are interested [in]."[98] Therefore, editors and reporters created news that met what they believed to be the demands of a mass black readership.

NEWS IN THE BLACK PRESS

Readers opening up weekly black newspapers in the 1920s and 1930s could expect to find a little something for everyone in the mélange of images and topics that directly and indirectly pertained to different groups within the black community. Most papers maintained a similar layout, which made reading different black papers a shared, ritualistic process. Spanning anywhere between fifteen and forty pages and divided into two main sections, the first section of black newspapers often contained what editors and publishers considered the most significant and breaking news coverage of the week. This included both domestic and international events that related directly to black life. This meant that the Black Press allocated space to events in Africa and the Diaspora. The editorial page, often appearing in the first section, featured letters to the editor while regular columns appeared in the second section of the paper. By the Great Depression, many papers were forced to reduce the number of pages published, though most had rebounded enough to feature twenty pages or more of news by 1940. However, like most news editors, black papers' editors moved sections around to generate reader interest and improve the likelihood of consumers purchasing the paper.[99]

Despite the efforts of editors to create different paper layouts, placing crime stories on the front pages remained consistent across the Black Press landscape. Social worker Melissa Mae Elliott's master's thesis, "News in the Negro Press," reported that coverage of crime dominated the front pages of black papers. In this regard, African American newspapers similar to other early-twentieth-century American papers typically led with crime stories. In the case of black papers, stories about white criminal acts against African American victims received more attention and editorial commentary. This coverage, according to Elliott, offered psychological relief to readers bombarded with negative stories about African Americans in the white press. "It gives the Negro a certain amount of satisfaction to note the shortcomings of the race which has set the pace for him."[100] The *Defender* and other papers, including the *Chicago Tribune*, regularly ran statistical data on lynching, which they covered as crime as opposed to some white northern and southern papers that either ignored the events or reported on them in a matter-of-fact tone.[101]

"Violently race-conscious" editors used considerable newspaper real estate to document the achievements and accomplishments of African Americans.[102] Elliott's study pointed out that behind coverage on crime, "inspirational news" appeared the most frequently on the front pages of black papers.[103] The Black Press was "the only instrument to bring to the attention of the Negro population stories of heroism by members of its race," remarked Lewis H. Fenderson, assistant professor of English at Howard University. Inspirational stories that chronicled individual and collective successes offered a model to which striving and working blacks might aspire. This coverage was aligned with the objectives of the earliest black papers to combat negative stereotypes of African Americans. News about black achievement, big and small, provided a corrective to the complete omission and distortion of black life in white newspapers.

African American newspapers, before anything else, functioned as a subaltern counterpublic sphere that allowed black people to "secure a status in the white world to which no stigma or inferiority attaches."[104] By retaining the staple objectives of the original Black Press, golden-age African American newspapers remained invested in a collective ideology that racial progress would be attained by broadcasting the merit of black humanity.

Along with publicizing positive aspects of African American life, Black Press editors believed they were also responsible for insuring that African Americans possessed sufficient health and educational information. Dr. A. Wilberforce Williams's health column in the *Defender* directly addressed health issues relevant to newly urbanized African Americans. Williams advised, "All poor mothers should purchase not only a house thermometer but a fever thermometer and learn how to use, read, and interpret it." The *Tribune* introduced a health column in 1924, which, according to the editor, would "help in the improvement of the conditions affecting my people." Many of the columns dealt with public health concerns and diseases such as syphilis and tuberculosis. As with much of the coverage in black newspapers, health editors often framed health issues according to racial ideology. Taking care to remind their readers that the "race health problem" retarded social advancement, doctors combined practical health advice with recommendations for building strong race psychology and physiology.[105] The *Courier's* weekly, "Let There Be Health," written by Dr. B. S. Herben of the New York Tuberculosis Association, offered the most all-purpose advice on matters related to general health and well-being. More than likely a syndicated column written by a white physician, "Let There Be Health" still offered readers coverage about communicable and social diseases that threatened black communities in particular. Many migrants, for example, were unprepared for harsh winters that often left them vulnerable to illness. Poor and overcrowded living conditions also made migrants susceptible to disease.[106]

Despite African American newspapers' objective to uplift the race, they also revealed and fostered a black leisure and recreation culture. In their discussion of athletes such as boxer Joe Louis, reporters for black newspapers combined race pride with news about sports, which demonstrated the centrality of sports in black communities. Regular theatrical columns and stories informed African Americans of various stage and movie house productions. Black newspapers' coverage of these activities indicated that northern migration had not simply offered southerners opportunities for economic advancement but a larger variety of recreational and leisure pastimes. Advertisements for—and reviews of—nightclub acts along with news reports of number runners, gambling operations, and rent parties represented a burgeoning group of readers who availed themselves of these recreational delights.[107]

Black newspapers contrasted these "lowbrow" leisure activities with "high" social events that could be found in the society section. Society news also represented leisure culture but reinforced ideas of African American civility. Virtually every black paper featured a page or two that was devoted to covering black society. Fraternal and social club meetings, the latest functions, and the comings and goings of black elites, as well as a new group of middle-class African Americans, typically made the society page. People relied on society news to know who was who within different communities.[108] Still, this area of the paper, while often derided by whites as well as notable black figures such as sociologist E. Franklin Frazier as portraying African Americans in an affected manner, allowed readers to see themselves in ways that diametrically countered negative black stereotypes.[109] Society sections also highlighted elite clubwomen performing "valuable race work" or attending social functions to benefit charitable causes.

Positive representations aside, coverage of black society exposed class and gender stratification within African American communities as well as within the newspapers themselves. Women were most likely to report news that was social and domestic in nature. Society editors and correspondents Geraldyn Dismond, Marvel Cooke, and a host of other nameless female reporters kept readers updated with the latest entertainment and social events in many urban areas, particularly Harlem. Women's page editors Thelma E. Berlack, Bertha Perry Rhodes, and Julia Bumry Jones controlled the news and information found on women's pages in the *Amsterdam News*, *Tribune*, and *Courier*, respectively. The *Amsterdam News* columns—"The Feminist Viewpoint" written by Berlack and "The Decorator's Letter Box: Expert Advice on Home Decoration"—reflected editors' attempts to differentiate a growing readership and segment the market by class and gender. As the masses of African American women entered into the northern, urban workforce as domestics, factory workers, and teachers, the Black Press provided targeted coverage that spoke to their concerns and interests.

Even as black newspapers continued to fulfill the objectives of uplifting and informing readers, newspapers also served as a major source of entertainment by providing literary and amusing features. Papers regularly featured serial and short stories, book reviews, comic strips, and crossword puzzles. Readers could also find advice columns and personal advertisements that aided men and women wishing to improve their relationships and love lives. Editors placed these features in the second section of the paper, which sometimes included a special magazine insert with photographs of occasions such as baby contests, beauty competitions, and other social events. The *Defender* was savvy enough to market the paper to children by developing the Bud Billiken club and the "*Defender* Junior" page, which provided fun content for the younger set.[110] The entertaining elements of early-twentieth-century black newspapers proved that editors believed that their papers could be both useful and enjoyable. In this regard, the Black Press was well within the American style of journalism of the period. At the same time, African American newspaper editors remained distinctly aware of their influence and power to "exert great forces for good or generate dangerous anti-social influences."[111] In this sense, the burden of racial progress made the job of combining information with entertainment more significant for the Black Press.

Coverage about the black church was one type of news coverage that editors knew satisfied the twin of objectives of racial uplift and entertainment. The need to engage a mass black readership, at the forefront of many decisions on what editors chose to cover, strongly influenced papers to devote relatively sizable portions of the paper to church activities. Practically every paper had a column with the generic title, "Church News." Most readers could depend on papers to announce weekly religious services and corresponding church events and functions. Editors viewed churches from two standpoints. On the one hand, churches, represented one of the major avenues to black social reform in the early twentieth century. It made a great deal of sense from an editorial perspective to heavily report on sermons, church functions, and religious services. In short, editors understood the importance that religious expression held for readers. A 1927 *Tribune* article noted readers' desire for church news, "Once church news is given to newspapers, the editorial chiefs ask for it, phone for it. They realize that the people want it, that they read it."[112] It was no surprise, then, that black newspapers broke up the monopoly that church and religious newspapers had on publicizing church activities and news by increasingly reporting on these topics.

In turn, churches relied on the Black Press to serve as publicity agents for services and events.[113] The *Christian Recorder*, the African Methodist Episcopal Church's newspaper, of Philadelphia, indicated that ministers and pastors should encourage their congregations to read newspapers. "Indeed, every progressive pastor ought [to,] at least once a year, preach a special newspaper sermon and ought to invite the editor or editors of leading Colored papers in his vicinity to present their cause to the people," stated the paper. The idea that "progressive" church leaders should be responsible for promoting their churches in secular newspapers suggested that the *Christian Recorder* believed that despite their orientation, popular black newspapers could spread the gospel. The Black Press' commitment to covering black churches demonstrated the critical role they played in black communities.

Yet, in many ways, black publishers and editors also saw themselves as displacing the church's dominant voice in black communities. *New York Age* editor, T. Thomas Fortune, discussing the importance of the black newspapers almost one hundred years after the founding of *Freedom's Journal*, remarked, "the Negro Press has taken the place of the Negro Preacher." Leaders like Fortune understood that black papers played an equal, if not more significant, role with an emerging mass black readership than religious organizations did. An *Amsterdam News* article picked up on this significance in a bitter complaint about ministers expecting "Free [advertising] Space Without Contributing Anything." The writer ended his article by marveling that black papers reached larger proportions of African Americans than ministers who needed "a wider congregation than may be enclosed within the walls of a church."[114] Despite the *Amsterdam News* writer's rancor, black churches and African American newspapers formed a symbiotic relationship that relied on a diverse black populace that found value in both institutions.

In making space for church news and other specialized coverage, editors recognized the existence of a mass black readership that was made up of different groups of people. However, the belief that a critical segment of readers were working-class urbanites who sought sensational news drove editors' overall approach to coverage. This conception sharply departed from a previous generation of African American newspapers. It also helped to redefine the black newspapers, in one sense, as black sexual spheres even as they continued to function as organs of racial uplift.

SENSATIONALISM IN THE BLACK PRESS

From an editorial vantage point in the American news industry, sensational coverage of crime and sex sold papers. Practically every major newspaper employed sensationalism at the dawn of the twentieth century. Although mid-nineteenth-century newspapers developed yellow journalism, news reporting that used headlines and images designed to appeal to readers' emotions, the twentieth century's technological advancements produced innovative photography and tabloid style formats that allowed for more interpretive reporting. Even newspapers such as the *New York Times*, which long considered itself a "highbrow" news institution, used sensationalism, though to a smaller degree. In contrast, tabloids and other newspapers that viewed their target audience as urban and working-class maintained a philosophy of news coverage where sensationalism reigned supreme. William Randolph Hearst, one of the founders of twentieth-century sensational journalism and owner of a number of tabloid newspapers advised his editors: "Put important items and personal news about well-known people there [front-page]." He further remarked, "The most sensational news can be told if told properly." Sensational news often translated into stories about crime and sex. "Jazz journalists" of the 1920s, particularly, concentrated on love triangles and divorce trials of the rich and famous.[115]

Editors and publishers of papers targeting African Americans believed that their readers wanted and enjoyed sensational news stories no less than their white counterparts. Thus, despite its contradiction with the advocacy objective of the Black Press, editors argued that their main impetus for using sensationalism stemmed from their attempt to satisfy readers' base desires.[116] Prominent African American intellectual and journalist Kelly Miller explained the predominance of sensational headlines on the covers of black papers in this way, "The business of a newspaper is to print what the people will read. Murder, sex sins and theft are never failing sources of public interest." Miller believed that newspapers were following the desires of the masses, and he placed responsibility for black papers' sensational coverage on "the people for wanting what they do."[117] An anonymous 1930 editorial in the *Courier* echoed Miller's commentary: "Where an editor knows that his public is interested in crime and scandal, he would be a poor business man not to capitalize upon that interest."[118] T. Ella Strother's survey of the *Defender* between 1905 and 1975 reveals that scandal represented 58 percent of news stories that appeared on the front page of the paper.[119]

The *Defender*'s, as well as other newspapers, ongoing preoccupation with scandal was also typical of interwar black news coverage. "Since the Great War in their effort to 'sell' the reader and keep him informed about the current sensational news . . . crime, scandal, divorces, and other 'headline' events made the front page," observed ANP founder Claude Barnett.[120] The desire to attract readers overrode any reticence editors may have had in covering sensational divorce trials and sex scandals in the context of racial uplift and protest against discrimination.

Many black news editors believed that working-class African Americans made up a sizable segment of the black public that found pleasure in reading scandal. Describing the different classes of readers that the Black Press catered to, *Courier* columnist John Louis Clarke noted, "Here we have the largest single group to be found, who have little intelligence; indeed, are usually but little advanced above illiteracy." According to Clarke, these readers craved "crime news and items of sensational portent."[121] Clarke acknowledged that it was more than just the "lower strata" that consumed sensationalism. He noted that the "better classes" read sensational news coverage but with less interest. In his critique of black society's refined pretense in Washington, DC, poet and author Langston Hughes wrote, "There appeared, also, to be the same love of scandal among the best folks as among the lower classes."[122] Both Clarke's and Hughes's comments negated Black Press editors' correlation of sensationalism with working-class readers. Instead, they suggested that the appeal of news stories that revolved around sexual intimacy and crime operated in a much wider domain that transcended class boundaries. This meant that not only news stories but any sensational content that touched on similar themes gratified a mass black readership of southern migrants as well as northern working-class, middle-class, and elite African Americans. Short and serial stories, comic strips, advice columns, and photographs—all features of journalism that suffered from the same working-class marginalization as sensationalism—functioned as black sexual public spheres.

Henry F. Arnold, a writer for the *Afro-American*, attempted to soften black newspapers' sensational coverage by observing that white papers often paid for disparaging information about "America's foremost white citizens" while black newspapers waited until the scandal hit the courts before reporting on it. "When the party or parties are carried before the courts, the disgrace has already arrived," stated Arnold. Referencing the ongoing debates in the early twentieth century surrounding whether black papers should publicize scandal, Arnold noted that it was a matter of giving the public what they desired and what they needed in terms of moral edification. Predicting the demise of papers that refused to report scandals, Arnold warned, "No newspaper can long survive if it fails to give the public news of the things which the public wants."[123] If, as Arnold suggested, black newspapers' existence depended on an ongoing relationship with their readership, then it was essential for Black Press editors to develop a deep sense of early-twentieth-century African Americans' desires and interests.

Determining what readers wanted, however, was easier said than done. Many readers angrily protested the coverage of crime and sexual scandals. In his 1943 study of readers' attitudes to the news in the *Defender*, Lincoln University

(Jefferson City, Missouri) journalism professor and *Defender* correspondent Consuelo C. Young indicated that the biggest complaint among the readers she sampled was the sensational coverage on front pages.[124] In an article for the *Afro-American*, Arnold wrote, "Considerable apprehension is felt among members of the race about the scandals, which appear in our papers."[125] In other instances, local leaders held forums to discuss what they believed was the disproportionate amount of space devoted to scandal in the Black Press.[126] These topics were misaligned with what they believed black newspapers should be and do. "I believe a community has every right to be informed of local and national and world-wide happenings," commented Carnes McKinney to the editor of the *New York Age*, one of New York City's more well-known black papers. He continued, "But why not select better news for front pages and headlines?"[127] McKinney's views reflected the ongoing tension between the historical racial uplift mission of the Black Press and its evolution into entertaining news sources for the mass black readership.

Some black newspapers agreed with readers who complained about sensational news stories. Notably, the newspaper, *Norfolk New Journal and Guide* made it clear to their readers that they would not engage in sensational tactics to reports news. An editorial in the paper stated, "Sordid details of crime or scandal which offend public decency have no place in a news story, regardless of how important the story is itself."[128] Unlike many of its counterparts, the *Journal and Guide* determined that it would take a more conservative approach to journalism it believed was conducive to their mission in uplifting African Americans.

In the minds of many editors and reporters, nonetheless, working-class and minimally educated blacks who desired crime and sex scandals continued to represent the reading public in the 1920s and 1930s. Whether this was actually true or not did not strike editors as particularly important. When commentators such as Miller and Clarke deemed it good business sense to cater to readers' interests, they implicitly imagined the power of a mass black readership in constructing what black newspapers were and would be. Although personal editorial philosophy influenced the ways in which these readers' interests were understood and conveyed through coverage, editors also took into consideration their perception of working-class readers' interests, if only to make sure that black newspapers remained profitable. The trick, then, for golden-age black newspapers was to continue to participate in racial uplift and reform while expanding its coverage to engage a mass black readership they imagined found pleasure in reading content about sexuality.

AN AFRICAN AMERICAN MASS READERSHIP
AND BLACK SEXUAL PUBLIC SPHERES

Since the antebellum period, readers equated black newspapers with racial uplift and the protestation of their mistreatment at the hands of white people. This history gave early-twentieth-century readers hope that newspapers would continue to advocate for them in similar ways. However, early-twentieth-century Black Press editors faced with an increasingly segmented reader market viewed their jobs in more expansive ways. Accordingly, editors used sensationalism in the interwar period to draw readers to their newspapers. A greater emphasis on crime and sex shared space with coverage intended to improve black life. Some readers and Black Press critics believed sensational news, particularly with its emphasis on sex, contradicted the ideal of black newspapers as organs of protest and uplift. Whereas crime could be written off as the product of poor education and lack of opportunities, sex was a much more problematic issue. Many readers became less sure that black newspapers would be instrumental in the advancement of the "race." These readers vehemently protested the inclusion of sexual representations in black newspapers.

Nonetheless, coverage of sexual topics transformed black newspapers into a variety of black sexual public spheres in which journalists and readers engaged each other about sexuality. Readers' responses and debates about sexuality indicated deeper class and political distinctions among golden age black newspapers as well as conceptions of a mass black readership. The Black Press drew on these conceptualizations to develop black sexual public spheres that reached beyond respectability to provide a space for readers' pleasure.

Chapter 2

DIVORCE TRIALS AND SEX SCANDALS

Black readers across the nation unfolding their weekly issue of the *Defender* on July 18, 1925, took in the headline "Bare Scandal in Divorce Case" and learned, by reading the article right below, that Dr. I. Garland Penn Jr., pastor of a church in Chicago, had filed for "absolute divorce" from his wife Mrs. Helen G. Penn for "extremely lewd and lascivious behavior" with a "prominent Louisville" man.[1] According to the article, "local circles" reported that the Penns had long experienced trouble in their marriage, but senior religious members in the community ordered them to "patch up" their domestic troubles. Unable to resolve their marital discord, however, Penn Jr. filed for divorce in Jefferson circuit court in Louisville, Kentucky, where he and Mrs. Penn still maintained a legal residence. While the vast majority of readers taking in the details of the case had never met Garland Penn Jr. or his wife, the *Defender* chose to run their divorce as its lead story. Why the paper's editorial staff made this decision had less to do with the details of the case, though they, salacious in nature, might have been of great interest to readers. Rather, it was Penn Jr.'s social status that catapulted his private life onto the *Defender*'s front page.

In 1925, Penn Jr. represented the epitome of an educated, refined race leader. As the son of prominent clergyman and journalist, Dr. I. Garland Penn Sr., and a minister himself, he was the progeny of an old black guard. He and others of similar status viewed themselves as members of a New Negro class that represented the better elements of African American life. Indeed, Penn Jr.'s friction with his wife came to light just four months after Alain Locke, "father of the Harlem Renaissance" and philosopher, wrote his essay "Enter the New Negro." In the essay, Locke broadly referred to the power of writers, artists, and other leading African Americans in the 1920s to overhaul retrograde images of "aunties," "uncles," and "mammies" with cultural productions.[2] An era of unparalleled production of writing and visual images demonstrated the weight different media formats sustained in demonstrating African American humanity. On the surface, Penn Jr. certainly did not fit the profile of the writers and artists that Locke and others viewed as ushering in the age of the New Negro. Instead he was more representative of an "old-line" black Protestant leadership that had emerged in early-nineteenth-century northern cities.

Nonetheless, a new generation of black religious leaders had to contend with growing a mass black readership who participated in a consumer marketplace and challenged the "natural" primacy of ministers, professionals and businessmen.[3] To this end, Penn Jr. and other early-twentieth-century middle-class and elite blacks found it difficult to keep unsavory details of their lives from public view in the Black Press. The open display of Penn Jr.'s private life through the coverage of his court case complicated, if not countered, his ability to live up to the parameters of respectability demanded of the African American elite and middle classes. At the same time, the coverage of his divorce appeased the imagined interest of a mass black readership that desired scandalous news about ministers.

This chapter discloses how the coverage of divorce and sex scandals, through the examination of select cases, in the Black Press between 1925 and 1930 functioned as a black sexual public sphere. The Black Press fed their audience a steady diet of front-page articles that detailed private intimate and sexual matters between middle-class and elite black couples during what is commonly known as the New Negro movement and the Harlem Renaissance. In keeping with emerging class categories within migration and urbanization, Black Press editors imagined a working-class readership who desired this coverage and sought to challenge the moral authority of middle-class and elite blacks.

Coverage of sex scandals and divorce trials did not appear in a vacuum. News reports on the latest divorces and the principal parties involved overlapped with an emerging discourse about the urban working class and poor black masses and their immorality relative to their "better-heeled" counterparts. An equally significant promotion of black folk cultural behavior and expression in response to the effort to center the black middle class coincided with front-page stories about sexual strife and conflict between couples. Closely examining Black Press coverage highlights class tensions, evolving sexual mores, the role of medicine and forensic sciences, the position of the Black Press in private matters and respectability, and community dynamics in the early twentieth century. Together these things reveal that contests and struggles over sexual matters within lower civil courts were heavily imbricated with class frictions that rested on the social changes between African Americans wrought by migration and urbanization.

Historically, African Americans' relationship to the judicial system has been largely conceptualized through their struggles for civil rights and social justice. However, the Black Press's extensive coverage of civil court trials demonstrated that readers were also interested in cases that involved infidelity and betrayal. Just as importantly, attention to sex scandals and divorce trials in the Black Press demonstrated how black institutions, such as Howard University in the case of Washington, DC, enabled black elites to define themselves as moral and chaste in contrast to poor and working-class African Americans.

While editors did not reveal evidence from readers that indicated their desire for news stories about divorce and sexual misdeeds, the concurrent rise of the "black folk" and the "better classes" of African Americans transformed this coverage into a black sexual public sphere that brought black class tensions into sharper relief.

CLASS, URBANIZATION, AND MIGRATION

Heavily publicized narratives about divorce and sexual indiscretion within the lower civil courts highlighted the Black Press' conception of a black sexual public sphere that was wrought by the twin driving forces of migration and urbanization. By virtue of the coverage that Black Press editors and publishers chose to feature on their front pages, they created a black community that was united in its recognition of the growing class divisions among themselves. In this regard, divorce trials and sex scandal coverage disclosed sexuality and class as important factors that disrupted the social privilege of elite and middle-class African Americans in the early twentieth century. Black newspapers used considerable space to document the achievements and accomplishments of African Americans. They were "the only instrument to bring to the attention of the Negro population stories of heroism by members of its race," remarked Fenderson. Inspirational stories that chronicled individual and collective successes offered a model to which striving and working blacks might aspire. The idea behind this coverage reflected the objectives of the earliest black newspapers to combat negative stereotypes of African Americans. However, the impetus for the stories also coincided with the belief that black papers were social and educational instruments dedicated to "inculcate race pride, loyalty, solidarity, and ambition" among the black masses.[4]

Early-twentieth-century editors' belief that readers longed for stories about people's personal sexual transgressions coincided with the transformation of cities into places where heterogeneous groups of African Americans lived and worked. As southern migrants poured into urban communities, the distinction between the "pre-migration upper class" residents and other African American city dwellers became less clear. Growing numbers of black businessmen and professionals (physicians, lawyers, teachers, journalists, and so forth) developed companies and organizations that capitalized on migrants' needs and desires for services and goods that most African Americans could not obtain from white businesses as a result of racism. In 1930, one Chicago black physician stated in reference to migrants, "I do not believe that this office building would have been here today if it had not been for those Negroes who came from the South. In less that thirty-eight years we have increased from five to two hundred and fifty doctors."[5] Business and professional classes of African Americans gradually supplanted old settlers and emerged as a new black "cream of society." Still, some old settlers, unwilling to relinquish their social status, continued to claim that they reflected the *true* upper class based on their education, social status, or length of their residency in cities if nothing else.[6] In some sense, then, migration helped many African Americans achieve their desire for class mobility. Larger numbers of southern migrants with thick accents and country clothing milling around urban areas offered elite and middle-class blacks tangible proof of their status and social standing.

Urbanization and black migration also produced a market for human-interest stories about elite and middle-class blacks who represented themselves as diametrically different in behavior and culture from other African Americans among a growing mass black readership. Rural migrants' entrance into cities between 1915 and 1940 instituted class boundaries between African Americans that had not been in place in the late nineteenth century. "Old settlers," servants of wealthy whites, and a small group of successful politicians, business, and professional men and their families frequently viewed southern migrants with disdain for their lack of sophistication and country airs. An upper-class African American woman in early-twentieth-century Chicago revealed her anxiety regarding southern newcomers:

> When the Negro started coming to Chicago, I didn't know what to do. I would run to see Mr. X (a leading colored man) and say to him, "X what are we going to do with all these Negroes from the South coming in here?

They look terrible. They sit down on the street car beside white people and I am sure there is going to be trouble." He would always tell me that these were my people but I would always answer him that I didn't belong to any such people.[7]

The woman was concerned that "Negroes from the South" might fail to abide by the de facto laws around black–white relationships. Many blacks, like this woman, considered themselves old settlers who proudly cited their family's presence in northern cities as far back as a hundred years or more and defined their class though their ability to delicately navigate their blackness without overstepping racial boundaries.

Angst over what was perceived as southern dress and expression particularly drove old settlers' objections to migrants.[8] As far as longtime black city residents were concerned, southern identity was synonymous with backwardness and uncouth behavior, while they defined themselves as respectable and refined. Behavior such as wearing head rags, bedroom slippers, and overalls automatically proclaimed a person's migrant status. Other conduct such as speaking loudly and hanging out on street corners was also associated with city newcomers.[9] The *Defender* regularly published lists of "Do's and Don'ts" to teach Chicago migrants, uninitiated in the ways of black northerners, how to behave properly. The paper, along with members of the Urban League and other black social reformers, designated themselves as the arbiters of respectability and highlighted its incongruity with southern behavior.[10]

Because the economic circumstances could vary widely between and within the different groups living in close proximity, people could not always reach common ground on who was in and who was out when it came to specific class groups. African Americans particularly viewed codes of appropriate behavior as the steps on the path to full citizenship. Whether one worked in a professional setting or in a labor-intensive environment, elite and middle-class African Americans theoretically subscribed to a set of behaviors they believed set them apart from the black masses who made up the majority of the black population.[11] What middle-class and elite blacks shared with each other and with their white counterparts, however, was an allegiance to mores and social rituals dependent on public decorum.[12] Thus, status and comportment, as for earlier generations, also helped to define middle- and upper-class segments of black communities in the 1920s. Individuals who possessed both economic and social means to formally and informally espouse and practice uplift ideology characterized what it meant to be elite. Swedish economist and sociologist Gunnar Myrdal described the black elite as the most race conscious. They provide the leadership and often almost the entire membership of the nationally established Negro defense organizations, such as the local branches of the N. A. A. C. P. But they sometimes feel great difficulty in identifying themselves with the Negro masses whose spokesmen they are. . . . Their social ambition is to keep up the distinction. In private they are often the severest critics of the Negro masses.[13]

Economic wealth as well as personal conduct characterized elite status in white society. While middle- and upper-class African Americans often earned more than working-class and poor blacks, they lacked the institutional and material wealth of affluent whites. This meant that residential and social segregation between classes was out of the question for most African Americans. Eugene Gordon remarked, "That is why, in any large gathering of Afro-American elite, the sheep are found rubbing noses with the goats."[14] Negative descriptions of working-class and poor blacks as "goats" aside, Gordon touched on the unique aspect of social class among African Americans.

In an effort to establish greater primacy over African American newcomers, longtime residents of cities established clubs that catered exclusively to individuals that could prove their families' long-term residence in urban areas.[15] Manners and customs reflecting respectability could be actualized in social clubs and associations found in many African American communities in the 1920s. To some degree, membership in a club or association marked a person's class position more than a professional position or occupation. Clubs provided a space for the "leisure-time of the leading social classes of Negroes."[16] While working-class blacks also joined clubs, their upper- and middle-class counterparts were much more likely to participate in clubs with bylaws and constitutions that emphasized public deportment and restraint to its members. In principle, clubs disciplined and asked members who did not comply with these conventions to leave the organization. Elite and middle-class blacks believed they set the moral tone for behavior for all African Americans. Making this case, African American anthropologist and sociologist St. Clair Drake wrote:

> Associations and churches thus become significant indices to economic class and status levels, and through the sanctions they exert become the guardians of the standards of "refinement" and "respectability," and the *modus vivendi* for upward social mobility.[17]

In this sense, elite and middle-class African Americans believed that social clubs and organizations helped to inculcate upper- and middle-class values as well as delineate them from the masses of poor and working-class African Americans.

Newspapers, in this regard, aided in the development of black middle-class society. St. Clair Drake and Horace Cayton reported that in Chicago, "'Society' publicity is highly prized. Every social club has its reporter who must see that notices of club meetings are inserted in the weekly press and that favorable accounts of dances and other special events, accompanied by pictures, will get into the papers."[18] Society news reinforced ideas of African American civility. Virtually every black paper featured a page or two committed to covering black society. Fraternal and social club meetings, the latest functions, and the comings and goings of black elites as well as a new group of middle-class African Americans typically made the society page. This area of the paper, while often derided by whites as portraying African Americans in an affected manner, allowed readers to see themselves in ways that diametrically countered white-constructed racist stereotypes.[19]

Much of the demand for news about black society came from the quarters of the elite and middle class who sought acknowledgment and confirmation of their ability to perform a set of behaviors that differentiated themselves from the masses. Claude Barnett, founder of the ANP, remarked:

> Men and women scan the weekly newspapers for the personal notes which might include themselves; to become informed of latest or coming weddings, recital, convention or charity bizarre; to be apprised of the fashionable parties, banquets, and club activities. To know who is who . . . one reads the society pages of any leading weekly.[20]

Barnett's comments suggest that black elites and the African American middle class expected the Black Press to function as a public relations manager of sorts, crafting and manipulating their public image. However, unlike the conventional public relations firm, the Black Press answered to different constituencies. This meant two important things: (1) Black newspapers committed themselves to maintaining a positive relationship with a variety of readers, and (2) the representation of events and people in the Black Press could be widely interpreted.

Therefore, rather than black middle-class publicity being understood solely as a model for appropriate behavior, it confirmed some working-class African Americans' perceptions that middle- and upper-class African Americans behaved in pretentious and snobbish ways. Drake and Cayton wrote: "The double subordination of the Negro lower class means that some of their ritual condemnation will be focused on the Negroes above them."[21] Labeled as "dicty," "hinkty," or "muckti mucks" by many newly transplanted migrants and black workers, black society represented wealthy, snobbish, and uptight African Americans. The word "dicty" was especially popular and signified urban slang employed exclusively by ordinary African Americans in the 1920s and 1930s to capture their growing resentment of more prosperous African Americans.[22]

Harlem Renaissance artists' representation of working-class African Americans in relationship to the "Negro middle class" and the "high-class Negro" represented another expression of intraracial class tension in the early twentieth century. Discussing the challenge of the African American artist to create racially authentic art in his famous 1926 essay, "The Negro Artist and the Racial Mountain," Langston Hughes derisively described elite and middle-class blacks as "smug" and "aping of things white." Hughes viewed African American upper- and middle-class status as a rejection of black authenticity that could be found among the black masses or who he described as the "low-down folks, the so-called common element."[23]

The racialization of class stratification also appeared in Rudolph Fisher's and Zora Neale Hurston's writings. Their observation of Harlem's diverse black populace provided them with opportunities to comment on class conflict within African American communities. Hurston's valorization of dialect and Fisher's short stories often featured plots that highlighted the sharp geospatial class lines that physically separated the "rats," poor and working-class African Americans, from elite and middle-class blacks or "high-toned dickties" in Harlem.[24] Hughes's, Fisher's, and Hurston's own complicated class relationship with an older brand of African American leadership inspired them to reject the premise that artistic expression should eschew the working-class and poorer segments of black life and concentrate on a black middle class that was comparable to a white one. As the self-defined "Niggerati," Hughes and Hurston, along with writers Bruce Nugent and Wallace Thurman among others, mocked what they saw as the efforts of the African American bourgeoisie to transcend their blackness by cloaking it in respectable behavior as defined by white, middle-class values.

The notion of respectability is what rankled many working-class African Americans who described elite and middle-class African Americans as "dicty," or acting superior because of their class status. They viewed elite and middle-class blacks as putting on a "front" to hide their true selves from public view. A front was the idea that "decorous *public* behavior" should be stressed at all times despite any private behavior or activities that might counter one's public image. Working-class African Americans excoriated middle- and upper-class blacks who fronted, labeling them "hypocrites" and crowing with delight "at finding a chink in the 'stuck-ups armor.'" Sociologist and regular columnist and critic of the press Kelly Miller believed that black readers particularly reveled in the dressing down of people in high places. "He is delighted to see somebody 'roasted'; the hotter of the roasting, the keener the delight," wrote Miller.[25] Divisions between those who "stress conventional, middle-class 'American' public behavior and those who ignore it" defined class categories among many African Americans in the early twentieth century.[26]

CLASS AND MARRIAGE

Marriage also helped draw a sharper line between African American social classes and offered a pathway to respectability and racial uplift.[27] Late-nineteenth-century black reform correlated racial progress with marriage and emphasis on family life. Whereas marriage had once been a way for people to demonstrate their civility, the early twentieth century saw it increasingly become a site in which men and women forged compatible sexual and romantic relationships with each other. Men and women, white and black, pushed Victorian values aside as they developed and merged new values to coexist with traditional conceptions of marital relationships. Easier access to birth control and shifts in women's social status stressed "companionate marriage" where both partners embraced emotional compatibility and mutual physical attraction and sexual enjoyment.[28] Marriage, then, reflected a process of changing values and ideals in which romantic and sexual relationships could be worked out between men and women.

Nonetheless, marriage remained a political mechanism in the twentieth century for African Americans to stress their suitability for full citizenship even as it offered elite and middle-class African Americans opportunities to make manifest their respectability. Highlighting one's morality was particularly important in the midst of a growing consumer culture that emerged out of rapidly urbanizing areas filled with migrants from the South. Movie theaters, dance halls, and spaces of leisure, which allowed men and women to occupy the same social spaces, upset traditional definitions of morality. The increased visibility of black life in places such as Harlem created more opportunities to sexually fetishize black life.[29] Moreover, a growing sociological discourse about the urban poor, unwed mothers, and "fathers on leave" in the early twentieth century made marriage an even greater piece of the picture of middle-class black respectability.[30]

Viewing marriage as a path to racial progress, however, became increasingly complicated. More people dissolved their unions in lockstep with the ideal of companionate marriage. Americans' migration to cities and participation in industrialized labor created greater opportunities for people, particularly women, to maintain their autonomy outside of traditional marital relationships.[31] At the beginning of 1920, one in six marriages ended in divorce. More men and women, believing that the purpose of marriage was to achieve happiness and personal satisfaction, availed themselves of different opportunities to end their marriages.[32] Many contemporary male critics strove to explain the higher rates of divorce by pointing to women's suffrage and their larger presence in educational institutions and various labor fields. Indeed, women's decreasing economic and political dependence on men offered numbers of women avenues of escape from unhappy marriages.[33]

Social reformers and sociologists alike, however, believed that the "natural" evils of city life made it virtually impossible for marriages to survive in an urban context.[34] It seems that everyone had a theory on why divorce rates continued to rise in the first part of the twentieth century. While black social reformers paid more attention to marriage in conduct and advice manuals, divorce was a topic largely left up to popular music and fiction to cover. Zora Neale Hurston's short story "Monkey Junk: A Satire on Modern Divorce," which appeared in a 1927 issue of the *Courier*, demonstrated how narratives about marital discord served as sources of critique and humor. The story chronicles the marriage and divorce trial of a young woman and a man in Harlem and poked fun at urban divorce.[35]

BLACK SOCIETY JOURNALISM

Black newspapers were not reticent in discussing divorce, particularly when it involved elite and middle-class African Americans, within a much larger context of coverage on the upper classes. Ironically, the desire of upper- and middle-class African Americans to document their social activities and achievements also enabled black papers to unveil their private sexual lives, not only to their peers but to working-class readers. Newspaper coverage of the sexual infidelity of the most "respected" members of early-twentieth-century African American communities confirmed that news editors believed that their readers gained pleasure from their exposure of black society's most private matters. Coverage of prominent black people's sexual lives in the Black Press reflected the rise of celebrity culture in American society. T. Ella Strother's study of the *Defender* indicates that the "personality story" dominated the paper's news coverage between 1920 and 1940.[36] Many *Defender* news stories that revolved around famous or well-known people placed them in the center of a particular scandal. Most black newspapers in this regard did not vary from white papers, which also featured the peccadilloes of the rich and famous in the early twentieth century.

"Celebrity journalism," the idea that "names make news," peaked in the 1920s and 1930s. "Everyday" figures deemed newsworthy by their participation in certain activities or institutions were also included in celebrity coverage. By the end of the nineteenth century, most newspapers had a well-established pattern of news coverage that involved editors assigning reporters to a "beat." These beats or areas of life—the urban public—included city hall, the courts, churches, high society, and theaters along with other arenas of leisure and recreation. Reporters often considered individuals or groups involved in matters within one of these areas to be newsworthy and developed stories around them.[37] Such new stories transformed people who were considered unremarkable by most standards in the nineteenth century into public figures of the early twentieth century.

Newspapers, then, made specific people "visible" and created an aura of notoriety around them that fed readers' growing interest in their private lives. The typical markers of fame and status at the turn of the twentieth century began to include a person's involvement in the growing entertainment and sports fields as well as politics. Newspapers informed readers of these figures' accomplishments, identifying them as famous or as celebrities. However, modern journalism developed and shaped readers' definition of what defined a public figure by covering "well-known" people from a wider segment of society. For instance, late-nineteenth-century newspaper column titles such as "People Often Talked Of" and "Millionaire Society" featured news of people well-known in high society but often unrecognizable to the average reader. Consequently, these columns shaped readers' consciousness of who was famous and important. Celebrity journalism not only mirrored readers' conceptions of fame and fortune but also helped to create them.[38]

When it came to early-twentieth-century African American life, class and prominence were also bound up together. Within the Black Press, professional and middle-class blacks, along with entertainers and sports figures, were considered newsworthy. Editors and journalists' attention to these groups meant that they devoted considerable front-page coverage to their private sexual lives. Melissa Mae Elliott viewed readers' interest in the divorce of figures such as W. E. B. Du Bois's daughter Yolande Du Bois and Booker T. Washington's son's marriage a reflection of a developing sophistication among African Americans.[39] Ironically, a mass black readership's pride in middle- and upper-class blacks' ability to "equal the Caucasian at his own game of snobbery" fueled news coverage of African American society."[40] Stories about divorce scandal also functioned as a black sexual public sphere, a space in which editors imagined that a mass black readership found pleasure in witnessing the shortcomings of elite and middle-class African Americans.

DIVORCE TRIALS

Black newspaper editors imagined that their readers wanted as much news as possible about preachers. Historically, preachers represented some of the most prominent black leaders in both rural and urban communities. Simultaneously serving as politician, teacher, and spiritual guide, the "negro preacher" was the consummate race leader of the late nineteenth and early twentieth centuries. Even more, black preachers played an essential role in aiding migrants to find jobs, housing, and food as they adjusted to the vast differences between the North and South. The changing landscape of African American life, where formal education became integral to leadership positions, placed many ministers under the scrutiny of newspapers as well as their congregations. An ANP article, written by William Pickens and featured in all three national papers as well as in the *Amsterdam News*, noted the frequency with which news about preachers appeared in newspapers. "The preachers are occupying entirely too much space in the bad news of the front pages nowadays," commented Pickens.[41] His comments did not indicate whether he believed ministers actually committed more sexual misdeeds than other public figures or whether newspapers simply documented their misdeeds in greater proportion.

Some newspaper critics suggested that the Black Press unfairly focused on scandals involving African American religious figures. A year before Pickens's comments, Eugene Gordon, a black columnist for the *Boston Globe*, stated, "[black] newspapers themselves are often scornful in their attitudes toward brothers of the cloth and are generous with space publishing their falls from grace."[42] Reverend Councill M. Harris of Portsmouth, Oregon, also believed that newspapers paid undue attention to his colleagues. Directly responding to Pickens, Reverend Harris stated "there are thousands of preachers who never get on the front pages when they are doing good—it is only when the preacher stumbles that he becomes the talk of the country."[43] Papers, then, emphasized preachers' involvement in scandals, underscoring, in some cases, the slowly eroding authority of the Black Church and the growing secularization of African Americans. Growing numbers of black men and women in places such as Chicago viewed the Black Church as a "racket" and found that ministers often did not practice what they preached. Heavily scrutinized by both church members and nonmembers, pastors who served black communities faced "continuous community criticism."[44] Thus, coverage of preachers captured their influence in various quarters of black life as well as the editors' belief that news of ministers' private affairs, especially sexual ones, generated readership.[45]

Papers devoted much of their attention to pastors of large urban churches with sizable congregations. Reporters could not be bothered with covering the numerous smaller, "lower-class" storefront churches, which dotted many city blocks. Any coverage of storefront ministers usually dealt with their legitimacy as ordained ministers. The black elite and middle-class often viewed storefront churches, heavily attended by poorer and working-class blacks, as inferior. Many middle-class ministers wished to see these churches disappear. Storefront church congregants' propensity to "get happy" and feel the spirit move them to their feet in ecstatic praise embarrassed middle-class ministers. This sort of worship did not comport with the modern image that New Negro ministers desired for the masses of African Americans. Black newspapers like the *Defender* supported this position, remarking, "We have passed the store front age. The pastor should represent a capable and dignified leadership in the community."[46] This sort of expectations as well as the high profile of ministers, particularly of larger congregations, meant that the Black Press viewed their activities and personal lives as sources of interest to their readers. In light of this, sexual scandal involving ministers regularly appeared on the front pages of early-twentieth-century black newspapers.

In 1925, Pittsburgh's Central Baptist Church (CBC) maintained a congregation with over 6,000 members and was one of the largest denominations in Pittsburgh.[47] It is not difficult to imagine, then, that the *Courier* believed that the church's prominence would draw readers' interest when the paper featured a January 25, 1925, front-page exposé on its minister, Reverend W. Augustus Jones. The paper reported that Reverend Jones had publicly accused his wife, Edna Jones, of extramarital relationships with a series of men, including several other leading churchmen. The *Courier* also revealed that Mrs. Jones, among other accusations, smoked Pall Mall cigarettes and called men "hot papas."[48] Readers also learned that she had four husbands, including one who was white, prior to her marriage to Reverend Jones.

The *Courier* further shaped readers' perceptions of Mrs. Jones with another front-page article that reported on Mrs. Jones's appearance before the Deacon's Board. It described her as telling a "pathetic 'sob' story" and "clad in a soft clinging gown, her lovely face radiant, her eyes liquid and luminous with tears."[49] In the weeks following Reverend Jones's initial charges, both the *Courier* and *Amsterdam News* reported a CBC meeting in front of several hundred church members who greeted Mrs. Jones's "impassioned plea" for mercy and her counter charges against Reverend Jones for committing his own infidelities with "hisses, impertinent laughs, and shouts of derision."[50] In making the church members' responses to Mrs. Jones known to readers, black newspapers both represented and re-created a sense of community that many migrants had experienced back home in the South. News in small black southern towns was typically shared through the "grapevine" or informal networks of information that included everything from information about threats of white violence to who was "stepping out" with someone's woman. In the context of the Black Press, the grapevine served to lay bare—to a mass black readership—preachers and their spouses' sexual foibles. It, then, became a black sexual public sphere, opening up potential dialogue about the sexual behavior of respected community members in the private spaces of readers' homes. The reports of Central Baptist's church members' unsympathetic response to Mrs. Jones suggested that a court of public opinion put little stock in the charges she launched against Reverend Jones. Later newspaper accounts reprinted a letter from church council members suspending any action toward Reverend Jones regarding his wife's charges until the divorce proceedings could be heard and decided upon in court. The council reasoned that it would do little good to publicly disclose more charges that would harm both Jones and the church. The church council members' decision to "wait and see" before a final determination about Reverend Jones's status underscored the eroding influence that the Black Church had on African American life, including marital and domestic matters. Instead, many of Pittsburgh's black residents gathered and convened at places such as the YMCA and libraries rather than churches and held a "distinct apathy" to attending regular religious services.[51] Coverage of the Jones's case operated within African Americans' shift from the Church as the sole center of civic and social life.

Increasingly, African Americans no longer viewed the Black Church as possessing the unique power to enforce moral standards. Cheryl D. Hicks argues that early-twentieth-century black working-class families strategically used the courts and New York State laws to control young women's behavior.[52] While black churches and ministers continued to hold sway over private matters in African American families, the courts attenuated their power. The Jones case further confirmed this change by demonstrating that civil courts, *not* the Church, played a larger role in resolving infidelity in ministers' marriages. Overall, newspapers played an important part in the increasing value placed on civil courts to resolve private matters in black homes. Coverage of court proceedings normalized their role in adjudicating disputes between family members. The coverage of the Jones case concluded with reports one year later that local courts had granted Reverend Jones a divorce on the grounds of "indignity to the person" stemming from Mrs. Jones's alleged extramarital affairs.[53]

Readers followed other extensive newspaper coverage of ministers' divorce proceedings throughout the 1920s. In the *Flipper v. Flipper* case, papers reported that Pearl Flipper filed for divorce from her husband, Rev. Dr. Carl Flipper, pastor of the AME Church of St. Louis, Missouri, in August 1927, for his sexual dalliances with a local high school teacher and another woman.[54] As the daughter of a former member of the North Carolina Legislature and son of an AME bishop, the Flippers' combined status made their domestic trouble national news. Their case received front-page coverage in the *Afro-American, Defender,* and *Courier* along with local papers. For over six months between 1927 to 1928, papers reported on various court filings in the case that included accusations of sexual misconduct and behavior unbecoming to the sanctity of marriage. By April 1928, newspapers informed their readers that the courts awarded Mrs. Flipper a divorce and custody of the former couple's two sons. According to the *Afro-American,* a crowded courtroom eagerly anticipated hearing the specific details of the case but was treated only to the verdict. The Flippers had opted to have their testimony taken privately in circuit court. Their privilege and financial status afforded them an opportunity to reestablish the privacy the Black Press had removed in broadcasting their marital woes on the newspapers' front pages. Nonetheless, the damage, at least from the Flippers' perspective, had already been done. News coverage of their case certainly served up more discussions in a black sexual public sphere among readers about the associations between class, religion, and sexuality.

Even as the Flippers might have been dismayed with public accounts of their conjugal disputes, other African Americans involved in marital scandals played to the court of public opinion by calculatedly using the Black Press' coverage to their advantage. A 1928 front-page article in the *Courier* reported that Mrs. John F. Moore, wife of Reverend Moore of the Sharp St. M. E. Church in Sandy Springs, Maryland, filed charges with the trustee board against Mrs. Bishop, church choir leader. According to Mrs. Moore, Mrs. Bishop had carried on an affair with her husband that had "wrecked" her home.[55] Interviewed by the *Afro-American,* Mrs. Monroe spoke at length about her husband's participation in petting parties with Mrs. Bishop and his disregard for her feelings about the affair. A month later, Mrs. Bishop responded to these allegations with her own interview with the paper and filed legal action against Mrs. Monroe for slander. Mrs. Monroe, maintained Mrs. Bishop, "lived under a jealous delusion" and had accused many other women of conducting extramarital affairs with her husband.[56]

In taking their cases directly to the *Afro-American,* both Mrs. Bishop and Mrs. Monroe appealed to a mass black readership to leverage how their respective cases might be decided by the church's trustee board. Because the *Afro-American* was a national paper with audiences that largely spanned the eastern seaboard, the women's divulgence of their respective positions with regard to the case exceeded their local communities. Both women knew that readers found their case interesting and that it was the subject of much conversation among everyday black men and women. Their collective thoughts and opinions mattered. It is impossible to know exactly what readers thought about the case or any other case, for that matter. Nonetheless, the fact that principal parties in different cases either sought to obscure intimate details or make them available indicates how news coverage offered a black sexual public sphere to discuss as well as enjoy the sexual issues in divorce trials.

Black newspapers' treatment of the Jones, Flipper, and Bishop cases was emblematic of the attention paid to ministers' personal relationships. Reporters documented ministers' moral "stumbles," in part, because everyday African Americans viewed their preachers and churches in less sacrosanct ways. Ironically, papers' regular exploitation of clergy's private lives indicated that ministers continued to wield considerable influence and power among African Americans in the early twentieth century. Ministers' prominence deemed them sources of interest and news.[57] This prominence, however, came at a cost to many ministers since it cast their most unsavory behavior into the public eye. Moreover, the attention to ministers' private lives disputed the chaste, moral image that many ministers, particularly of sizable middle- and mixed-class congregations, wished to portray of themselves. Preachers often assailed lower-class African Americans, both adults and youth, for patronizing "jive joints" and imbibing alcohol, behavior that defied Christian principles.

Newspaper coverage made it difficult for middle-class ministers to uphold this desired image. In their effort to produce news that would incite readers' interest, black papers created a black sexual public sphere that challenged respectable preachers and, by extension, their churches. Within this space, readers could question traditional African American leadership bestowed in the guise of ministers and also form opinions about sexual behavior. Newspaper coverage remade venerable male ministers and their wives into disreputable and lascivious characters.

BLACK MIDDLE-CLASS DIVORCE

At the same time that preachers found their private lives displayed on the front pages, the Black Press made readers privy to the personal sexual details of an emerging black middle class. Sociologists Drake and Cayton's work on the black middle class in Chicago is emblematic of some of the growing class anxieties of African Americans aspiring to move further up the social ladder from the working class and poor blacks moving into cities. The notion of "getting ahead" and "advancing the race" dominated the minds of the African American middle class. In both instances, according to Drake and Cayton, early-twentieth-century African Americans sought individual social and economic achievement that reflected well on the entire race as well as advanced their specific personal interests.[58] Middle-class African American in this sense viewed not only their professional but their social lives as exemplars. They also confirmed their separation from the black lower classes. However, the adherence to a set of social codes and values made black middle-class couples vulnerable to public scrutiny if they experienced marital troubles or sought a divorce.

The Osbornes discovered this firsthand when they experienced issues in their marriage in 1925. Covered extensively by the *Afro-American* and the *Defender*, as well as reported by several other papers for nearly two years, the Osborne divorce case emphasized both the class and sexual dimensions of Washington, DC, that was a microcosm for similar issues playing out in other African American marriages, including those of ministers, in the early twentieth century. On November 7, 1925, the *Afro-American* and *Defender* announced the opening trial of the Osborne divorce trial and promised that it would be "one of the most sensational" divorce cases the public would witness.[59] James B. Osborne and Ruth A. Osborne, married on June 25, 1920, were parents of a four-year-old daughter, Gloria. The *Afro-American* revealed that they brought in a combined income of $270 per month. James Osborne worked in the veterans bureau while his wife was described as a temporary employee at the Navy's Bureau of Navigation. The Osbornes belonged to the "brown middle-class." People like the Osbornes had been able to benefit from the post–World War I expansion of the federal government. Increased public service employment opportunities in the 1920s allowed couples such as the Osbornes degrees of social and economic mobility.[60]

The Osbornes' connections with other prominent African Americans solidified their class and social status and helped dictate the amount and type of coverage the papers would devote to them. Mrs. Osborne was the sister-in-law of Fred Wilkinson, Howard University registrar, and one of her sisters was married to a Washington, DC, public school teacher. Society columns regularly featured the couple's attendance at social gatherings and travels in the region. Just a year prior to the announcement of their divorce, the *Courier's* "Eve Lynn Chats 'Bout Society and Folks" column listed the couple as one of the many society folks visiting relatives for the summer.[61] Another front-page article described the couple as "very popular in the social circles of the nation's capital."[62]

According to the *Afro-American* and the *Defender*, Mrs. Osborne had filed for a "limited divorce" as a result of Mr. Osborne's alleged cruelty and desertion. Mrs. Osborne stated that she had been hospitalized for a period of two weeks beginning on September 1, 1925, for a private operation. The only communication from her husband, via her sisters and their spouses, indicated that if she were to return home, "he would kick her down the stairs." Mrs. Osborne reported that she was unable to retrieve her personal belongings because her husband had locked her out of the marital home. Mr. Osborne responded with his own bill of divorce declaring that his wife had engaged in infidelity with Benjamin B. Pinn, a local real estate agent, between 1924 and 1925 and asked for a complete termination of their marriage. He denied having ever been cruel to his wife prior to learning that she had committed adultery. According to Mr. Osborne, he learned that the private operation his wife recently had was due to the "ravages of a disease" inflicted upon her by assignation with Mr. Pinn.[63]

Like the airing of preachers' private squabbles, the Osborne case revealed that divorce was not a private affair.[64] The community often held sway over familial matters within the confines of legal proceedings. The *Afro-American* reported that five neighbors of Mr. Osborne submitted affidavits in circuit court that Mrs. Osborne lacked the maternal capacity to care for the Osborne's young daughter. The neighbors also testified that they had observed Pinn, the real estate agent, regularly calling on Mrs. Osborne "day and night when no one else was there except Mrs. Osborne."[65] Despite the neighbors' testimony, Mrs. Osborne was awarded temporary custody of Gloria with regular visitation for Mr. Osborne.[66] On December 19, 1925, the *Defender* revealed that Mrs. Osborne won another bout in the legal battle against her husband. According to the account, Mrs. Osborne's attorneys, Raymond Neudecker and Bartrand Emmerson Jr. had successfully accomplished the removal of Mr. Osborne's accusation of his wife's adultery, including a charge that one of her affairs had resulted "in her physical condition which necessitated an operation," from the bill for divorce. Ironically, in reporting to readers that the offending paragraphs would be omitted, the *Defender* exposed the Osbornes' private life to a much wider audience than the court proceedings would have done.[67]

When the Osborne trial came up in district court in 1927, a little over one year had passed. The *Defender* continued to promote the case as one that shook Washington, DC's black society circles and rehashed for its readers the details of the case, helping readers understand the main issues that needed to be resolved for a judgment to be made about the case.[68] Dr. Carson, the attending physician at the private hospital where Mrs. Osborne received medical treatment, testified that he had performed an operation for appendicitis and inflamed urinary organs. He also indicated that he observed that she had a mild case of leukorrhea or discharge from irritated vaginal membranes. Thus, coverage of the Osborne case offered up the topic of venereal disease for public discussion. The subject of venereal disease, specifically syphilis, was the focus of national discussion about the health of soldiers during World War I. During the interwar years, public health officials continued to target vulnerable populations, including African Americans. Black and white social reformers promoted social hygiene—including an emphasis on moral behavior, abstinence, and education about venereal disease—to poor and working-class African Americans. An ongoing discussion about social diseases like gonorrhea and syphilis also occurred in medical columns in the Black Press and informed readers of hygienic practices to avoid them. Columns such as these introduced readers to definitions of sexually transmitted diseases. [69]

Social reformers educating the public about sexually transmitted diseases also targeted middle-class audiences. Reformers addressed these groups in an effort to prepare them to teach youth and less educated groups about sexually transmitted diseases. Most reformers associated social diseases with poverty and lack of education. They assumed that these afflictions did not greatly impact elite and middle-class African Americans.[70] Social reformers almost always correlated sexually transmitted diseases with poor and working-class blacks. Drake and Cayton pointed out that the rate of sexually transmitted diseases among Negroes in Chicago was twenty-five times higher than the rates of whites. However, the two sociologists, like other black elites, believed that it was necessary to stress that these rates did not mean that disease should be viewed as synonymous with black life. Black health officials and reformers stressed that environmentally related poverty and familial disorganization stemming from slavery were the primary culprits of social diseases. These factors, they believed, made it unlikely for middle-class and elite African Americans to contract sexually transmitted diseases.[71]

The Osborne divorce, however, cast sexually transmitted diseases in a different light. Instead of being characteristic of the "black bottom" or poor African American neighborhoods, sexually transmitted disease had cropped up among Washington, DC's most socially prominent members. Typically, prominence and middle-class status offered families such as the Osbornes a veil of privacy about sexually transmitted diseases. Unlike the masses, the Osbornes could afford private medical treatment. The cost of treatment for syphilis ranged anywhere from $305 to $1,000. Whites were much more likely to see private physicians who often did not report these cases to public health officials.[72] Private black physicians were probably even more reluctant to account for patients with sexually transmitted disease because of the stereotypical and racist perceptions associated with the black body. As a result, middle-class and black elites were often left out of the black public discussions of sexually transmitted disease. The black sexual public sphere provided by the press was not as discriminating and expanded the association of disease to elite and middle-class blacks.

The *Courier* and *Defender*'s coverage also involved the question of whether adultery had actually occurred between Benjamin Pinn and Ruth Osborne. In this regard, a partially damaged unsigned letter found by Mrs. Sarah Osborne, Ruth's mother-in-law, became a central piece of evidence. Mr. Osborne maintained his belief that Mr. Pinn had authored the letter to his wife. Despite its tattered state, enough of the letter's message could be read. Mr. Pinn denied writing it, although he acknowledged that the letter contained handwriting that looked like his own. All three newspapers published excerpts from the letter, which contained terms of endearment and referenced Mrs. Osborne's illness. Mr. Osborne and his attorneys argued that the letter served as proof that Mr. Pinn was guilty of adultery and the source of the sexually transmitted disease contracted by the Osbornes.[73]

Evidence of an adulterous affair, however, did not stop with the letter. Mr. Osborne's attorney called Joseph Templeton, a janitor, who testified that he observed Ruth Osborne and Benjamin Pinn rent rooms at a local rooming house where he worked over the course of 1923 and 1924. Mrs. Taylor, owner of the boarding house refuted the janitor's testimony, stating that she had never rented a room to Mr. Pinn or Mrs. Osborne. Indeed, she protested that she ran a respectable house and had housed two bishops on previous occasions, though she could not present the guest register attesting to this fact. Many readers understood the taint and implication of rooming houses; they had a dubious air surrounding them and were often associated with prostitution and other immoral behavior. The papers also informed readers that Emma Pinn, wife of Benjamin Pinn, testified on behalf of her husband while Fred Wilkinson, brother-in-law to Ruth, confirmed her side of the events.[74]

The coverage of key witnesses' testimony to the alleged adultery suggested that community and familial surveillance functioned to regulate and sanction sexual behavior. The Black Press reminded readers that their own private sexual encounters could be fodder for the public given the right set of circumstances. Christophe Regina states, "living in close proximity with one's neighbors offered many opportunities for watchful eyes to observe and comment on behavior in the street or behind closed doors."[75] African American newspapers further inscribed the power of working-class neighbors by designating the witnesses' occupations and social standing. The crime of adultery highlighted the tenuous class boundaries that existed, for example, between Mr. Templeton, the janitor, and Mrs. Taylor, owner of the boarding house. Normally, Mrs. Osborne's word would have carried more weight than Mr. Templeton's, but the accusations of adultery damaged her credibility.

The judge granted Jerome Osborne an absolute divorce from his wife on March 26, 1927.[76] The judge also awarded tentative custody of their daughter to Mr. Osborne and Maggie Wilkinson, sister of Ruth. People found guilty of adultery were often viewed as unfit parents. All three papers recounted the links in "the chain of evidence" used by the judge to render his decision. But the *Afro-American* published part of the memorandum of Justice Smith's decision. As the paper had predicted, it included the judge's opinion of the testimony of Joseph Templeton, the janitor. According to the opinion, Templeton's observation of Benjamin Pinn and Ruth Osborne's entrance into a room with a made-up bed and exit out of the room with a rumpled bed confirmed the accusation of adultery.[77] The final chapter of the case appeared in papers on September 24, 1927. In an effort to jog readers' memories about the case, the *Afro-American* claimed that the Osborne trial had caused a stir among DC elites and across the country. The *Afro-American* reported that Ruth Osborne would be appealing the judge's decision in an effort to regain custody of her daughter and to seek some form of financial support from her former husband.

The coverage of the Osborne case demonstrated to readers that issues such as sexually transmitted disease, infidelity, and violence—themes typically associated with poor blacks—could also be found among the growing numbers of the black middle class.[78] News coverage of the Osborne case made the private sexual lives of the black middle class public knowledge. Thus, the Black Press challenged the relationship between immorality and poverty cast by reformers and sociologists and exposed fault lines in this social framework. While black newspapers relied on the Osbornes' prominence and sensational coverage to attract readers, it also demonstrated that social status placed elite and middle-class African Americans within a black sexual public sphere in African American newspapers.

SEXUAL SCANDALS AND THE BLACK ELITE

The Black Press' coverage of sex scandals did not always feature the dissolution of a marriage. Between 1927 and 1930, the "Curtis case" involved twenty-nine-year-old Eva Fitzhugh, an African American woman proprietor of a tearoom, who sued a prominent dentist, forty-two-year-old Dr. Arthur L. Curtis and his wife, Helen Gordon Curtis, for $5,000 each for physically assaulting her. According to a 1927 affidavit Fitzhugh sent to the *Afro-American*, she and Dr. Curtis had developed a sexual relationship after an initial professional encounter in 1926 where he treated Fitzhugh for a medial ailment. Fitzhugh indicated that she became pregnant as a result of her relationship with Dr. Curtis. Unwilling to terminate the pregnancy, Fitzhugh stated that Dr. Curtis and his father, Dr. A. M. Curtis, forced her to have an abortion, which they performed together.[79]

Ms. Fitzhugh stated that shortly after the operation, Dr. Curtis's interest in her waned. Still, she responded to his request for her to come to his office. Ms. Fitzhugh reported her surprise to find Mrs. Curtis waiting there with her husband. Mrs. Curtis proceeded to beat Fitzhugh while Dr. Curtis prevented her from fleeing. Once allowed to leave, Fitzhugh filed a complaint with the police, but Dr. Curtis convinced her to drop the charges. Approximately two months later, Dr. Curtis requested another private meeting with Fitzhugh under the guise of discussing their relationship. He, however, physically assaulted her and called the police and charged that Fitzhugh accosted him. The police arrested and charged Fitzhugh with making threats and disturbing the peace. In turn, Fitzhugh refiled complaints against Dr. Curtis and his wife.[80]

Dr. Curtis categorically denied all of Fitzhugh's charges. Instead, he declared that she was insane and that all of her claims were an elaborate fantasy that she had concocted. The case did not go to trial until February 1930, almost three years after Fitzhugh's account to the *Afro-American*. All three of the national newspapers, the *Afro-American*, *Courier*, and *Defender*, along with the *Tribune* and *Amsterdam News*, reported on the trial. Out of the three papers, the *Afro-American* devoted the most coverage to the trial for several weeks in February. The paper published ten articles and two editorials on the Curtis case. In contrast, the other newspapers featured an average of two articles on the case with no paper exceeding three.

The overwhelming amount of coverage in the *Afro-American*, however, was connected to the geographical proximity of the case to the paper. With its main headquarters located in Baltimore and an office in Washington, DC, it was natural that the *Afro-American* took a greater interest in covering the story. However, the *Afro-American* was also associated with the case in another way. In the immediate aftermath of her encounter with Dr. Curtis and his wife, Fitzhugh sent the *Afro-American* a sworn statement detailing the events in question. Moreover, she sat for interviews with several journalists, including Laurence Lautier, a freelance reporter who often contributed to the *Afro-American*. The court subpoenaed Lautier and other reporters to testify to their knowledge of the facts in the case.

Moreover, Fitzhugh's attorneys asked representatives of the *Afro-American* to bring in the sworn affidavit and any pictures they had in their possession. The *Afro-American* operated as more than a black sexual public sphere for reporting the sexual issues in the trial; it became a part of the story.[81]

The Black Press' attention to the case assumed that a mass black readership was interested in the case's details due to the prominence of the principal actors, Dr. and Mrs. Curtis. The son of an established physician, Dr. Curtis obtained his medial training at Howard University and, after graduating, worked as a faculty member of the school. Curtis also operated a private practice and served as a visiting surgeon at the Freedman's Hospital, the primary medical establishment for blacks in the District of Columbia. With a record of serving in World War I as one of six black doctors at the field hospital in Dijon, France, Dr. Curtis represented the New Negro doctor.[82]

Helen Gordon Curtis, in her own right, was no less elite than her husband. Newspapers described her as a "leading society matron" and a manager of a shop in Detroit that often took her out of town. Both Dr. and Helen Curtis belonged to several social clubs and organizations. The Curtis's social affiliation also manifested itself in their selection of a defense attorney. Famed civil rights lawyer Charles Hamilton Houston served as their legal representation. A Harvard-trained lawyer, Houston held the position of vice dean and dean of the Howard School of Law between 1929 and 1935. Houston's participation as a defense attorney functioned as a larger backdrop for the development and professionalization of black lawyers educated at Howard. Howard produced more black law school graduates than any other institution in the early twentieth century and inspired Houston's landmark work on civil rights cases in the 1930s and 1940s. Nonetheless, Houston's connection with and defense of the Curtises in the district court demonstrated the social connections and processes that black elites drew on to guard their status and reputation.[83]

In fact, the cast of black elites who attended the trial in a show of support for the Curtises proved to be part of the story for newspapers covering the trial. Prominent businessmen, such as John R. Hawkins, banker and financial secretary of the African Methodist Episcopal Church, and Howard University faculty members, including the venerable Kelly Miller, well-known black sociologist and outspoken leader of the black community, attended the opening trial proceedings. No papers noted or remarked on people who might have attended the trial on behalf of Fitzhugh. It was clear that Eva Fitzhugh possessed less stature than either Dr. or Mrs. Curtis.[84]

The disparity in class between the Curtises and Fitzhugh was brought into full relief via expert testimony from African American professionals that included physicians, anesthetists, nurses, and news reporters from Washington, DC. The Curtis case established that this growing group wielded influence among blacks. Many of the medical professionals worked at Freedman's hospital, which served as the teaching hospital for Howard Medical School. With Houston serving as the defense attorney, along with the dean of Howard University Law School and the dean of Howard University in attendance, Fitzhugh had virtually taken on Howard University in her lawsuit against Dr. Curtis. Fitzhugh's lawyer, Austin F. Canfield, pointed out the class inequities in his closing comments when he remarked that he had to defend her from the entire professional field associated with Howard.

Indeed, for many, the class conflict that rose to the surface in the context of an alleged illicit sexual affair is what made the case so sensational. The papers played up the class differences. Despite being the owner of a tearoom that catered exclusively to whites, the *Afro-American* and other papers constructed Eva Fitzhugh as a poor, pitiable figure; headlines referred to her as either the "Tea Room Girl" or the "Tea Room Lassie." The papers, however, always referred to the Curtis couple as Dr. and Mrs. Curtis.[85] The Black Press also, on several different occasions, took extra care in describing the differences in both women's clothing. According to *Afro-American* writer, E. W. Baker, the sixth day of the trial opened with Mrs. Curtis dressed in a "chic and close-fitting black hat, cream colored hose, black shoes and kid clothes." In contrast, Baker described Fitzhugh as wearing "the same brown coat, brown turban hat, shaded brown hose and shoes that she has worn during several days of the trial."[86] The implication here was that Mrs. Curtis had not worn the same clothing over the course of the trial, suggesting that she maintained a more elite status. Reporters did not describe Mr. Curtis or any other man's attire in any of the coverage.

The contrast that reporters made between the two women did not stop at the color or style of their clothing. Some of the *Afro-American*'s reports described Fitzhugh as "olive brown" while Mrs. Curtis was considered "very fair in complexion." In making comparisons, the trial became more a contest between the two women. William N. Jones, staff writer, wrote in the opening paragraph of his news report on the judgment in the case: "Sitting inside the railing, just four seats apart, Monday morning two women steeled themselves for the final curtain, raised in the melodrama which has interested the nation's capital for a week."[87] Jones's juxtaposition of the two women highlighted an interracial contestation between black women that centered class and skin color as markers of power and privilege. The *Afro-American*'s coverage manifested into a black sexual public sphere that recognized readers' interest in class dynamics embedded in the case.

Despite the fact that the case was about an alleged physical assault that Fitzhugh allegedly suffered at the hands of Dr. and Mrs. Curtis, newspapers capitalized on the sexual elements of the case. The *Afro-American's* account of the testimony and the closing arguments highlighted private sexual matters. One of the more compelling parts of the testimony revealed that Dr. Curtis and his father had together performed an abortion on Fitzhugh. While Canfield made sure to tell the jury that neither he nor Fitzhugh sought compensation for harm she sustained from the procedure, he insisted that the sexual encounters and resulting abortion established a motive for the alleged beating.

Dr. Curtis adamantly denied performing an abortion on Fitzhugh, resulting in both lawyers devoting a great deal of time to this matter. The coverage of the testimony of the abortion inserted the subject into the public domain of the newspapers. Yet, the Curtis case was far from the only time the subject of abortion had appeared in early-twentieth-century black newspapers. The *Courier* republished the bestselling novel, *Bad Girl* by Viña Delmar which depicted the trials of a young woman's efforts to terminate her pregnancy.[88] Other papers regularly featured front-page headlines that announced the arrests of doctors who performed botched abortions on young women who had died from the procedure. These early-twentieth-century media reports on abortion deaths often served to warn women of the consequences of premarital and extramarital sexual relationships.[89]

The nature of the trial, however, extended the typical narrative on abortion in black papers. In the first place, the recipient of the abortion was alive and could give voice to her experiences. Most readers would have been acquainted with accounts of abortion where women's voices were silenced through death or overshadowed by judicial authorities' insistence that they disclose abortionists' names. Investigators often sought dying women's admission and disclosure of the physician responsible for the procedure.[90] Fitzhugh's affidavit revealed that she had been coerced into having an abortion against her wishes. Testimony also revealed the physical pain of abortion that was often absent from typical newspaper reports. Fitzhugh claimed that unable to withstand the pain, she "jumped off the operating table and went home" before the procedure was complete. She was subsequently taken to a hospital where Dr. Curtis and his father completed the abortion.[91]

Given that it was unclear who was telling the truth about the abortion and the lack of evidence confirming the surgery, Fitzhugh's attorney aggressively cross-examined Dr. Curtis on his testimony that he had not performed an abortion on Fitzhugh. To challenge Ms. Fitzhugh's assertion, Dr. Curtis noted that his father, Dr. A. M. Curtis, not he, performed a medical treatment on Fitzhugh.

To support his claim, one of Dr. A. M. Curtis's attending nurses, Mary Carter, testified that she was present when he treated Ms. Fitzhugh. According to her statement, Dr. A. M. Curtis gave Ms. Fitzhugh "tampon treatments" but not an abortion. Medical officials often used tampons to treat cervical erosions and vaginal discharge in addition to providing protection for menstrual cycles. The defense called on Dr. William Lofton, an African American anesthetist, to confirm the elder Curtis and his son's statements.[92]

An *Afro-American* editorial captured the trial's production of sexual knowledge and illumination of private sexual matters. The editorial stated that the case "serves to call attention to the high standards which the medical profession must observe to command confidence and patronage." Yet, unwilling to take issue with Dr. Curtis's father's revelation that Fitzhugh had come to him with a sexually transmitted disease, the editorial writer argued that this testimony was forced. Indeed, the writer congratulated the elder Dr. Curtis, suggesting that he could have very well stated that Fitzhugh suffered from a more "terrible ailment or two such ailments and our available scientific knowledge is still so lacking that no one could safely contradict him."[93] The *Afro-American* editorial affirmed and reinscribed the power and the authority of physicians, black and white, to produce sexual knowledge about everyday African Americans. The editorial, then, presented the case as a way to discuss the professional ethics of physicians who held private and personal knowledge about their patients' lives.

While the *Afro-American* editorial spoke to the African American medical field's influence, black papers as, a whole, reminded readers that whites continued to hold sway over civil and criminal matters among African Americans. Each newspaper noted that the judge, and jury, ten men and two women, were white. Whites also formed an active part of the proceedings: the star defense witness in the case was Benjamin Karpman, a white psychiatrist and clinical professor of psychiatry at Howard Medical School. Karpman had testified that Fitzhugh suffered from "hysterical insanity," thus the reason for her accusations against the Curtises.[94] Karpman's testimony captured a long and rich history of the medical establishment's diagnosis of women as hysterical. Sexual frustration was often viewed as the underlying issue.[95] In the Curtis case, accusations that Fitzhugh was "socially unclean" worked in conjunction with her depiction as hysterical. Fitzhugh's attorney, however, was able to undermine Karpman's testimony by pointing out to the jury that he was a biased witness due to his eight-year relationship with Dr. Curtis and his consultation with him about the case prior to the trial.[96]

By the end of the trial, Fitzhugh indicated that the negative publicity of the trial had forced her to close her business. Houston, the defense attorney, scoffed at this claim stating that only black papers had covered the story. Houston went on to note that Fitzhugh had not sent her affidavit to white papers. Whites, he declared would not have been privy to the coverage, leaving Fitzhugh to continue her business as usual.[97] Houston also suggested that Fitzhugh understood the power of the black newspapers to reach a mass public. Claiming that her intent in notifying the papers was to embarrass Dr. Curtis in front of his patients, Houston accused Fitzhugh of appealing to the court of public opinion. The *Afro-American* and other papers almost certainly ensured Dr. Curtis's embarrassment with their description of his behavior. One article portrayed Dr. Curtis as being accused of "violent love-making."[98]

Since the court spectators were exclusively African American, Black Press coverage constituted a black sexual public sphere that included both readers and court spectators. "An audience that has packed Judge Siddon's courtroom every day this week," proved to one writer, "that what a crowd wants is sensation and plenty of it."[99] The *Afro-American*'s extensive coverage suggested that a correlation existed between the desire of the actual audience attending the trial and an imagined mass readership's appetite for scandal. In truth, the case generated so much interest because it tapped into the tensions that had long existed between black elites and working and poorer classes of African Americans. It also allowed people to view and discuss issues such as abortion and sexually transmitted diseases.

After two weeks of hearings, the case ended. Most papers used their front-page to publicize the decision. "Dr. and Mrs. A. L. Curtis Must Pay Eva Fitzhugh for Alleged Assault—Capital Society Shocked at Verdict," announced the *Courier* to its readers on February 8th. According to the *Courier*, the judge in the case awarded Fitzhugh $5,300 following eight hours of deliberation by the jury. The *Tribune* also documented the verdict with a front-page headline, "Hubby Must Pay $5,300," and a paragraph recounting the decision alongside a picture of Mrs. Helen Curtis. The *Amsterdam News* also reported the judgment with a small paragraph on the first page to reestablish the importance of the case. The *Defender*, on the other hand, imagined that the story had lost some of its news value and placed the story on the first page of the second section where readers could find the editorial page, comics, and photographs.[100]

Unsurprisingly, the *Afro-American* published a front-page article reporting the verdict and devoted another full page to a series of articles that gave blow-by-blow details of the closing arguments and small pieces of information. For example, one article indicated that the windows in the courtroom were open during the hearing. A commentary written by William N. Jones that appeared on the paper's editorial page functioned as the *Afro-American*'s closing statement about the case. According to Jones, the Curtis case illustrated greater human civility and progress. He stated, "A few thousand years ago our ancestors would have settled such tangle with clubs and the struggle would have been to the death."[101] The Curtis case, Jones believed, demonstrated the utility of the court in arbitrating domestic issues. While he did not reference the displacement of the Black Church or community in adjudicating private matters, Jones's statements suggested that he and some African Americans viewed court cases on sexual scandal as a model for settling disputes. What Jones failed to consider, however, is that coverage of the Curtis case was just as important as the case itself. It functioned as a black sexual public sphere that offered readers a window into the private sexual life of the black elite and middle class.

CLASS AND THE PRODUCTION OF SEXUAL KNOWLEDGE AND NEWS

The Black Press's coverage of divorce trials and sex scandal cases put the sexual lives of the black elite and middle class on public display as well as revealed the changing class relationships within the black community. In constructing news from divorce trials and sex scandals that involved prominent African Americans, the Black Press became an extension of the public sphere of the court system. Yet, even as black papers exposed the affairs of black elites and the African American middle class, they reaffirmed that sexuality was "private." This is what made the headlines so satisfying and thrilling. Newspapers revealed and spoke about sexual matters that should not be aired in other public forums.

Because black newspaper editors and publishers built the business of black journalism on a mass African American population of readers, they geared much of their news coverage to an audience that they imagined desired private information about old settlers and an emerging middle class. Black papers did not publish letters from readers seeking news about divorce trials and sex scandals. However, editors chose to use newspapers' most valuable real estate, the front page, to feature news stories about divorce and sex scandals. In so doing, Black Press editors exposed their judgment about the importance they believed readers placed on divorce and sex scandals involving prominent black community members. Thus, black newspapers assumed a diverse and financially solvent readership that would purchase papers and enjoy coverage that scrutinized the black elite and middle class.[102]

Divorce trials and sex scandals helped black papers produce new knowledge about sexuality. In particular, coverage of doctors and specialists' expert testimony acquainted a mass black readership with modern language and ideas about sexuality. Sex scandals and divorce trials also helped to upset concepts of the sanctity of marriage as a marker of respectability. To this end, what was considered immoral and, most importantly, who made these judgments was turned on its head. In the end, these judgments were not simply made by the courts but also by black newspapers and their readers who upset elite black and middle-class morality and respectability by exposing and consuming news about their private sexual lives.

Black newspapers' belief that their readership desired coverage of black bathing beauty pageant contestants and winners and representation of everyday women sunbathing at beaches and public pools functioned as another black sexual public sphere, one that was primarily visual and offered respectable *and* sexual alternatives to the images of women constructed by elite and black middle-class values. Representations of black lesbians, however, indicated that images of healthy black female sexuality depended on images of a black lesbian within the same black sexual public sphere that demonized women's sexuality outside the boundaries of heterosexuality.

Chapter 3

BATHING BEAUTIES
AND PREDATORY LESBIANS

On May 24, 1930, a short eight months after the stock market crash, an animated debate over the sexual purity of black women occurred in the *Chicago Defender*. J. Wilson of Oakland, California, spurred the debate with a letter to the editor, commenting on the paper's regular protest of black women's sexual exploitation by white men. Wilson stated, "'Nigger' women are easy for them [white men]. Even those so-called respectable Colored women (there isn't no such animal) they even entertain them in broad daylight—these respectable ones." Wilson did not identify his race in the letter but implied that he was a "fine colored" man who had no chance with a black woman unless he had "a swell car and a good paying job and money in the bank."[1] In making this comment, Wilson tapped into the economic deprivation that pervaded many communities during the beginning of the Great Depression and had left many men, particularly African American men, feeling incapable of living up to the financial obligations of manhood. Moreover, Wilson's words marked black women's bodies as ones that could be bought and sold to the highest bidder.

Readers' letters commenting on Wilson's comments poured into the *Defender* in the weeks after its publication.[2] For a mass black readership, the issue was not so much that Wilson was wrong about black women. Many of the readers who expressed outrage at Wilson's letter grudgingly acknowledged that they believed that African American women in general were immoral. June Waytes, writing from Pittsburgh, stated, "Personally I do not agree with Mr. Wilson. . . . But I must admit that our women are backward in comparison with the white women when it comes to being sympathetical [sic], good natured, sociable and serviceable." Too many black women, according William Kegg Fisher, associated with the "white man in the dark." Nonetheless, Paul W. Moore of Oakland, California, believed that Wilson "most certainly has not had contact with the better element of Race women."[3] On its face, the association between morality and leisure in the fledgling decades of the twentieth century was hardly unusual and could be found among both white and black Americans. But tacit in readers' comments was the notion that while respectable black women existed, they were the exception to the rule. In this regard, Wilson's ideas about black women were mirrored by a mass black readership who merged images of black women in the Black Press with their own preconceived notions and ideologies.

Together, Wilson and the letter writers tapped into long-standing stereotypes about black women. These stereotypes were rooted in slavery and pervasive structural systems of racism that formed throughout the United States after emancipation and branded black women's bodies as hypersexual. White counterparts, by virtue of their whiteness, did not bear the burden of proving their sexual virtue. The deep irony that the Wilson debate reveals is that assumptions about black women's inherent sexual and immoral character were not isolated to white people. African Americans, particularly men, internalized many of the negative images about black women's sexuality.

These negative representations bedeviled many black women. How could they fight negative images and redefine themselves as respectable *and* sexual beings outside and *within* African American communities? In some ways, many African American women viewed the challenge of creating a respectable sexual image among other African Americans as more significant. Racial segregation often magnified gender tensions. As the Wilson debate showed, black women's morality, by virtue of their skin color, was not a given and had to be proven to whomever they came into contact. What, then, were the options for young working and middle-class black women who came of age within a larger cultural American framework of changing moral and sexual values in the early twentieth century? In part, the answers to this question, while not completely satisfactory, lay within the image of the black bathing beauty.

This chapter argues that black newspapers created a black sexual public sphere through their coverage of black bathing beauty pageants' contestants and winners during the 1920s and 1930s. The presentation of African American women's bodies in this setting created a space for an agentive sexuality within a frame of respectability. However, the black bathing beauty image was not free of sexual objectification. Rather, it was part and parcel of a growing consumer culture in which women's bodies were used to market and sell goods. The black bathing beauty's appeal rested on the power of her implicit heterosexuality that was woven into numerous photographs in black newspapers. The image was also fueled by the relatively few, but equally powerful, images of African American lesbians whom the Black Press drew as criminal and predatory. Nonetheless, the coverage of black bathing beauty contests created a sexual public sphere that shaped the gaze of black heterosexual women and provided African American women with a means to be at once respectable and sexual.

REPRESENTATIONS OF BLACK WOMEN AND SEXUAL DISCOURSE IN THE BLACK PRESS

Black women had long grappled with derisive and insidious sexual stereotypes by the time Americans began referring to a modern era in the 1920s. Viewed as hypersexual and immoral temptresses by white society, black women were the measuring sticks by which white women could gauge their own morality. In an effort to confront and then challenge these images, late-nineteenth- and early-twentieth-century elite and middle-class African American women strategically created a "culture of dissemblance" and shielded their private selves from a white public to defend themselves from the symbolic and literal sexual assaults on their characters and bodies.[4] Historians have sought to explain this strategy as a "politics of respectability."[5] This approach met the demands of a Victorian culture that required women, at least on the surface, to be passionless and embody sexual purity.[6] However, unlike their mothers, dissembling their sexuality was not the only option for young elite and middle-class African American women coming of age in the 1920s and 1930s.

As witnesses to the rapid commercialization of sex and the rise of consumption and recreation, young women were not exclusively indoctrinated with the industrial principles of thrift and personal sacrifice that their mothers were exposed to in the late nineteenth and early twentieth centuries. Instead, young black women of different class groups experienced an increasingly erotic world where sex was publicly discussed and observed in people's daily interactions.[7] Black leaders and educators' efforts to restrict more popular behaviors among young women—such as the consumption of alcohol and tobacco, dancing, and spending time with men—manifested themselves in students' strikes at places such as Howard and Fisk.[8] Resistance such as this, however, did little to quell the growing chasm between Victorians codes of sexual behavior and early-twentieth-century liberal ideals that offered young African American women greater latitude to experience pleasure.

Young black women turned to advice columns to deal with the contradictions between shifting sexual behavior and the expectations of parents and other community leaders. John D'Emilio and Estelle Freedman indicate that new definitions of dating and social relationships between men and women confounded post–World War I young adults. In an effort to demystify much of the confusion surrounding these issues, they wrote to various newspaper advice columnists for counsel about dating and sexual relationships.[9] Letters to advice columnists were a regular staple in American periodicals, including black newspapers, since the late nineteenth century. Many of these advice columns were syndicated and allowed readers throughout the United States to collectively experience the anxieties about intimate relationships that individuals writing to these columns expressed.

In contrast to their mothers, who understood that all premarital sexual acts were forbidden, young women were faced with the question of how far they should go sexually with boyfriends before marriage. Questions to advice columnists about sexual norms were partially prompted by the different values that grew out of urbanization. A writer identified as "Hopeless" wrote *Afro-American* advice columnist Julia Jerome, "I am in the biggest city in the world and I am, I think, the loneliest girl in the world." Wanting to know how she could meet young men without flirting, she asked Jerome, "Please tell me how is a decent girl to meet men if she doesn't flirt?" "My dear," answered Jerome, "necessity always overcomes convention." Jerome claimed that women were much more financially independent than women in the past. Therefore, flirting did not have the same negative connotation as it once possessed. Jerome recommended: "Hopeless, . . . go ahead and flirt, but do it modestly, sweetly, charmingly and naturally—not as if you were being terribly wicked—for you are not."[10] Jerome, though, failed to explain exactly how young women might flirt and yet maintain their respectability. "Hopeless" and other young women were more than likely left with as many, if not more, questions about the appropriate way that respectable young black women should behave if they were attracted to or wanted to meet young men.

Young black women not only relied on the Black Press to address their concerns and questions about the new sexual values that defined the 1920s and 1930s but also about sexual behaviors that included physical contact and touching. With the introduction of a new lexicon for describing a range of sexual behaviors, black girls and women posed questions to advice columns on what their appropriate behavior should be in the context of relationships between themselves and young men.

Dear Aunt Phyllis,

There is so much said about girls who pet. However, we girls who do not pet are not very popular. My mother is always telling me to be ladylike, yet when I am, I seem to be left out of everything.

Josie[11]

Like Josie, other young women desired assistance with negotiating modern sexual behavior with traditional views about sex. However, many of them were reticent in specifying the sexual behavior in question as Josie had. This was more than likely due to fears of appearing immoral.

Violet, a young woman, asked *Courier* advice columnist Mary Strong in 1927: "Is it true a woman has to be 'modern' in her sex morals to get along?" Writing that her boyfriend said that she was too rigid, Violet sought Strong's counsel. While Violet did not specifically identify what she meant by modern (perhaps she did not know), her boyfriend's criticism stung enough to prompt her to write for advice. Strong cautioned Violet that her boyfriend was not interested in her in a way that was honorable. A respectful man would be happy that Violet was above what Strong called "latter day social activities," which most likely referred to petting. Strong went on to advise Violet that she should bide her time, suggesting that her boyfriend may be testing her to see if she would submit to his wishes. Girls did not need to be modern in their sex morals, argued Strong. She maintained that girls who were not modern would receive more marriage proposals if they followed traditional views. Conversely girls who chose to follow modern morals would only receive "a mere evening's pleasure."[12]

Strong's response was unremarkable and the standard response that most young women could expect to receive to the question Violet posed. Violet's letter reflected many young women's struggles to behave in ways that were consistent with traditional values in a world that was rapidly redefining black womanhood and sexuality. Violet's final question captured the confusion that she may have felt about her boyfriend's criticism of her as "rigid." Strong's answer affirmed social reformers' views in which sex before marriage was considered immoral. Yet, a more significant detail is that Strong suggested that men will often test women's morality with requests for them to engage in sexual relations. In this instance, women who resisted men's sexual overtures would be rewarded with offers of marriage. Strong's response demonstrated that inasmuch as advice columns gave voice to young black women's questions and concerns about evolving sexual values, the answers they received continued to be framed in conventional and heteronormative understandings of women as chaste and pure prior to marriage.

Advice columns also attempted to help young African American men, albeit to a lesser degree, resolve issues around sexuality. Middle-class codes of manliness among early-twentieth-century African American men were no less radically different than for their female counterparts. Young black men coming of age amid the jazz age found it progressively more difficult to abide by their grandfathers and fathers' allegiance to the "disciplining of the body" and "curtailment of their consumption and leisure practices."[13] Advice columnists often gave young men dramatically different advice from young women, counseling them that they should be socially assertive in their relationships with women. "Women Prefer Bold Men," stated a 1928 headline of Jerome's column, "Art of Love." Advising that women "always admired bold and direct men," Jerome responded to Harry H's request for assistance about expressing feelings for a female friend of his. Jerome, though, cautioned men from exhibiting overly hasty or aggressive behavior.[14] Resembling the advice that she gave young women, Jerome attempted to provide guidance to men that bridged the emergent divide between traditional gender codes and modern sexual values and protocols for men. In either case, sexual guidance to women or counsel to men, advice columns informed young middle-class adult readers that their struggles to be respectable while enjoying newly discovered leisure and recreational activities, laden with sexual connotations, were not theirs to bear on their own.

Yet, even as men experienced the tension between "old-fashioned" gender and sexual ideals, it was young black middle-class women who stood the most to lose if they did not strike the appropriate balance between respectability and sexuality. While advice columns in the Black Press provided a space for women to pose questions about moralizing discourses and express apprehension concerning women's sexual freedom, it did not allow them a way to remedy the images of black women's morality and their bodies. While questions about the way black women should comport themselves were vital to racial progress, how black women's physical images were represented were just as important and preoccupied early-twentieth-century African American women. In general, from the late nineteenth century, African Americans have relied on the camera to document black respectability. However, photography in black print culture, particularly in the form of the Black Press, went beyond personifying respectability. Photography also contributed to making publications profitable. Thus, when it came to black women, the images of their bodies in print served a variety of purposes that intersected with questions about black women's sexual morality.

IMAGES OF AFRICAN AMERICAN WOMEN

To say that African American women have a troubled history with photography is to profoundly understate the ways in which the camera has been used to manufacture images to define the black female body as the antithesis of womanhood. Prior to photography, negative representations of African women circulated via sketches and paintings that exaggerated black women's physiognomy to bolster the gross falsehood that they were less than human. A rich body of work has documented photography as a technology for making visual African American women's inherently laborious and sexually deviant body as pictured in the white mind.[15] While these degraded portrayals of black women would have a jump start, late-nineteenth- and early-twentieth-century advances in photography allowed African American photographers to turn the eye of the camera on themselves to depose stereotypes of black life. Positive visual representations of African Americans could do far more than the written word, for they offered a concrete and tangible witness to black humanity.[16] The era of the New Negro, where many blacks viewed themselves outside the image of servility and inferiority, inspired elite and ordinary African Americans to reinvent themselves. Upper- and middle-class African Americans commissioned photographs of themselves, collaborating with the photographer to redefine images of blackness.[17]

The rise of a mass black print culture in the early twentieth century furthered African Americans' efforts to transform their likeness and the negative associations with it. In 1924, John W. Baddy, editor of the political and literary magazine *The Messenger* (1917–1928), declared to his readers that the publication would present only "Negro women who are unique, accomplished, beautiful, intelligent, industrious and successful."[18] These descriptors rejected white allegations that African American women were unattractive, licentious, and savage. *Crisis: A Record of the Darker Races* (1910–), the official print arm of the NAACP, and *Opportunity: A Journal of Negro Life* (1923–1949), the organ of the National Urban League, also used physical images of women to cultivate and reflect African American pride and accomplishment. Many of the *Crisis* and *Opportunity* covers in the 1920s featured sketches of the faces of attractive black women. Profiles of black women and their social accomplishments through biographies and obituaries within the magazines demonstrated black women's virtue. Customary for the time period, women's bodies often remained invisible to *Crisis*'s middle-class readers. By the 1930s, *Crisis* and *Opportunity* began using photographs of motion picture actresses, college graduates, teachers, and clubwomen to adorn the covers of the publication.[19]

Besides offering redeeming depictions of black womanhood, magazines also demonstrated that early-twentieth-century African American women's physical beauty was an important measure of the race.[20] But it was not just any black woman that could embody the criteria of black womanhood worthy of being featured on or in magazines. Physical features such as skin color, hair texture, and, to a lesser degree, facial features such as size of nose and lips mattered. Many of the women appearing on the covers of magazines possessed mixed-racial facial features and light skin color. They functioned as the magazine editors' attempts to document the truth about black women's moral character.[21] These photographs suggested to readers that the prerequisite for black female beauty and respectability was an African racial heritage that included other racial phenotypical characteristics. Early-twentieth-century black women grappled with hegemonic conceptualizations of beauty and sexual desirability that deemed lighter skin as more attractive. Writing for the *Defender*, Roscoe Holloway observed, "I have heard efficient, attractive brown-skinned girls say to each other when talking of certain men: 'It doesn't do any good to make eyes at that man—you're too dark for him.'" The message was clear to black women that not only did they have to contend with skin color politics outside African American communities but that their fiercest and most painful battles might be fought around the "color line within the race."[22]

Messenger, Crisis, and *Opportunity,* as well as most African American magazines in the early twentieth century, were run by men and were published for middle-class audiences. Conceptions of black womanhood in these instances, then, hardly represented a critical mass of African American women. In contrast, publications such as *Half-Century Magazine* (1916–1925), edited and owned by a black woman, published content that was relevant to the masses of black men and women throughout the country. *Half-Century* made efforts to feature darker-skinned women and children on its covers and in the magazine. With diverse skin tones and dressed in the latest fashions, the magazine portrayed black women as sophisticated and urbane. In reality, as much as the magazine's editor purported to create a publication so that the "masses may read and understand," the clothing and lifestyle it highlighted remained out of the reach for the vast majority of migrant and working-class women.[23] Moreover, the magazine struck a rather conservative tone in its approach to the representation of women by placing them in scenes of domesticity and consumption. Nonetheless, the images in *Half-Century* magazine suggested that when black women controlled their own images, they were more mindful of the diverse landscape of black women readers.

Like magazines, black newspapers focused on recuperating images of black life and shoring up the image of black womanhood specifically. Many black newspapers featured profiles and photographs of attractive women on the front pages of their papers. Unlike magazines that were often ordered through the mail and received monthly or semi-quarterly, readers purchased their papers from newspaper boys on street corners and local stores and newsstands. Front pages mattered for they drew in readers, enticing them with sensational headlines and attractive pictures. Black Press editors and publishers relied on images of beautiful black women to draw a mass black readership to their papers. In some ways, pictures of attractive women served as sources of aspiration for black female readers. For example, the *Defender*'s December 12, 1936, issue showcased seven photographs at the top of the front page with the headline "Beautiful Women—From Colleges, Social Circles and the Home." The *Defender* included a mini-biography under each woman's photograph.[24] Images such as this called out African American women's physical beauty and intellectual capabilities for men and women readers.

Percival Prattis, editor and manager of the American Pictorial Publishing Company (APPC), the photo service branch of the ANP, stressed the importance of female beauty within black papers. Prattis dedicated the APPC's short-lived monthly photo supplement, *The National News Gravure*, which appeared in newspapers such as the *Tribune*, to featuring "beautiful pictures of beautiful persons and pictures, which will show something of the progress that Philadelphia Negroes are making." However, Prattis, like other news editors, gendered his quest for images of "beautiful persons" when he asked Theus Photo Service, "What about the pictures of pretty girls? Haven't you any that you might mail in to us this week?"[25] Physical attractiveness also played a role when Ira Lewis, manager of the *Courier*, strongly suggested to publisher Robert Vann that the paper feature photographs of "beauty queens" on the front pages of the paper. Lewis's push for coverage of beauty queens reflected the larger impetus to amend white perceptions of black women. However, featuring appealing women in the Black Press was never just about uplift and progress. The pressure to sell papers, a constant factor in the black newspaper business, meant that images of black women were easily commodified. Neither Prattis nor Lewis was oblivious to the notion that attractive women on the cover of the paper might increase the paper's circulation.[26]

Black papers also tapped into the growing acceptance of the images of black women's bodies in the entertainment world. Within the pages of the Black Press, readers discovered partially dressed women in alluring poses who beckoned readers to purchase the latest Bessie Smith record or to attend a chorus-line production. These advertisements and black women's work as entertainers were often the subject of ministers and social reformers' criticism.[27] However, some of the fiercest debates around the image of African American women was reserved for the chorus girl.

THE CHORUS GIRL

True for both white and black early-twentieth-century female performance, the chorus girl was a "central obsession of American popular culture."[28] The chorus girl's visibility reflected the growing entertainment culture of theater, and later film, among everyday Americans. Troupes of women dancers had emerged in London during the mid–nineteenth century. By the early twentieth century, chorus-girl lines had become a regular feature in stage entertainment in theaters and variety halls across the United States.[29] Often nameless and poorly paid, chorus girls made up a requisite component of successful theatrical productions. However, images of chorines symbolized the anxiety over the evolving role of women in the early twentieth century. The chorus girl was emblematic of women's modernity in an urban context and mass culture even as she was a threat to an orderly and well-maintained society of women who might be managed and controlled.[30]

Within African American culture, discourses on black female performance through the trope of the chorus girl had long existed in early-twentieth-century African American literary expression such as poetry. The chorus girl's lighter skin did not necessarily suggest the morality that it did when it was a characteristic of women featured in magazines and newspapers as paragons of black womanhood. The visual marker of light skin possessed by many of the chorus girls operated as a tangible reminder for some of the oppressive relationship between African Americans and whites. Writer Zora Neale Hurston castigated the chorus line as a "bleached chorus" that reflected white interests and desire rather than that of African Americans.[31] Therefore, the color hegemony that persisted within the world of African American representational politics, which used light skin to overhaul a negative image of all black women, ceased to exist when it came to the chorus girl. Instead, within the context of the entertainment marketplace, it became another type marker of hypersexuality because light skin carried with it the stain of miscegenation.

The complexity and mystique of the chorus girl image made her interesting enough that black newspapers found ways to feature chorines in discussions and news as well as to profile individual performers throughout the 1920s and 1930s. The *Courier* went as far to include sexual innuendo in many of their features. The "tongue in cheek" claim that "cute little chorine, Florence Wilson, is one of the reasons for the Negro migration to Harlem" exemplified the approach the paper took toward chorus girls.[32] The *Tribune's* series, "Confessions of an Ex-Chorus Girl," which spanned over three months in 1929, treated its readers to one twenty-four-year-old young woman's "road to ruin" by relating her experiences as a chorine. Told in first person to columnist Orrin C. Evans, the unnamed woman informed her readers about her sexual encounters and consumption of alcohol and drugs in the hopes "that some of the younger girls who are preparing to travel over the road I have travelled will see the moral in this story of shame."[33] Ironically, the series ended abruptly without the female protagonist revealing the exact moral disgrace she suffered. Instead, "Confessions" presented young female readers with a lively woman who was able to successfully navigate a succession of events in her travels as a chorus girl. Similar to the way formula stories about the female migrant functioned, "Confessions" was entertaining reading that highlighted the Black Press's belief that readers sought representations of women's sexual agency and pleasure even if they were packaged in a moralizing form.

Prior to the 1920s, moralizing stories such as "Confessions" and coverage that stigmatized the life of a chorus girl might have gone unchallenged. However, in an age of migration, urbanization, and the concurrent development of a black readership that consumed and participated in the entertainment industry, one-dimensional representations of the chorine were unsustainable. Eva Jessye, the first African American female director of a professional choral group, wrote a lengthy article in the *Courier* defending the chorus girl as "the most active medium in presenting the beautiful racial types." In 1928, when she wrote the article, Jessye was the manager of the Dixie Jubilee singers in New York and regularly encountered chorus girls on the theater circuit. Jessye claimed that the "chorus girl has forced recognition of the beauty and charm of the colored woman, not only from the outside, but has awakened the Negro woman herself to her own possibilities which feat may be considered the greater accomplishment." Jessye saw the chorus girl as a trendsetter, helping to inform modern African American women about fashion, makeup, and overall physical attractiveness. Citing shows such as *Shuffle Along*, *Rang Tang*, and Lew Leslie's *Blackbirds*, Jessye remarked, "Can you imagine any sane woman not rushing home to experiment in various shades of powders . . . holding counsel with herself on the advisability of shortening her skirt a wee bit, deciding that landlord or no first of the month will pinch off the price of a marcel and massage and that with a little care as to diet and exercise she could have a cut figure like the saucy little pony on the left end?"[34] Jessye reconfigured the chorus girl in her comments, noting that she often was college educated and from a good family. Indeed, Jessye saw the chorus girl as a professional and not as consequence of a woman's inability to find work in more respectable fields. She viewed the chorus girl as a powerful influence over "thousands of women" who "are taking better care of their bodies, using reliable aids to beauty and health, developing that air of well-being and self-satisfaction that is the foundation of poise."[35] Jayna Brown argues, "For a black constituency during the 1920s, black chorus women were important figures of hopeful migratory movement, urban ebullience, and promise." Jessye, recognizing the power and influence of chorines, stated that the "Chorus Girl Has Helped Glorify Modern Woman."[36]

Male columnists added their voices to Jessye's support of chorus girls. *Defender* columnist Maurice Dancer also viewed the chorus girl as representing the modern woman. He noted, "I do not believe that any other branch of society contains women whose ingenuity skill and self-possession can rival hers." He also described the chorus girl as "an out-and-out individualist, working as hard as she can work for what she wants."[37] *Afro-American* theater editor Ralph Matthews chastised his readers for assuming that a chorus girl by virtue of her profession had the "stamp of a harlot and Jezebel upon her." He added: "All chorus girls are not 'gold diggers,' ready to vamp every woman's husband as [a] nonprofessional would have the public suppose."[38] Both Dancer's and Matthews's comments undercut the popular perceptions that readers maintained about chorus girls specifically and the world of female entertainers more broadly.

The defense of the chorus girl and other female entertainers in the press extended to what was worn or not worn on the stage. By the early twentieth century, mass-produced magazines and newspapers, in conjunction with a wider readership, helped to expand popular conceptions of permissible sexual images of American women.[39] Known as "cheesecake," images of scantily attired women began to appear in popular publications across the nation in the 1920s and 1930s. Rapidly changing sexual mores of the opening decades of the twentieth century introduced readers to partially nude women's bodies in a range of contexts that included advertisements to everyday women in swimwear sunbathing on beaches. Whereas nineteenth-century values remanded displays of women's sexuality to "underground" and "illicit" channels of commercial sex found in notorious urban districts such as the Bowery (Five Points) in New York, early-twentieth-century periodicals fostered highly visible sexual representations.

A long, complex history of black women's nude bodies foregrounded the Black Press' coverage of the issue. Deborah Willis argues that a certain level of tolerance for the sexualization of black female performers already existed in the early twentieth century. Dancer Josephine Baker's legendary banana skirt and exposed breasts simultaneously challenged and affirmed stereotypes of black women's exotic and unruly sexuality. Black newspapers testified to this as they regularly published photographs of nearly nude black women performers throughout the 1920s and 1930s. Still, many Black Press readers viewed female performers' entertainment and bodies as one step removed from ill repute. Between 1926 and 1928, *Courier* reporters asked chorines and readers, "What do you think of nudity on the stage?" Ironically, the *Courier* and other papers did not question whether it was proper for the newspaper to publish seductive pictures of performers in advertisements. Black newspapers published black female performers in revealing costumes with no serious moral qualms.[40] The question of female entertainers' nudity on the stage, according to the *Courier's* reporting, divided black public opinion. Displayed on one page, the *Courier* organized the opinions of a range of African Americans, including people who worked in the theatrical world, who voiced different positions on the nudity.

By presenting divergent points of view together, the paper reinforced for readers that it was a forum for deliberation over the appropriate sexual representation of women's bodies.[41] The *Courier* took an active role in surveying chorus girls to get their voices on the subject on record. One reporter asked Miss Spencer, "a pretty chorus girl," to state her assessment of nudity on stage: "I think a colored girl has as much as right [to] show a beautiful form as a white girl."[42] Spencer's comments racialized the debate making nudity not about immorality but the rights of African American women to present their bodies in whatever manner they liked and have the same perceived autonomy as their white counterparts. The *Courier's* coverage of the question of nudity and reader survey demonstrated one of the many ways that the Black Press specifically created a black sexual public sphere for African Americans to opine about sexuality.

Even as Jessye's, Dancer's, and Matthews's avid defense of the chorus girl, along with some readers' views, indicated a growing space for black women's sexuality that existed somewhere on a moral–immoral continuum, the chorine was widely viewed as sexually dangerous. As a result, the chorus girl was not an image that could incorporate enduring values of respectability. Celebration and condemnation of chorines, however, coexisted to create an opening for an image that could be both sexual and respectable. The black bathing beauty offered an image that was sufficiently different from the controversial chorus girl but retained enough of her sexual agency and independence to capture readers' attention. However, coverage of bathing beauties offered a model of black womanhood to middle-class African American women who refused to dissemble their bodies and sexual selves from public view even as they retained their respectability.

THE BLACK BATHING BEAUTY

The black bathing beauty pageant grew out of local beauty competitions and celebrations in nineteenth-century American society. Transformations in standards of physical attractiveness and a burgeoning national interest in beauty contests and pageants in the 1920s influenced black newspapers to cover these events. Beauty competitions had been part of local community celebrations in nineteenth-century American society. The confluence of an increasing interest in women's physiques and facial features and a rise in consumption of beauty products produced the first Miss America contest in 1921. The competition suggested that a national standard of beauty could be determined. As expected, whites excluded African American women from the pageant, implicitly suggesting that black women's beauty could not represent the nation.[43]

Like whites, African Americans held beauty competitions prior to the twentieth century. Black newspapers often covered and held beauty competitions to help increase their circulation. Nonetheless, newspapers' infusion of racial uplift ideology into their periodic searches for the "Most Beautiful Afro-American Woman" fit into a broader emphasis on women's beauty and sexuality. Papers regularly featured beauty contests that required entrants to submit photos to be judged by their physical beauty. Similar to magazines, black newspapers used women's physical images to make claims of racial pride and value. Black papers fought debased and distorted images with what they believed were representations of the ideal race woman.[44]

The popularization of bathing beauty pageants added a sexual dimension to the measurement of African American women's beauty. Beauty competitions have always straddled the line between, as Angela Latham argues, "soft pornography and family entertainment."[45] However, contest producers' emphasis on facial beauty attempted to override the sexual elements of the pageants. The rise of the bathing beauty competitions toward the end of the 1920s redirected the focus from women's countenance to their bodies. The proliferation of bathing beauty competitions largely stemmed from the unprecedented amounts of leisure time that Americans possessed in the early twentieth century. Public halls and street corners all served as gendered sites of leisure at the turn of the twentieth century. Public bathing areas operated in similar ways. Both white and black Americans capitalized on newly unstructured leisure time and could be found indulging in recreational activities, of which swimming was one. The popularity of "sunbathing" at beaches and radical changes in swimwear placed bathing beauty pageants center stage for the emerging consumer culture.

This new attention to consumerism, leisure, and pleasure grew alongside a rise in the idea that athletic activities and sports benefited women's health and beauty. Despite continued anxieties and concerns that sports and physical activities harmed women's "natural" feminine disposition, scientific and medical literature in the years preceding World War I advocated "moderate" exercise for women. Black newspapers echoed this advice. A 1915 *Tribune* issue urged females "to retain your beauty" by engaging in "systematic and stimulating exercise." Recommendations such as this paved the road to women's participation in organized sports in the 1920s and 1930s. Women found greater acceptance for their competition in sports such as swimming, tennis, and basketball. Early female athletes, however, gravitated more toward swimming, relative to other sports. The popularity of streamlined bathing suits and the success of swimming star Annette Kellerman influenced a generation of primarily white female swimmers in the 1920s.[46] While African American women also increasingly joined sports teams and organizations, they were less likely to take up swimming. Sports coverage of girls' basketball teams in black newspapers proved that this sport was more popular among young African American women. Some newspapers such as the *Tribune* even sponsored girls' basketball teams (the Tribune Girls). Yet, many black papers chose to marginalize female athletes, focusing instead on male athletes and male-dominated sports such as football and boxing. When it came to women, they preferred to feature bathing beauties over the female athlete.[47]

The standalone black bathing beauty contest was born on August 17, 1926, in Harlem's Savoy Ballroom. The management's decision to create a bathing beauty contest correlated with the rise of the dancehall as a central social institution in Harlem. Large numbers of African Americans turned out to attend the contest and watch contestants vie for a first prize of an all-expenses-paid week in Atlantic City and a second prize of a $100 bill. Six months later, the Savoy, recognizing the financial benefits of the contest, began to hold weekly contests on Saturday nights in subsequent Augusts. Mirroring the success of the Savoy's contest, other cities, in the North and South, began to host their own bathing beauty contests. Local institutions and organizations quickly realized how profitable that bathing beauty pageants could be and used them to fundraise.[48] Organizations also held bathing beauty contests for girls as young as two. The *Defender*'s annual Bud Billiken picnic and parade in Chicago hosted the biggest children's bathing beauty pageant.

Like images of scantily clothed chorus girls, photographs and sketches of bathing beauties from across the United States became a staple in black newspapers. However, they did not seem to pose concern for black papers or its readers as did images of female entertainers. Ironically, social reformers, intent on "policing" working-class women's bodies publicly said little about bathing beauty pageants or photographs of women in swim attire appearing in black newspapers. While some white clubwomen argued that "Bathing Girl Pageants Impair Morals," black club women focused more on women's presence in cabarets, dance halls, and speakeasies and appeared to overlook the sexual overtones of bathing beauty pageants.[49] In absence of moral outrage, black papers imagined the black bathing beauty as wholesome. Indeed, she increasingly became an integral part of fraternal organizations and women's clubs.

Black colleges as well as uplift clubs and organizations organized local bathing beauty competitions. The *Courier* presented Little Rock, Arkansas' Parent-Teacher Association's first bathing beauty contest in 1929. Describing the pageant as the "most brilliant social event of the season," the *Courier* revealed that all twenty-eight of the contestants were selected among "socially prominent maids and matrons of the city." One of these maids and winner of the contest, stenographer Hazel R. Sherwood, smiled into the camera with a hand on her hip.[50] Various branches of the NAACP also sponsored bathing beauty pageants. The *Defender* featured the 1933 winner of the Northeastern Ohio NAACP's contest, which was associated with their annual picnic. Ironically, *Crisis*, the official publication of the organization, did not feature the winners of these pageants in the 1920s and 1930s. Instead, *Crisis* chose to highlight winners of popularity contests such as college homecoming competitions and the winners of baby and children's beauty contests. These photographs were in keeping with *Crisis*'s self-imposed boundaries of respectability.

In addition to participating in pageants, clubwomen served as chaperones to the contestants. The *Courier* promised contestants in the "Big Beauty Pageant and Bathing Beauty Revue" held at the Falcon Club in 1929, in which "prominent ladies from different cities will look after your welfare from the time you arrive until the contest is over." Parents could rest assured that their young daughters would remain safe and chaste despite the sexual overtones of the competitions. Chaperones made respectable what would have been in another context profane.

Unlike chorus and showgirls, the presence of a chaperone guaranteed the bathing beauty immunity from attacks on her character. If necessary, the chaperone could verify the bathing beauty's moral constitution. Clubwomen sometimes directed pageants typically sponsored by male organizations or companies. The *Courier* revealed that Mrs. Charles Webster, "a prominent society matron," had been chosen to oversee the competition. Clubwomen's involvement in bathing beauty pageants demonstrated that new definitions of respectability, which included sexual attractiveness, had surfaced not necessarily to displace older ideas but to coexist with them.[51] The role of clubwomen in beauty pageants also represented the traditional roles of protector and reformer. Nannie Burroughs, leading member of the Women's Convention of the Black Baptist Convention, placed many young working-class women under her watchful eye as director of the National Training School for Girls. Organizations such as the Detroit Urban League believed female migrants' physical appearances were inconsistent with the organization's notions of respectability. The League's Dress Well Club, founded in 1917, intended to address the "almost nude women . . . standing around in the public thoroughfares."[52] Yet only a decade later many clubwomen and social reformers accommodated their ideas of respectability to public displays of African American women's bodies. Almost nude women were perfectly fine in the milieu of black newspapers' coverage of bathing beauty pageants.

Photographs of alluring young women clad in bathing attire were located among articles and photographs documenting racial progress in black newspapers. A 1928 issue of the *Defender* featured a photograph of clubwomen in attendance at the annual meeting of the National Federation of Women's Clubs in Washington, DC. A large group of women could be seen sitting modestly with their legs demurely crossed. Just below the photo, a series of three photos displayed the winners of the Appomattox bathing beauty contest. All three women wore bathing suits that showed off their physiques. One winner smiled with one hand on her hip and the other tucked behind her head to accentuate her body for viewers. In this instance, the *Defender*'s placement of the two photos on the same page proved that editors believed that both images of black womanhood could inhabit the same respectable space.[53]

The *Defender* and other papers continued the trend of including photos of bathing beauties with other visual representations of racial advancement through the 1930s. The paper placed the brown-complexioned winner of Royal Duke's 1932 bathing beauty contest in Des Moines, Iowa, among pictures such as a photograph of the Fisk Jubilee singers, an African American aviator's flight from New York to Haiti, and the twenty-one-year anniversary of the Phalanx Forum club, an interracial group of federal employees. Photographs of bathing beauties that were placed in the midst of uplifting news about black life demonstrated how newspapers chose black women's bodies and sexuality to be presented as a source of accomplishment and pride.[54]

Nonetheless, black clubwomen's accommodation of women's partial nudity in pageants rarely spilled over to the women-centered areas of the paper as few photographs of bathing beauties appeared on the women's page. Older African American women deployed dissemblance to retain control over black women's sexuality in this area. The "Women's Activities" pages of black newspapers regularly depicted middle-class African American women as paragons of "respectability." Respectability was often correlated with sexual restraint, thrift, and industriousness. Articles and photographs presenting women as wives, clubwomen, and social reformers reflected these ideals.[55] A highly gendered space, the woman's page characteristically contained discussions of household management, childcare, cooking, and society gatherings. Relatively few in number, visual images on the women's page were strikingly similar to the ones found in *Crisis* or *Opportunity*. Thus, despite their active participation in the pageants, black women took care to control displays of women's sexuality in the sections of the newspaper they controlled. Photographs and discussions of fashion shows appeared more often than pictures of bathing beauties on the women's pages of black newspapers. The relative absence of bathing beauties and the presence of pictures of fashion parades in the women's pages indicates that women viewed fashion as more than a simple mechanism for presenting themselves as attractive. Therefore, fashion shows helped foster positive images of women and aided readers in imagining "what respectable blacks [particularly women] should wear."[56]

The predominance of images of bathing beauties on pages not devoted to women's issues also suggests that male editors more than likely placed them in these areas to attract men. Black women readers certainly gazed at bathing beauty pageant contestants and winners. Like the image of the "Beautiful Women—From Colleges, Social Circles and the Home," photographs of bathing beauties may have inspired black readers, giving them a visual idea of what respectable sexual desirability looked like. LaKisha Michelle Simmons argues that young African American women in early-twentieth-century New Orleans developed aspiration models of love and romance by reading the magazine *True Confessions*.[57] The visual images of bathing beauties extended the pleasure African American girls and women found reading fiction in black newspapers and in *True Confessions*. The bathing beauty demonstrated to a mass black female readership how to present their bodies in ways that embraced their sexuality. It also offered up opportunities for black women with same-sex desire to enjoy the eroticism of the black female form.

Nonetheless, black women did not appear to be the target audience for photographs of bathing beauties. Far outweighing black women journalists in number and power, black male publishers and editors made the ultimate decision on how, when, and where black women's bodies would be displayed in their papers. Bathing beauty pageants' advertisers made it clear that men made up a sizable portion of the audience attracted to images of bathing beauties. "See World's Dazzling Cuties in the Flesh" announced a 1931 *Amsterdam News* advertisement promoting the Savoy's weekly Saturday night bathing beauty pageant in August. Another Savoy advertisement promised that the pageant would take place with "scores of the prettiest and shapeliest girls in town." The bottom of the same advertisement directly addressed male readers, "Good to look at boys,—A sight for sore eyes."[58] In this sense, photographs of bathing beauties and women in swim attire coincided with similar photographs of white women in white publications. Sarah Banet-Weiser argues, "The beauty pageant always assumes the heterosexual contract, an unspoken but omnipresent commitment."[59] This commitment helped both black and white newspapers sell papers as newspapers editors and publishers assumed heterosexual men's interest in women's bodies to increase circulation. Black newspapers, specifically, helped interpret the black female body as one that was sexual and marketable.[60]

Other coverage of the bathing beauty winners also demonstrated that black women's bodies were commodities that could be exchanged for goods and monetary prizes. The *Defender* informed young women vying to be crowned "Miss Defender" at the national bathing beauty contest at Dreamland Gardens in Chicago that noted filmmaker Oscar Micheaux would give the winner a part in his next film. The *Courier* ran a picture of a "classy Whippet sedan" that would be awarded to the winner of the 1929 bathing beauty contest at Falcon Park in Pittsburgh. Other prizes consisted of cash, gold, and trips to foreign locations such as Paris. Bathing beauty pageants offered women access to material goods and opportunities to travel, things they normally might not have had without the competitions. Contrary to white stereotypes of black women's bodies as sites of immorality, these pageants suggested to black women that sexual desirability and attractiveness would be rewarded with monetary and material rewards.[61] The commodification of women's bodies in other public spaces, such as the streets and brothels, allowed women opportunities to escape domestic and other mundane work. Pageants also served women and offered occasions for socially sanctioned "sexual fulfillment" in ways that were comparable to buffet flats and apartment parties.[62]

Over time, papers increasingly utilized more space for pictures of bathing beauties. By the mid-1930s, newspapers promoted various contests by publishing photos of the contestants in the preceding weeks of the pageants. In a photograph titled "They Couldn't Be Cuter," the *Defender* featured two contestants for the *Chicago Defender* and 101 Ranch cabaret beauty contest in New York City. Seven different Pittsburgh bathing beauties competing for the title of "Miss Bronze America" captured the attention of the *Courier* in 1940. The *Courier* asked its readership, "On a hot summer day what can be a better pickup ... how can one get a better lift than by looking at such a display of bronze beauty as pictured here?" Descriptions of each woman included words such as "sparklingly," "vivacious," and "statuesque."[63] Words such as these indicated that pictures of bathing beauties were not simply published to announce winners of beauty contests or simply to reflect black accomplishment. Readers could also find pictures of the losers in newspapers. In a photo centered on page 4, the *Defender* suggested that the woman in a bathing suit with her face resting slightly on clasped hands while she lay on her stomach with legs crossed casually behind her was "Pretty, but Not Pretty Enough" to win a recent bathing beauty contest. However, the *Defender*'s placement of the picture in the newspaper two weeks after the competition indicated that she was surely attractive enough for its readers.[64]

However, the power to decide how bathing beauties would be presented did not rest solely in the hands of Black Press editors. While most of the photographs of the women served the Black Press's conception of their readers' interests, the contestants' ostensible willingness to place their bodies on display in the context of the pageants suggests an agency that could be read in the poses many of the women struck. Aware of the camera lens, winners and contestants alike posed seductively making sure to accentuate their figures for audiences.

Editors also imagined readers were interested in viewing the bodies of black women who were neither entertainers nor bathing beauty contestants. During the summer months, newspapers often promoted and covered recreation and leisure on black beaches and at racially segregated public pools. Summer fun was often coded "female" as newspapers began publishing pictures of "everyday" women caught sunbathing at beaches across the United States. Very few images of men in swimwear appeared on the pages of newspapers—unless attractive women accompanied them. The pictures identified women dressed in swimming attire and frolicking in water as teachers, students, wives, and mothers. Historically, these terms, "teachers, wives, and mothers," marked African American women as middle-class, respectable, and devoid of outward displays of sexuality.

While women who performed sex work in private and public spaces also saw themselves possessing socially accepted identities such as these, communities rejected their efforts to maintain "complex, lucid and conflicting outlooks on sexual labor and sexuality."[65] The bathing beauty, however, offered African

American women a chance to maintain their class status and morality even as their bodies were viewed as sexual objects. Women's apparent willingness to pose provocatively and show off their bodies to readers and pageant audiences reflected both a new era of sexual liberalism and public acknowledgment of black women's sexual desirability outside of the entertainment arena.

As in the photographs of bathing beauty contestants and winners, many of the images of everyday women indicated that black papers imagined a male viewership. Provocative and teasing headlines such as "Chicago Beaches Offer More than Relief from Heat" were meant to catch men's attention and introduce them to groups of attractive women in bathing suits smiling for the camera. The caption noted that the photos offered "indisputable proof that Chicago watering places have more to offer the vacationist than relief from high temperatures." The *Defender* jokingly disclosed the benefits of Chicago's black bathing areas through the sexualization of women for an assumed male reader.[66] Other papers also alluded to male audiences. The *Afro-American* featured a photograph titled "What Happens at Druid Hill Park Pool on Hot Days." The photo displayed a group of young women in bathing suits resting on their stomachs with legs poised in the air. The photo also included an insert of two additional women, clothed in swim attire, in the far right of the picture. The caption of the photograph revealed that the women's "shapely figures attracted the cameraman."[67] The nature of the photographs suggests that the Black Press viewed photographs of women in swimsuits in gendered ways that cast women's bodies as sources of pleasure for male readers.

Headlines and captions of photographs of bathing beauties promoted and reflected a particular ideal of heterosexual black womanhood. A fit body, healthy sexuality oriented toward men, and physical attractiveness reconfigured the face of respectability into one that incorporated sexuality. Black women's bodies, however, also signified black progress and accomplishment. If the Miss America pageant served as a national symbol of beauty and refinement, then the bodies of black women stood in for the entire race.[68] The publication of bathing beauty photos, then, created a visual black sexual public sphere that transformed the image of black women from ugly and immoral to beautiful, educated, and refined. Most importantly, the photographs proved that sexuality was a vital component in images designed to uplift the race. In short, black women could be sexual in the context of racial uplift, thereby creating a modern conception of African American womanhood. Therefore, images of attractive black women in bathing attire simultaneously satisfied typical male-centered societal expectations that viewed women's bodies as sexual objects but also helped to alter the negative public image of all African Americans.

However, the stances and poses that women struck in the photos suggest that they understood themselves and their bodies as being more than simply objects in service of the race. The images of bathing beauties revealed African American women's delight with their bodies and ability to express sexual agency. The black bathing beauty brought together the overt sexuality of the chorus girl with the qualities of the virginal schoolgirl and respectable wife. The merging of these polarities captured the essence of an understanding of respectability that allowed women to traverse gender and sexual borders but remain unscathed and above criticism. The key to the balancing act, however, also rested less in who the black bathing beauty was and more in who she was not. Thus, in order for readers to accept the image of black bathing beauty that reflected the embodiment of respectable sexuality, they needed to view and accept its embodied inverse, the predatory lesbian.

THE PREDATORY LESBIAN

The Black Press found it difficult to conceptualize reader interest that warranted devoting substantive attention to female homosexuality and women's gender-nonconforming dress. Therefore, relatively few images of lesbianism appeared in black newspapers during the 1920s and 1930s. Mabel Hampton, Harlem dancer and later lesbian activist, recounted taking special measures to protect herself and accompanying women from men who might question them about the gender-nonconforming apparel of pants in working-class neighborhoods. Women who exhibited gender expression or sexual behavior that could not be translated into a heteronormative framework were also vulnerable to verbal or physical assault by men in the community.[69] In sharp contrast to a black sexual public sphere of male homosexual coverage, as described in Chapter 5, little commentary, positive or negative, on black lesbians existed in the Black Press. While it is clear that, in general, most early-twentieth-century African Americans viewed homosexuality as a taboo subject, many people reserved special hostility for female gender-nonconforming and lesbian expression.

When black papers chose to feature news about "women loving women," it was largely cloaked in violence. Stories like the one in a 1922 issue of the *Defender*, which reported that the police arrested women of the "unusual type" for fighting, were emblematic of the coverage on black lesbians. Articles about violent encounters between women stood in for the gaping chasm of a running commentary on female homosexuality in the Black Press as well as the silence on the topic in black sociology. Reports of violence criminalized black women, which supposedly occurred between women vying for the attention of another woman. In this way, the Black Press mirrored white sociological discourse that observed that women in homosexual relationships engaged in violent confrontations that involved "fist fights, hair pullings, trumped-up stories that put the rival in punishment, and every other conceivable type of trouble making activity."[70] The *New York Age* ran a story with the headline "Women Rivals for Affection of Another Woman Battle with Knives, and One Has Head Almost Severed from Body" that might have served as an example of any medical or scientific study of women who expressed same-sex desire.[71] Representations such as these reflected late-nineteenth- and early-twentieth-century sexology, which formed the basis for how many understood female homosexuality in the Black Press.[72]

The prevailing theme of violence fit sexologists' characterizations of lesbians as possessing an inverted sex role or the physical and mental qualities of the opposite sex. Any woman who engaged in sexual relationships with another woman was automatically viewed as taking on the trappings of manhood. In turn, men who dressed or behaved as women were understood to have a female constitution and were treated as such (Chapter 5 discusses male homosexuality and gender-nonconforming expression). Medical and scientific experts conflated gender with sexual behavior.[73] Already a complicated concept, sexologists' conception of inversion took on an even more problematic definition when it came to black women. By white standards, black women already fundamentally lacked the necessary qualities of femininity to qualify for normative womanhood. Sexologists, then, believed that black women, whom they already characterized as naturally mannish, were more likely to exhibit sexual inversion. They were the consummate inverts.

Conversely, feminine women were naturally submissive. Their sexual desire for men could easily be perverted by the female invert who, in interracial contexts, was typically constructed as the black other. Since the female invert suffered from masculine tendencies, her masculinity was unhealthy and pathological; it was viewed as naturally violent or predatory.[74] The narrative of the predatory lesbian illustrated the menace of female homosexuality and took on a decidedly more dangerous tone in comparison to gay men. Within white publications, the narrative was used to undermine the burgeoning social and political independence of women. As white women begin to attain higher political and social status, a discourse of dangerous female heterosexuality *and* homosexuality arose to counter any threat that might disrupt white male hegemony.[75] However, this explanation is race-specific and reflected early-twentieth-century white women's experiences. African American women who attained higher educational and social status were generally viewed positively as their accomplishment was thought to be instrumental to the overall advancement of the entire race. Images of African American predatory lesbians served other purposes in black newspapers.

The African American predatory lesbian is largely missing from black sociological studies of sexuality. No collective African American medical and scientific discourse exists to pathologize her in a historical black context. Inasmuch as the African American predatory lesbian existed at all, she occurred in the popular imagination of the Black Press. An *Afro-American* front-page story on March 1, 1930, informed readers that girls at the Industrial Home for Colored Girls in Melvale, Maryland, "indulged in homosexual practices."[76] According to the paper, older girls introduced younger ones to "abnormal" sexual activities once they arrived at the facility. The story disclosed that one girl cut another girl with a razor. Moreover, the paper not only connected female homosexuality with violence but also associated it with mental retardation and antisocial, primitive behavior by noting that 75 percent of the young women had the intellectual capabilities of three- and four-year-old children and "eat with their hands." With stories such as this, readers found it difficult to see lesbians as anything but degraded.[77]

The image of young innocent girls institutionalized in Melvale would have struck a chord with working-class mothers and fathers with daughters. Many early-twentieth-century African American parents expressed great consternation with girls and young women's morality and vastly changing sexual values, which they had difficulty reconciling with their own. Wayward daughters could easily find themselves in places like Melvale on the request of parents who sought help regulating girls' behavior.[78] Infractions that ranged from staying out past curfew, shoplifting, and petty theft to premarital sex and prostitution could merit institutionalizing girls and young black women. Many parents also requested state support for saving daughters they feared might be harmed through their poor choices. Nonetheless, families' decisions to cede control of their daughter, granddaughter, sister, or niece to the state meant that they lost control over the length and type of punishment granted to the young woman.

The *Afro-American's* coverage of Melvale was situated in the anxieties of black reformers and families alike about the future of black womanhood in the era of the "New Woman." Like so much of the concern about young black women, as expressed in Chapter 2, sexuality was at the heart of the issue. The *Afro-American* imagined that homosexuality predominated the concerns about young women's sexuality. Parents, already under pressure to block the unrelenting and increasing number of leisure activities, which, to older generations, appeared to be brimming with sexual associations, read the article about Melvale in horror.

While the point of the article was to highlight the dysfunction of Melvale, the topic of homosexuality was central to the degeneracy of the institution. Every girl of the 100 that were housed at the facility, according to the report, had experienced some form of homosexual experience. The *Afro-American*'s emphasis on abnormal sexuality made sense in the context of the horrific descriptions of the institution and was just as significant for the Black Press's overall coverage of female homosexuality.

The paper's depiction of sexual and moral depravity at Melvale was far outside the norms of many readers' experiences. For middle-class and elite black families, the moral turpitude that existed in reformatories such as Melvale was of no concern to them. In this sense, their daughters had little to fear and were out of the reach of the homosexual threat. However, because she was largely unseen and silent, the African American predatory lesbian was still dangerous. Paradoxically, her invisibility meant that she could materialize in the most innocuous contexts, such as churches and schools. Thus, when news of the predatory lesbian emerged in a 1929 *Amsterdam News*' front-page article on female "Sex Circuses" at P.S. 136, a public school located on 135th street in Harlem, readers learned that lesbianism was not isolated to reformatory institutions. The article reported, "It is the practice . . . of a group of girls of abnormal sex habits to wait outside the school and make dates with girl students."[79]

The *Tribune* also warned female students in Philadelphia about the predatory lesbian. Kenton Jackson, *Tribune* columnist, reported that homosexuals represented a particular threat to high school girls who were vulnerable to "some underworld denizen" who was "watching their every move." To prove the danger that "sex perverts" posed for young women, Rita, a student at a local high school, related her story to *Tribune* readers. After attending a show with a young man, Rita went to a house where he left her with an older woman. Rita stated: "While he was gone, the woman came over to me and asked me my age. I told her. Then she kissed me. I was astonished. I was amazed. She then kissed me again and again." It is only when the older women "attempted to perform an orgy" with Rita did she resist.[80] The article ends with a moralizing tone, advising readers that Rita's story was representative of many girls' experience. Directly addressing young women, Jackson stated: "It pays to keep your eyes open and don't get caught in vice dens. No one knows what may happen." The exposé and its depiction of an "actual event" through Rita's story fueled the power of the narrative even further for readers.

Other types of news writing in black papers further reinforced for readers the idea of the violent, predatory lesbian. This time she was in the entertainment world. Ralph Matthews, city editor for the *Afro-American*, highlighted same-sex relationships between women as particularly "freakish" and "violent" in Harlem nightlife. According to Matthews, young, naive chorines faced the likelihood of being wooed by more senior chorus girls. He stated, "A hardened chorus girl, abnormally bent, first wins the confidence of the rookie by words of encouragement." Girls, who fall under the spell of a "female invert," commented Matthews, faced a life of degradation and despair from which there seemed no return or solace.[81]

Matthew's commentary on homosexuality among female entertainers suggested that it was not so much the display of their partially clad bodies or sexuality that was cause for concern but that it could be misdirected to women by rapacious lesbians. As both an editor and writer of "Looking at the Stars," a column on the black entertainment industry, Matthews undoubtedly had firsthand knowledge of female homosexuality in the theater world. Popular lesbian performers such as Gladys Bentley were mainstays on the stage and served as the female invert Matthews referred to in his comments. While Bentley was not a chorus girl, the man's tuxedo that she wore in her performances disclosed her homosexuality and branded her a "mannish woman."[82] This automatically marked her as a sexual aggressor and made any woman she might encounter as sexual prey.

Because the Black Press depicted predatory lesbian behavior as a threat toward young "innocent" women, it not only touched on the schoolgirl but also reflected black social reformers' anxiety about the naive migrant girl trope in tandem with the chorus girl. Two consecutive issues of the *Afro-American* in 1934 featured a serial story, titled "She Wolf," that captured the challenges of a female southern migrant looking to make it "big" in Harlem's entertainment world (Figure 3.1). The protagonist, Ruby Roberts, a young woman from a small North Carolina town, manages to obtain a singing gig at one of Harlem's hottest nightspots, the "Bronze Club," through her encounter with Tandy Shaffer, an orchestra leader. Ruby develops a nonsexual relationship with Tandy as he becomes a "protector" of sorts since she is still unsophisticated in the ways of urban life. Tandy tells Ruby, "North Carolina towns are so different from Harlem." After her encounter, Ruby meets Pert Fleason, the "She Wolf" who, unbeknownst to Ruby, is a well-known lesbian performer at the club. Over a short period of time, Ruby and Pert develop a friendship; Pert shows Ruby the attention that she longs for Tandy to give her. It is only when Pert kisses Ruby and reveals her sexual motivations for befriending her that Ruby is faced with the dilemma of whether she should continue her friendship with Pert.

The first installment of the story ends with Tandy catching Pert "forcefully" kissing Ruby and a reference to Radclyffe Hall's 1928 lesbian novel, *Well of Loneliness*: "What happened to Ruby Roberts? Does she fall into the well of loneliness, the haven of twilight women?" Matthews imagined a readership that would have read Hall's work, which chronicles the life a young Englishwoman

Figure 3.1. "She Wolf," November 17, 1934. Courtesy of *The Afro-American Newspaper*.

who suffered from being a female "invert" and the social stigma of loving women.[83] Even if readers were unfamiliar with the novel, a black sexual public of women understood that loneliness and isolation was a consequence of female homosexuality.

When the second installment begins, readers are informed that Tandy believes that Ruby and Pert are lesbians. Ruby, unaware of Tandy's belief, is confused by Tandy's new animosity toward her. Only after agreeing to visiting a house that is a cover for Lilith's, a lesbian bar located in the basement, with Pert does Ruby finally understand the meaning behind Tandy's hostile attitude and behavior. There, Ruby overhears conversations between women threatening to harm each other over their struggle for the affections of a mutual love interest. Realizing that Pert has led her into a "den of she-wolves," she runs out of the bar. Safely out of harm's way, Ruby goes to Tandy's and apologizes for her naiveté. Tandy also expresses his remorse for believing that Ruby and Pert were involved in a homosexual relationship. The story ends with Ruby's pledge always to keep Tandy near as a protector.

"She Wolf" embodied the predatory lesbian in the character of Pert Fleason. The second installment of the story featured visual illustrations of Pert with a wolf's head and a female body reclined on a chair while Ruby anxiously looks at her. Ruby observes Pert staring intently at her with overt sexual interest, "Her dark eyes had traveled from her trim ankles which had protruded from the edge of her booth, up her well-formed thighs to her breast." Pert's obvious sexual attraction to Ruby disrupted early-twentieth-century gender conventions that positioned men as sexual aggressors. Tandy, Ruby's male benefactor, and other club performers recognize Pert as competition. Using language familiar to discussing a predatory animal, a performer states: "What chance has he [Tandy] got against Pert when she really sets her cap for a wren. Did you ever watch a cat creeping along a limb after a canary?"[84]

However, despite Matthews's depiction of female homosexuality as predation, "She Wolf" opened up the potential for the existence of female desire and sexual pleasure outside of heterosexuality. In an attempt to persuade Ruby to leave Tandy, Pert "bitterly" argues: "A woman is a fool to trust any man. There is only one way to attain real happiness. One way to get real love and devotion. Only a woman understands the cravings of another woman's heart." Pert offers Ruby the love and physical affection that she desperately sought. Ruby also demonstrates a sexual energy that makes her an agent, in part, of her own circumstances. Frustrated at the lack of physical attention paid to her by Tandy, Ruby thinks: "She enjoyed his company, but God! She was human. She was young; she wanted caresses; she wanted loving." Ruby's desire reflected the changing concept of female sexuality, where women could appropriately express sexual desire as long it remained in the domain of heterosexuality.

Matthews's characterization of Ruby fit this new paradigm and resonated with young women who wrote into advice columnists, participated in bathing pageants, and performed as chorus girls in theaters. Yet, the story also allowed readers to imagine what sex between women could be. The story's narrator conjured the image with the lines: "She was standing very close to the girl now. Her negligee had dropped open and Ruby could feel the warmth of her velvety flesh pressed against her own."[85] Nonetheless, Matthews mostly casts Ruby as the helpless victim of Pert writing, "Ruby tried to pull herself together, but the force of the woman so close to her seemed to crush her spirit." While "She Wolf" was a risqué story that was designed to titillate *Afro-American* readers, male and female, with scenes of female homosexual desire, its ultimate objective was to warn of the danger of female homosexuality and to restrict female sexual desire and independence to heterosexuality.[86]

Perhaps the most arresting visual representation of a predatory lesbian in black papers occurred in a race record advertisement for the infamous

Ma Rainey song, "Prove It on Me Blues" (Figure 3.2). Rainey's ode to lesbianism defiantly claimed:

> They said I do it, ain't nobody caught me
> Sure got to prove it on me
> Went out last night with a crowd of my friends
> They must've been women, 'cause I don't like no men.[87]

Listeners often found clear allusions to homosexuality in other blues women's music. In another song titled "Sissy Blues," Rainey laments that she has lost her man to a "sissy," named "Kate." Here, Rainey reveals the existence of sexual relationships between men. Lucille Bogan, more commonly referred to as Bessie Jackson, also sang about sexual relationships between women in the 1930s. In her 1935 song, "B. D. Blues," Jackson (Bogan) sang: "B. D. women you sure can't understand They got a head like a sweet angel and they walk like a nach'l man." B. D. in the context of the song referred to a masculine-behaving lesbian labeled "bulldagger" or "bulldyke." Sometimes, male performers also made references to female homosexuality in their music. Willie Borum recorded the song "Bad Girl Blues" that included the following lyrics: "Women loving each other and they don't think about no man. They ain't playing no secret no more, these women playing it a wide open hand." George Hanna's song "Freakish Blues" also reflected a lesbian desire.[88]

The advertisement of Ma Rainey's song "Prove It on Me Blues" amplified the aural representations of female homosexuality but placed it within the ominous framework of the predatory lesbian. The ad displayed a likeness of Rainey standing on a street corner dressed in a jacket, suit, hat, and tie. She seems to be flirting with two women dressed in gender-conforming attire while a police officer observes her interaction with the women. The text of the advertisement read: "What's all this? Scandal? Maybe so, but you wouldn't have thought it of Ma Rainey. But look at that cop watching her! What does it all mean?"[89] This question, despite it being rhetorical, called on readers to interpret symbols such as dress and behavior to understand the image.

Rainey's mannish stance and clothing, for some readers, signified gender transgression. With one hand on her hip and the other placed on the vest of her three-piece suit, Rainey exuded an air of confidence and assurance that would have normally been associated with males. Her confident smile from beneath her rakish wide brim hat added to her carefree demeanor. Ma Rainey's physical appearance in the advertisement, then, fit into a larger narrative of female homosexuality in the Black Press. The scrutiny of the police officer in the ad suggested that Rainey's intentions toward the women were at the very least immoral if not criminal. Moreover, the advertisement positioned Rainey

Figure 3.2. "Prove It on Me Blues," September 22, 1928. Courtesy of *The Chicago Defender*.

as the aggressor while the other women seemed to be unwitting targets of her untoward affection. The ad, then, reinforced the idea of the predatory lesbian and provided a visual image of female homosexuality that was consistent with the textual images that black papers published.

THE NEGOTIATION OF THE CULTURAL DISSEMBLANCE

The combination of textual and visual representations of the bathing beauty and the predatory lesbian constructed interdependent black sexual public spheres. Both images were the recalcitrant offspring of dissemblance. While turn-of-the-twentieth-century black bourgeois values demanded that African American women "dissemble" their sexuality to meet the demands of respectability, new generations of African American women, in part, rejected outmoded Victorian representations of women. Rapidly changing cultural and sexual values, which emerged with urbanization, industrialization, and consumer culture made dissemblance untenable for modern black women moving and socializing within black spaces. The black bathing beauty, an expansive category that included everyday women relaxing and sunbathing, widened the boundaries of respectability to sanction the pleasure of viewing black women's open displays of their bodies and sexual agency.

Images of the black bathing beauty also drew on revolutionary ideals of sexual liberalism and were at once middle-class, heterosexual, respectable, and seductive. The bathing beauty allowed interwar African American women, in the context of black newspapers, to carve out modern sexual identities that upended dissemblance and broadened the parameters of respectability within the confines of sexuality. Nonetheless, the radical transformation wrought by the bathing beauty was not without cost. Black papers helped to transform respectability by imagining the predatory lesbian as the antithesis of the bathing beauty. African American female homosexuals emerged as the sexual deviants of the black community. They were not sites of pleasure.

Together, both images, the bathing beauty and the predatory lesbian, created a black sexual public sphere that reinforced the gendered nature of sexuality by demonstrating that all black women, irrespective of their heterosexual or homosexual behavior, would be measured by sexuality. The Black Press constructed a different but equally significant black sexual public sphere to help a mass African American readership discuss and visualize interracial sexual relationships and their status in early-twentieth-century African American life.

Chapter 4

THE QUESTION OF INTERRACIAL SEXUAL RELATIONSHIPS AND INTERMARRIAGE

Readers thumbing through the pages of the July 1, 1933 issue of the *Afro-American* would have landed on page 13, which was completely devoted to photographs and stories of well-known, many of them wealthy, black–white interracial couples, including boxer Jack Johnson and his wife, along with dancer Josephine Baker and her white husband.[1] The page's banner headline, "Lawmakers Legislate, Lynchers Lynch, but Interracial Love Affairs Go On," framed the coverage as a challenge to early-twentieth-century racist ideology that advocated for the social separation between African Americans and whites.[2] The *Afro-American's* decision to spend considerable space on chronicling a short history of intimate interracial relationships of famous couples touched on many of the same themes that motivated black papers' coverage of divorce trials and sex scandals. Editors believed that readers appreciated the growing celebrity culture that dominated the American psyche in the 1920s and 1930s. Marriage, however, between African Americans and whites held an even greater significance for a mass black readership that faced antiblack racism.

Black newspapers regularly published news, commentaries, fictional stories, and readers' letters on interracial relationships between blacks and whites. Based on their perception that readers were interested in the topic, black newspaper editors devoted a great deal of space to these issues relative to other sexual matters. In so doing, the Black Press created a space for readers to voice their opinions about love and sex across the color line. Newspaper fiction that featured plots about romantic and sexual relationships between blacks and whites was heavily debated among readers. Nonetheless, editors situated these stories and readers' responses in a larger black sexual public sphere of newspaper coverage that, in part, determined that a mass black readership held diverse views on interracial sexual coverage and content. Put into conversation with African Americans race leaders such as W. E. B. Du Bois and George Schulyer, *Courier* columnists, readers incorporated pleasure and desire into the broader meanings about interracial marriage and romance.

This chapter discloses the Black Press' editorial imagination of readers who desired images and discussions about interracial marriage. Editors and reporters constructed a visual and textual black sexual public sphere on interracial marriage. It manifested African Americans' diverse views about intimate relationships between blacks and whites. Black Press coverage and short stories on interracial sexuality subverted and challenged white ideologies about interracial relationship. In part, readers' debates about representations of interracial intermarriage in newspaper fiction offered another view on the subject that was predicated on the pleasure of reading and viewing images about marital unions between people of different races.

INTERMARRIAGE AND THE FEDERAL MARRIAGE BILL

Lynching and rape and their relationship to interracial sexual encounters between white and black people left an indelible mark on African Americans and influenced their thinking about intermarriage. Indeed, the history of lynching loomed like a threatening storm cloud over interracial relationships between black and white people, particularly between black men and white women in the early twentieth century. The literal danger of these relationships—not just in the South but throughout the nation—pervaded African Americans' sensibility about love and sex with white individuals.

Lynching and rape in African American communities meant that a cultural and social preoccupation with interracial sexual relationships between blacks and whites plagued the black public consciousness. Black leaders, however, attempted to avoid publicly discussing black–white sexual relationships in the early years of the twentieth century.[3] Depending on the audience and channel of communication, the topic was fraught with controversy and the threat of violence if one were to speak about it among whites. Nevertheless, the early Black Press regularly covered extralegal murder of African American men by hanging for alleged crimes of sexual assault and relationships with white women. As lynching and antimiscegenation laws in the late nineteenth century developed, the image of the savage black male beast and his lust for white women percolated throughout the South. The Black Press not only reported on these atrocities but created antilynching imagery to protest and advocate for the federal government's intervention.[4] Most famously, Ida B. Wells used journalism to challenge the "threadbare lie that Negro men rape white women."[5] Wells and other nineteenth-century black journalists set a precedent for the *Defender* and twentieth-century black newspaper's running commentary and reports on lynching.

Notably, the *Defender* in its early years treated its readers to front-page sensationalistic headlines and photographs documenting "southern white gentlemen" who lynched African Americans by burning them at the stake. Some articles in the paper made it clear that white women's false accusations were at the root of the violent white mobs. The *Defender* reported that Reverend Grant Smith was brutally beaten by a group of white men for casting doubt on the credibility of two white women who accused two black men of sexually assaulting them.[6] By the mid-1920s, papers reported the decline of lynching in the United States. Nonetheless, papers continued to report on lynching, making sure to remark on white women who falsely accused African American men of sexual assault in articles such as the *Afro-American*'s report "Virginia Mob of 1000 Seeks Fake Rapist."[7] Many readers were already aware of the history of white women's fallacious charges against black men. Black newspapers simply reaffirmed a narrative about black men–white women's sexual relationships that had already been passed down from one generation to the next.

A smaller but strident coexisting discourse about the sexual assault of black women by white men also circulated in the Black Press. Black women expressed concern in newspapers about the lack of protection afforded them by the law. Believing that they had to rely on themselves, many African American women such as writer Victoria Constance chose to construct chaste images of black womanhood as coats of armor to protect them from white men's verbal and physical assaults. Constance stated in a piece titled "Need Chivalry for Colored Women Also, Says Md. Mother" in the *Afro-American*:

> I take particular pains to attract no attention to myself by voice, gesture, or costume anywhere in public. Yet, I have been insulted by white men, North and South so often that I cease to feel anything beyond a dry contempt at their money-jingling insistence and filthy comments. The idea of anyone being lynched for insulting me would probably move your most rabid lynch advocate to laughter.[8]

Like the dissembling mothers of the bathing beauties discussed in Chapter 3, Constance's comments would have resonated with the *Afro-American's* and other black papers' readership who experienced or witnessed firsthand negative views about African American women's bodies. White men's street harassment and sexual attacks on black women were common occurrences. Readers read frequent reports of theses outrages with little to no justice meted out by judicial systems in the South or the North.

In voicing her disgust, however, Constance tapped into black readers' ongoing debates surrounding black women's morality (examined in the Chapter 3). The idea that black women were inherently immoral often formed the basis of discussions on sexuality. Even as many African Americans expressed outrage about the attacks against black women, all too many subscribed to the view that they were morally compromised. This attitude, in addition to the cultural prohibitions against respectable women speaking about sexual topics, meant that far less coverage in the Black Press was devoted to black women's voices on the topic of white men's sexual assault. Nonetheless, black women wrote to black papers forcefully arguing that they were not afforded the protections that came with white womanhood. They injected their voices into a nexus of coverage about interracial sexual violence in a black sexual public sphere. However, their inability to completely remove the stain of sexual stereotypes made it difficult for black women to be viewed as proper victims of rape by white men and seek justice for the crime.

The narrative of lynching and rape informed many African American leaders' public positions on legislation designed to outlaw interracial marriage. Repeated proposals by Northern states to ban marriage between people of different races raised the ire of leading African Americans. One of the most notable figures was W. E. B. Du Bois who stood firmly against antimiscegenation laws. Du Bois extensively wrote about his views on interracial marriage as an editor of the *Crisis.* Many of his editorials challenged the suggestion that African Americans were unfit to marry and have sexual relations with whites. Du Bois, in a 1920 *Crisis* editorial, stated, "As to the individual right of any two sane grown individuals of any race to marry there can be no denial in any civilized land."[9] For Du Bois, people's right to select their spouse, racial difference aside, was at the heart of his argument against laws against intermarriage. Moreover, Du Bois as the leader of the NAACP understood that fears about racial integration were at the root of legal injunctions against intermarriage.[10]

Ironically, although Du Bois opposed legal prohibitions that made it a crime for people of difference races to marry, he objected, in practice, to individuals transgressing the color line with regard to romantic and sexual relationships.[11]

Du Bois believed that cultural compatibility made it difficult for couples of different races to raise children and develop healthy familial units. Rather than focusing on marrying outside of their race, African Americans, Du Bois argued, should concentrate on building a "great black race tradition of which the Negro and world will be as proud in the future as it had in the ancient world."[12] Du Bois went even further in his comments and stated:

> THE CRISIS, therefore, most emphatically advises against race intermarriage in America but it does so while maintaining the moral and legal right of individuals who may think otherwise and it most emphatically refuses to base its opposition on other than social grounds.[13]

As editor of the *Crisis* and director of publicity and research for the NAACP, as well as one of the founders of the organization, Du Bois's stance symbolized a broader position maintained by many race leaders who opposed miscegenation laws but refused to support or promote intermarriage.[14] Therefore, Du Bois was less invested in connecting his platform on interracial marriage to critical numbers of African Americans.

As far as race leaders were concerned, miscegenation laws unfairly punished African American men for crossing the color line but allowed white men to do so with impunity. In this sense, race leaders framed a great deal of protest of antimiscegenation laws around the idea that the protection of black women's virtue was at stake in the continued fight against laws that banned marriage between various racial groups.[15] Du Bois wrote:

> [antimiscegenation] laws leave the colored girls absolutely helpless for the lust of white men. It reduces colored women in the eyes of the law to the position of dogs. As low as the white girl falls, she can compel her seducer to marry her. . . . We must kill [antimiscegenation laws] not because we are anxious to marry the white men's sisters, but because we are determined that white men will leave our sisters alone.[16]

Laws against intermarriage meant that white men, in the estimation of Du Bois and other race leaders, could sexually coerce African American women with no consequences. In an early-twentieth-century black bourgeoise moral value system that correlated women's worth with their sexual virtue, black women's honor might be salvaged by marriage if she experienced a sexually exploitive relationship with a white man.

The Black Press echoed Du Bois's views on intermarriage and constructed a much more expansive discussion on racial intermarriage than what appeared in the *Crisis* and other small publications. A *Defender* editorial reported in 1923 that a federal antimiscegenation bill placed before the U.S. Senate was a "blow designed to remove all semblance of legal protection that the women of the Race, long the prey of Southern libertines, have been able to avail themselves of in the fight to maintain their womanhood." In 1925 the *Philadelphia Tribune* republished an editorial from a Louisville black paper that stated, "Whenever colored people oppose anti-marriage laws . . . the claim is made they want 'social equality,' whatever that is. But the truth is colored men want to see their women protected." Black male readers tended to agree with this premise. Oliver B. Hardon of Bordentown, New Jersey, wrote to the *Defender*: "Intermarriage is the only method by which our women can be protected in the South."[17] The Black Press's coverage of intermarriage aligned with Du Bois and other race leaders' view that black women's protection served as a major focus of the battle to halt the passage of anti-intermarriage bills.

The 1930 Uniform Marriage Bill also received special attention from the Black Press. While the law was designed to federally regulate marriage and divorce in all forty-eight states, many black leaders writing in the Black Press feared that federal regulation of marriage and divorce would lead to a national ban against intermarriage. With twenty-nine states in 1930 already stipulating against marriage between whites and nonwhites, Kelly Miller, of Howard University, prominent African American intellectual and journalist, noted, "any such [uniform marriage bill] legislation will in all human probability involve a nationalizing antimiscegenation provision."[18] The Black Press's coverage of intermarriage through its discussions of legislation involved relatively few readers' voices. Nonetheless, it provided readers with opportunities to understand the social and civil rights implications of proposed bans against interracial marriage.

While Miller, like other leading vocal opponents of miscegenation laws, did not promote marriage between blacks and whites, George Schuyler, writer and *Pittsburgh Courier* columnist, regularly commented on the benefits of intermarriage and advocated for it. As the husband of a white woman, Josephine Cognell, Schuyler envisioned race mixing as a way to solve racism. In 1928, Schuyler wrote an article titled "Racial Intermarriage in the United States: One of the Most Interesting Phenomena in Our National Life." It first appeared in *Parade* magazine but later was published as a little blue book, a publication for working-class audiences. Schuyler debunked rhetoric that characterized intermarriage as abnormal tragic unions between the lower classes of both blacks and whites. Divorce rates, according to Schuyler, were lower among interracial couples. He believed their struggles against racial obstacles made typical marital struggles easier to manage.[19] It was a theme that he would continually strike over the course of his career as a journalist in other white publications.

Almost one year after the publication of "Racial Intermarriage in the United States," Schuyler wrote about similar ideas in an *American Mercury* article. In an attempt to answer his own question, "What is ultimately to become of the colored brother in America?" Schuyler saw interracial intermarriage as a solution to racial discrimination and oppression and took pains to point out that that no natural antipathy existed between the two races. Thus Schuyler believed at a basic level that prohibition of intermarriage was designed to consolidate economic and social power in the hands of whites.[20] His view sharply departed from Du Bois and other race leaders, Peggy Pascoe argues, who, when speaking to whites, "softened their objections to miscegenation law with assurances that most Blacks always had and always would prefer to marry other Blacks."[21] Conversely, Schuyler argued that an organic sexual desire that was repressed through unnatural antimiscegenation laws retarded the natural evolution of relationships between people of different races.

Schuyler shared his ideas about intermarriage in his *Courier* column, "Views and Reviews," in the late 1920s and 1930s. Extolling the benefits of intermarriage on different occasions, he noted, "there is no more fierce loyalty than that of the parties to a mixed marriage."[22] In bringing his views on marriage across racial lines to the Black Press, Schuyler contributed a distinctly black sexual public sphere that was outside of the white publications he wrote for in earlier periods. Schuyler's thoughts on intermarriage and his own marriage to a white woman infuriated some readers and was praised by others. *Courier* contributor writer, Andrew Larson, of Cristóbal, Canal Zone, wrote in reference to Schuyler's position, "Intermarriage is just as perfidious to the Negro race as Mr. Schuyler is today." Readers often expressed their dismay with Schuyler's unapologetic promotion of intermarriage, arguing that it amounted to racial betrayal. Readers who countered Schuyler's detractors defended his position. They made it clear that marrying outside one's race, particularly to a white person, had less to do with a rejection of one's identity as a black person and more of a person's individual right to marry whom one pleases.[23]

Readers' contrasting perspectives on Schuyler's thoughts on intermarriage cast it in a serious tone that lacked the connotation of pleasure that it would have when the *Afro-American* framed the subject in night life and drag balls. Regardless of the different positions that Du Bois and Schuyler took on intermarriage, both men expressed popular positions among prominent African American men, including the Black Press editorial perspective, and made the topic a political symbol. Readers also politicized interracial marriage. However, the coverage of lynching, rape, antimiscegenation legislation and black leaders' thoughts on intermarriage was also significant in that it primed a mass black readership to participate in a black sexual public sphere that allowed it to connect pleasure with interracial social mixing and romance.

INTERRACIAL MIXING IN BLACK AND TANS AND DRAG BALLS

Coverage of race mixing in urban nightlife incorporated a good deal of black papers' objections to northern de facto laws against whites and blacks fraternizing in public spaces. Whites who enjoyed performances by black entertainers almost exclusively attended establishments like the well-known Cotton Club in Harlem. In fact, club owners regularly barred African Americans from entering their doors as patrons. The *Amsterdam News* remarked on the phenomenon of whites participating in Harlem nightlife with the comment, "Eleven o' clock Saturday night, when the throngs are out for hours of joy, the Avenue is the Uptown White Way." Eleven o'clock Sunday morning, when the multitude are bound for worship, the street is Tan Town's Holy Way. . . . What a difference a few hours make."[24] In many nightlife spaces, however, it was rare to witness racial mixing. Blacks and whites were literally separated into performers and spectators where most blacks either served or entertained white audiences.[25]

Alternatively, black and tan clubs were nightclubs that allowed whites, African Americans, and Asians to dance, drink, and socialize with one another.[26] Almost always located in black urban neighborhoods such as Harlem or Bronzeville in Chicago, the taint of immorality hovered over the socialization between whites and blacks in these arenas. Black and tans were associated with a lower element of African American life and contained entertainment characterized as sexually provocative. The illegal consumption of alcohol, a part of the scene, placed black and tans outside the lines of respectability as well as made them illegal.

Some middle-class African Americans voiced concerns that black and tans reinforced negative stereotypes about black sexuality, although they were staunchly against laws that prohibited blacks and whites from socializing with each other.[27] Like the topic of intermarriage, African Americans viewed social interactions between blacks and whites as a political symbol. Nonetheless, popular representations of black and tans and other integrated urban nightlife spaces challenged black elites and the middle class to fully support them. Novelists represented interracial encounters in urban nightlife. Books such as Carl Van Vechten's *Nigger Heaven* and Claude McKay's *Home to Harlem* featured descriptions of black nightclub entertainment that catered solely to whites. Wallace Thurman's *Infants of the Spring* and *Blacker the Berry* portrayed Harlem black and tans as hosting interracial sexual liaisons. White audiences primarily consumed novels such as these and saw them, in part, as travel guides to "downtown" life. However, many African Americans viewed books like Van Vechten's as an obstacle to black advancement. Literature helped to foster the idea that urban nightlife served as one of the few arenas of early-twentieth-century life that truly allowed blacks and whites as well as other racial groups to socialize with one another.[28]

Many black newspapers commented negatively on the increasing tide of middle-class whites in black neighborhoods "slumming" or wanting to witness firsthand the "primitive" sexual nature of blacks.[29] At the same time, black papers took a more apologist tone toward the existence of black and tans and viewed them as an avenue to more racially liberal attitudes. The *Defender*, for example, harshly criticized authorities for threatening to close the Sunset Café, the most popular black and tan cabaret in Chicago, in the early twentieth century. A 1922 article stated:

> Both the newspapers and the authorities have referred to the Sunset time and time again as a black and tan resort. It is a well-known fact that the dances and entertainment as well as the mode of operation at this place is on a par with that of any and all so-called "smart" cafes, cabarets, etc. Murders have been committed in the notorious dive which is located across the street from the Sunset—Tearneys—and not a word has been said by either the police or state officials.

According to the *Defender*, Tearneys was allowed to operate without sanction because it was a "lily white joint." The *Defender* argued, "the Sunset should be left alone."[30] The paper highlighted how authorities' threat to put the Sunset club out of business was predicated on the club's policy for admitting blacks and whites.

To further make its point about racial discrimination against black and tans for allowing whites and blacks to socialize together, the *Defender* featured an editorial cartoon sharply criticizing white attitudes and policies toward the clubs' interracial policies. The first of a three-panel cartoon depicted several interracial couples dressed in respectable formal attire. The second panel displayed another interracial couple. Again, dressed very well, the couple shares a meal. The final panel shows a black couple making their way up the steps of an establishment with the title "Café" on its entrance. The *Defender* placed the word "If" above the first panel and placed the following three lines under the three panels respectively:

Those cafes where races mingle for dancing and pleasure are to be called "black-and-tan dens of immorality,"

And men and women of both races who patronize them are "lewd and immoral"

Then why do not our "pure and holy" white friends treat us to a moral lesson by opening the doors of their places to ALL Americans?[31]

The editorial cartoon reworked popular images, which reduced interracial cafés to indecent sites of entertainment and leisure, into respectable sites of recreation and leisure. The *Defender*'s editorial pointed the finger at whites and argued that the moral responsibility rested at their doorsteps since they refused to allow blacks to enter white establishments.

The visual representation of the interracial couples in the cartoon also conveyed to readers a specific conceptualization of racial mixing. All the interracial couples depicted in the cartoon were black men and white women. This imagery upset widely held white ideas about interracial sexuality where African American men possessed unbridled, savage lust for white women. Representations of black male–white female couples reinforced the *Defender*'s front-page coverage of barbaric white violence toward black men falsely accused of sexually assaulting white women, in effect countering negative stereotypes that cast black men with brute intent on ravishing white women's bodies.[32] This view of interracial social mixing between men and women depended on a mass black readership that understood this history in order for the cartoon images to have meaning.

Similarly, the *Defender*'s images of black men with white women imagined a readership that recognized the history of white men's sexual assault on black women. To show white men dancing with black women would have evoked the image of white men's regular sexual exploitation of African American women. There was no place for consensual relationships between white men and black women in the *Defender*'s imagination. In this regard, the paper resonated with some of its black male readers who believed white men had unfettered access to black women's bodies while they were restricted from the same with white women. One reader wrote: "If we Colored men could exploit their women for the purpose of amalgamation and ours would remain 99 per cent un polluted instead of the case being vice versa I could champion your feeling."[33] The reader's comment affirmed a Black Press editorial perspective and belief that a mass black readership viewed interracial relationships between white men and black women as synonymous with sexual exploitation.

The *Courier* followed the *Defender*'s lead in defending the Sunset Café's reputation five years later when it reported that police raided the Sunset and the

Plantation Café, another well-known black and tan club, to stop the "Yuletide merriment of 500 men and women—white and colored" in the midst of celebrating the holiday season. The report revealed that the police described the clubs as "scenes of heavy drinking and wild dancing." The *Courier* offered readers an alternative account of the club with a story by reporter "Sally O'Brien" who purportedly visited the place one Saturday evening in April 1927. More than likely the name "Sally O'Brien" was a pseudonym used to poke fun at white anxieties about young white women attending black and tans. No other articles appeared in the *Courier* with this byline. O'Brien described the scene as a "kissing epidemic" with both blacks and whites embracing and kissing.[34] In addition to the sexual overtones of black and tans, black newspapers envisioned them as symbolic of racial liberalism and harmony. Articles like the one featured in the *Courier* indicated that interracial clubs allowed blacks and whites to engage in *consensual* and enjoyable sexual relationships. The Black Press imagined a mass black readership that embraced black and tans. Yet, even as the coverage on black and tans referenced the pleasure that African Americans and whites experienced in these spaces, much of the coverage about black and tans functioned as a black sexual public sphere that condemned white law enforcement's surveillance of interracial relationship.[35] A mass black readership's pleasure, then, was attenuated by the criminalization of interracial relationships in public spaces.

Race leaders such as Du Bois took a much more Victorian and moralistic attitude toward sexual encounters of any sort outside of marriage, including interracial ones in black and tans. In fact, race leaders believed that anti-intermarriage bills contributed to premarital sexual encounters, otherwise viewed as immoral, between whites and African Americans, particularly white men and black women, in black and tans. Unlike the Black Press editorial perspective on black and tans, traditional race leaders and social reformers had a more difficult time seeing these nightspots as sites of healthy or pleasurable relationships between the races. Kevin Mumford, writing about early-twentieth-century Chicago and New York, notes, "Within the black urban sociological tradition, then, the implicit, unquestioned stigma of interracial relations was pervasive, virtually a foundation of the discipline."[36] Despite many black newspapers' toleration, if not promotion of black and tans, some black papers such as the conservative *New York Age* imagined less receptive readers to interracial mixing in night clubs.[37] As the Depression began to take its toll on the discretionary income of both blacks and whites, patronage of black and tan clubs dwindled. The *Defender* reported the closure of the Sunset Café in 1930, suggesting that the downturn in the economy was responsible for its demise.[38]

Nonetheless, black and tans' closures did not halt interracial leisure spaces or black newspapers' representation of them. The coverage of drag balls offered other occasions for the Black Press to imagine readers' interest in interracial mixing in public spaces, though these events would generate white judicial reprobation that the Black Press protested. As discussed in Chapter 5, black papers devoted prime real estate to drag balls, gender-crossing masquerade affairs where men dressed as women and competed for prizes for the best female impersonation in front of heterosexual and homosexual audiences. Drag balls were often interracial affairs that included white men who dressed in women's apparel. Jennifer Terry argues that the interracial encounters between black and white men at drag balls were cause for concern for sexologists and the police in the early twentieth century who attributed the rise of "male homosexual perversion" in cities to the increase of African Americans and foreigners.[39] Combined, the criminalization of gender-nonconforming expression and homosexuality and the social disapproval of racially integrated nightlife meant that drag balls were more likely to be subject to police intervention.

Tribune reporter Randy Dixon informed readers that racial mixing played a role in the attention the drag ball received from authorities who sought to break up the Philadelphia affair. According to Dixon, the 12th Street Philadelphia police captain, George F. Kronbar, and his force broke up a "pansy" ball with "revolvers and blackjacks" sponsored by the "Other Fellows, erst-while 'Fairies' organization" and carried "19 patrol-loads" to the local jail.[40] A great deal of Dixon's coverage focused on the arrest of some of Philadelphia's most respected African Americans, including reporters, that were swept up in the raid. Dixon also made sure to expose the inequity in reporting that the white women in attendance were released while black women were allowed to go only after being retained for some time.

The same newspaper issue, which featured Dixon's report, included an editorial that stated:

> There is a hard and fast unwritten law in Philadelphia, that wherever white and colored people are gathered at a dance or public party it is the duty of the police to break it up. That is the thing which is the back of the raid. The mixing of races is the cause for police seeing red and raving like mad bulls.[41]

Both Dixon and the *Tribune's* editor agreed that the police raid on the ball was not due to the gender-nonconforming and homosexual expression. Instead, it was targeted for being a site of interracial pleasure. Consequently, the *Tribune*, normally a conservative paper that imagined female impersonation and homosexuality as a scourge or something to be ridiculed, overlooked the problematic nature of the drag ball. Just two years prior to the raid, the paper had reported with disgust and consternation that, "groups of pansies, white and colored, parade proudly along the paved pathways."[42] However, the paper, in the instance of the ball, defended its existence: "Your reporter did not see a single act during the short-progress of the dance that warranted the intervention of the police."[43] The *Tribune's* report and editorial on the raid indicated that despite the ball's inclusion of gender-nonconforming and homosexual expression, readers most likely would have felt similar indignation at the police for breaking up the ball.

Other newspapers also highlighted how the police scrutinized drag balls based on being sites of interracial mixing. The same month and year that the *Tribune* reported on the raid in Philadelphia, the *Afro-American* reported that the Atlantic City branch of the "Other Fellows Association" chose to cancel a drag ball named the "Black and White Ball" rather than follow the orders of the police to refuse admittance to whites. Atlantic City police officials issued the ban of whites based on the fact that they had received letters from white parents objecting to the ball. The *Afro-American* countered the authorities' statement and noted that many of the letter writers actually stated their opposition to the ball was due to its gender and sexual transgression and not its racial composition. The account went on to laud the "Other Fellows Association" for "coldly turning down the segregated dance proposition."[44] Despite the ball's cancelation, the reporter highlighted the fact that one could observe, on the night of the scheduled ball, "several groups of mixed black and whites" striding "up and down the sands with graceful, lady-like steps and gestures." The *Afro-American* politicized the cancelation of the ball and the interracial gathering of men dressed like women who congregated in absence of the ball, noting, "Perhaps their example set the non-segregation precedent."[45]

Coverage of the balls was caught between issues of morality and the potential that the balls held as sites of progressive interracial mixing. Columnists such as *Courier* theatrical editor, Floyd G. Snelson, grudgingly remarked that the balls, despite being a "humiliating field of degeneracy and indecency," possessed no color line. Snelson went on to describe in vivid detail the racial composition of one ball's participants: "Complexions varied from the chalky pale white of a Caucasian dope fiend . . . to the pure deep blackness of a native African. Browns, taupes, high-yellows and reds were to be seen but whites were in the profusion." Even the more conservative *Defender*, when it came to covering drag balls noted, in reference to the 68th Annual Hamilton Lodge Ball, "Members of both races mixed."[46] While the paper did not explicitly celebrate the interracial configuration of the ball, the fact that the paper mentioned it suggests that editors imagined that this detail would have been of interest to its readers.

The *Amsterdam News* even factored race in their discussion and treatment of individual female impersonators participating in balls. The paper backed Bonnie Clark, a well-known African American female impersonator against a white contestant in a female impersonation competition. Clark claimed that judges treated black female impersonators much more harshly than they did white ones and "always arranged for the white girls to win."[47] Bonnie backed up these claims, noting that in the seven contests in which she competed none of them had a black judge, causing white female impersonators to win in each of these cases. Not only did the *Amsterdam News* allow Clark to speak about racial discrimination in the context of the ball, the paper also verified her claims of unfair treatment, stating: "Perhaps there was some justification for Bonnie's accusation of undue roughness at Friday night's affair . . . scores of contestants were forcefully booted from the small platform which had been erected for the display of gowns"[48] In taking seriously Bonnie's mistreatment by the white judges, the *Amsterdam News*, like the *Tribune* and the *Afro-American*, imagined that racial inequities within interracial drag balls took precedent over any moral qualms the readers might have about gender-nonconforming and homosexual expression.

Coverage of black and tans and "pansy" balls, while not explicitly about interracial sexual relationships and intermarriage, incorporated this topic into articles and visual representation on the subjects. Black Press editors and reporters understood that prohibitions about interracial interactions held a particular resonance for a mass black readership. The connections that the Black Press drew between drag balls and interracial intimate relationships made the coverage a black sexual public sphere for politicized discussions of the topic. Like the news about the uniform marriage bill and Schuyler's columns, coverage of interracial relationships in black and tans and pansy balls became serious political symbols of African Americans struggle for civil rights.

REPRESENTATIONS OF INTERRACIAL RELATIONSHIPS IN THE BLACK PRESS

Beyond reporting on interracial relationships through miscegenation laws, black and tans, and "pansy" balls, the Black Press, particularly the *Afro-American* and the *Courier*, placed real and fictive interracial marriages and sexual relationships in the context of love and pleasure. Editors featured many of the news stories celebrating real interracial couples on the front pages of their papers, indicating how important they believed interracial love stories were to a mass black readership. Readers could find fictional stories about interracial romance and relationships in the second section of the paper. In both instances, black newspapers' coverage focused on the aspect of love and romance in interracial relationships.

Initially, black papers covered personal relationships across the color line that reflected the political symbolism of antimiscegenation laws and racial progress. One of the most sensational intermarriages covered in the Black Press involved the union between Kip Rhinelander, a wealthy white man, and Alice Jones, a woman with black ancestry, from White Plains, New York, in 1925. Black newspapers' coverage of Kip Rhinelander's request for an annulment based on the argument that he had no knowledge of his wife's ancestry absorbed readers' interest over the course of several years in the mid-1920s. Most black papers' vehemently defended Jones from what they believed were her husband's lies that he was unaware of her racial background. Black newspapers' attention to the Rhinelander case fit within many of the issues around class and celebrity discussed in Chapter 2. However, rather than the attention to the case operating as a symbol of class tensions, Black Press editors used it to address readers' anxieties over the arbitrary construction of race in American society.[49] The coverage of the case, then, fit within other coverage in the Black Press that constructed interracial marriage as a means for exposing racial injustice. Indeed, the Black Press often referenced the Rhinelander case in the years following its resolution to discuss issues such as passing and anti-intermarriage legislation.

The serious nature of intimate interracial relationships meant that most black newspapers continued to cover the issue through the lens of news about scandal, legislation, and social commentary throughout the 1930s. However, the photograph of stage performer, Clarence (Tanny) Johnstone, and Stella Sandler, his white married lover and wife of British violinist, Albert Sandler, that appeared in the *Afro-American* in April 1934 departed in some significant ways from the Black Press' customary treatment of famous interracial relationships.[50] Black newspapers had covered the transnational clandestine love affair of the couple for months. Like the divorce cases of prominent black doctors and ministers, the *Afro-American* and other papers imagined that the couple's notoriety would attract readers' attention. Yet, unlike the Rhinelander case, the *Afro-American* used an image of the couple to frame a discussion that asked a mass black readership what they thought about fictional depictions of interracial sexual relationships. The paper asked its readers, "Where Is Your Boiling Point on the Race Question?" (Figure 4.1). According to the *Afro-American*, while they were "duty-bound" to report news of interracial romances and marriages, they had been turning down fictional stories that centered on sexual and intimate relationships between whites and blacks. "We thought our readers did not want their stories too sexy," remarked the *Afro-American*. However, the

Figure 4.1. "Where Is Your Boiling Point on the Race Question?" April 7, 1934.
Courtesy of *The Afro-American Newspapers.*

Afro-American wanted to know if their assumption about readers was accurate. "Send in your answer at once so we can print or reject the stories—after all, it's your paper," instructed the *Afro-American* to its readers.[51]

The paper's invitation to readers to submit their thoughts on fictional stories about interracial relationship fostered an intentional black sexual public sphere on sexual relationships between people of different races. Even more, the *Afro-American* interjected "sex" into the discussion, a topic within discussions of intermarriage that Du Bois and other race leaders referenced only in the context of white men's exploitive relationships with black women. Addressing the sexual elements in interracial relationships was dangerous territory as it potentially moved public discussions toward antiblack discourse that defined black men as sexual degenerates. Nonetheless, Du Bois and other race leaders' emphasis on white men upset notions of black sexual degeneracy and displaced the basis of legislation designed to protect white womanhood. The *Afro-American*, on the other hand, placed interracial relationships in a pleasurable context by referring to stories that represented these relationships as "sexy." The paper's question removed the violence and terror from interracial sex. In its place, the *Afro-American* asked readers to judge stories about interracial relationships on the merits of whether they were too exciting or sexually provocative.

To be clear, the *Afro-American's* question was not whether it should continue to publish news about the Johnstone-Sandler affair as the *Afro-American* believed that it was "duty-bound to print the facts." Rather, the paper asked its readers whether it should change its policy of "turning down fiction stories dealing with love affairs between the races" and "rake up the snappiest black and tan tales" they could find.[52] Although black papers covered interracial relationships such as the Rhinelander and the Johnstone and Sandler cases, the *Afro-American's* question suggested that it was uncertain about a mass black readership's reception of newspaper fiction that featured interracial romantic relationships. Fiction, unlike news stories, suggested a voluntary and intentional effort to promote marriage between whites and blacks. It also offered opportunities to develop far more creative, pleasurable narratives about interracial relationships than the news stories that focused on civil rights and legislation.

Contrary to its statement that it had a policy of turning down such stories, the *Afro-American* took pride in the fact that it published short stories about interracial intimate relationships. The paper certainly recognized the controversy of publishing stories with interracial sexual and romantic content, but it made sure to let readers know that they accepted stories that white publications turned down. The *Afro-American* published "Her Father Was Colored" in a 1932 issue, two years prior to the question the paper posed to readers about featuring interracial romantic fiction. Celebrating the fact that the story was first rejected by white publications, the *Afro-American* printed the letter the white author, Ruth St. John, received. The paper also included the statement, "National Magazines Will Not Accept Stories of Interracial Lovemaking."[53] In announcing that it published a story deemed unacceptable to white audiences, the *Afro-American* suggested that its mass black readership was far more modern and progressive in attitudes toward stories about interracial romance and love.

The *Afro-American*, then, posed the question to assess readers' views on interracial romantic fiction as well as to incite a vigorous discussion around interracial romantic relationships. In many ways, the *Afro-American*'s question about a mass black readership's thoughts on intermarriage was unoriginal. In 1933, a year before the *Afro-American*'s question, the *Defender*, in its weekly feature, "What Do You Say about It?" queried their readers, "Do you favor intermarriages between the races as a solution to all racial problems?" Couched in racial uplift terms, the *Defender*'s question narrowly structured the issue of interracial marriage around civil rights and racial equality.[54] To stress the seriousness of the question, the *Defender* presented five well-formulated responses from readers that all advocated for intermarriage. Although the *Defender* invited readers to dialogue and present differing viewpoints, the letters they chose to feature advocated for marriage between people of different races.

The *Afro-American* did something very different than the *Defender* in that it went beyond the politics of intermarriage to create a debate about the pleasure of reading fictional stories about intermarriage. The paper was successful in its efforts. Readers' letters poured into the *Afro-American*'s office responding to its question and sparked a public discussion in the paper around the question of interracial romantic and sexual relationships and its position in the *Afro-American* and the larger American society. The paper published readers' responses over the next three months. Most of the readers encouraged the *Afro-American* to publish sexy black and tan tales. Reader Joseph Lourie wrote, "I'm very anxious to get my vote in and counted on the 'yes' side of the editorial policy dealing with black-and-white love and sex stories." Lourie continued, viewing the question as a matter of modernity: "I am sure a large portion of your young and more modern subscribers will enjoy at least one such story or article each week." Leroy Pullum of Atlanta responded, "I can stand several pages of it, one right after the other. It does me good to know what the white man and white woman are doing about crossing our line." Nelson O. Johnson simply stated, "I think the stories dealing with black and white love affairs are all right and I would like to read them."[55] Readers' ability to express their desire for fictional representations of interracial romantic relationships provided a voice that expanded the tepid support of race leaders like Du Bois. Whereas some readers suggested that their support for short stories about interracial relationships was tied to civil rights, others simply indicated that they enjoyed reading them.

Some readers used their letters not only to express their desire for interracial sexual stories but also to speak positively about their own interracial relationships. The political stakes of interracial sexual relationships made individual experiences particularly powerful and helped the *Afro-American* dramatize them for a mass black readership.[56] "I love to read inter-racial love stories. Of course, I am white and have a colored husband," remarked Mrs. Clara Collins from West Virginia. She continued, "I love my husband. We live happily together." Mrs. Sarah Livingstone, also white, wrote that many of her neighbors in her Philadelphia community would be "delighted" to read interracial love stories. Framing her interracial relationship around class lines, Livingstone claimed, "I have been married for five years to one of the finest gentlemen that ever lived even though you would classify him as colored. We live in a fine neighborhood." Another white female reader described interracial relationships as "the most thrilling type of romance and love obtainable." She revealed, "My husband is sealskin brown and I am ash blond of English extraction."[57] Notably, none of the letter writers who discussed their personal interracial relationships were black. Although the *Afro-American's* question created a black sexual public sphere for representations of interracial relationships, the lack of letters from African Americans spoke to the power and relatively security white people maintained in their ability to publicly discuss the topic. Even more significantly, the notion of a black sexual public sphere was disrupted by white people's voices expressing pleasure over stories that validated their personal relationships with African Americans.

However, it was more than just whiteness that influenced who received space to give voice to their interracial relationships. Gender played a critical role. No letters from white men expounding on their relationships with an African American appeared in the *Afro-American*. Letters from white women about their black husbands, however, spoke to the broader news coverage of interracial couples that the Black Press presented to readers. As stated earlier, editors, like race leaders, viewed sexual relationships between white men and black women as inherently exploitive. It is impossible to know whether or not white men or black women wrote letters to discuss their relationships and editors chose not to publish them. What is clear is that the editorial perspective of the *Afro-American* demonstrated that narratives about mutually pleasurable relationships between black women and white men were inconsistent with the views of a mass black readership.

The *Afro-American* also did not publish any letters from black men celebrating their relationships with white women. Conversely, readers cautioned fellow readers on the danger they believed that interracial love and sex posed for African Americans. One letter writer suggested that relationships with white women were particularly hazardous by noting, "When we think of the thousands of colored men, women, and children who have been tortured and lynched because of lying whites it seems to me that the average colored person upon finding himself alone with a white woman would hide his face and run." One southern reader, despite his love for interracial romance stories, acknowledged that, "but down here where I live no colored man makes love to a white woman; and probably won't for a long time." Signing his name as "President Stratford" and listing his address as "1 Cemetery Street," the reader may have avoided using his actual name for fear of being lynched. The reference to cemetery signified the possible place an African American man involved with white women in the South might find themselves.[58] However, readers did not need the letter to remind them how dangerous sexual relationships, real and purported, could be with whites. A photograph of the deceased body of Andrew McCloud, age 24, appeared on the front page of the *Afro-American* during the same span of months that the paper published the letters debating the virtues of interracial relationships. The newspaper reported that he was lynched after being arrested on suspicion of attempted assault on a white woman.[59]

While some letter writers discussed their personal experiences in interracial relationships, other readers indicated that black papers such as the *Afro-American* participated in truth-telling by publishing stories on interracial love. As one reader put it, a white newspaper "suppresses or distorts news of interracial love affairs. . . . I say print those interracial love stories that you have been doing so much talking about because after all they represent the truth." Another reader living in Atlanta believed that the *Afro-American's* interracial love stories gave him the opportunity to learn information he did not have access to ordinarily. "I live down South where I haven't a chance to learn what is going on unless you tell me, so I read everything in your paper every week and enjoy it all," informed James Thomas. Another reader alluded to the fact that white papers did not represent interracial sexuality. "If I don't get it through my colored press—I haven't a chance to get it through any other," commented Adrian Wells.[60] Letters such as these illustrated the trust that a mass black readership had developed in the Black Press during the Great Migration. In this instance, readers not only counted on the *Afro-American* to provide them with an honest portrayal (ironically enough) of interracial romantic relationships through fiction, but they also expected the paper to provide a space for people to express their views on them.

Letter writers also vocalized their opposition to fictional representations of interracial relationships with as much fervor as did its supporters. Mrs. Lou Ella McNorton stated, "I wish to be listed as one who objects most strenuously to 'black-and-white' love affairs being made a special feature of the AFRO-AMERICAN." Describing herself as a "constant reader" Mrs. McNorton asked the *Afro-American* to "keep the paper clean enough so that we may put it into the hands of our girls and boys. . . . I do not see any good it will do us as a race to read the love affairs of the two races in our wonderful paper. I will be glad when the mess is cut out."[61] Race pride, for some readers, represented the crux of the issue in publishing fictional accounts of interracial romance. "To encourage them [interracial love affairs] by printing stories about them is to threaten radical solidarity, and on this ground alone I oppose them," advised E. Thornton Talbot. Captain John H. Woods observed, "I am colored and I married a colored woman. I can take her any place and feel proud of her. Let me see those married to a white woman go where I go; see if they will be proud of their white wives." Another reader stated, "The white man thinks it is a disgrace to include interracial stories in his paper. Why can't we feel the same way?"[62] Readers who were disturbed about interracial stories viewed them as morally and racially dangerous to African Americans. Narratives about sex and love between people of different races was not simply about pleasure and enjoyment. Instead, they were tied to morality, racial pride, and uplift, according to readers who rejected their placement in the *Afro-American*. Readers who did not support the stories' publication in the paper, however, did not object to interracial relationships in practice. The issue for them was the ways in which interracial romantic fiction departed from what they viewed as the mission of the Black Press.

The *Afro-American* editors did not announce their decision to begin publishing interracial love stories but it began to feature them soon after they posed their initial question. The story, "Empress: A True Love Story of the Love for an Ofay Lad for a Brown Girl," appeared in the paper on April 28th, three weeks after it asked readers, "How Much Could They Take?" Along with the stories, the *Afro-American* also began to display more photographs of real-life interracial couples on its front page. A photograph of a Washington, DC, couple, Mr. and Mrs. James Clark, who boasted "three years of interracial marital bliss" graced the front page of the *Afro-American*. The paper also chose to feature the story, "Paradise Lost: An Interracial Love Story" on the same page as the picture of the couple.[63]

The connection that the *Afro-American* editors wanted to establish between reality and fiction was not lost on readers. One reader, noting the increase in front-page stories devoted to interracial relationships, pointed out that he and his colleagues now saw the *Afro-American* as "second-class because of the fact that for several weeks, you have carried as front-page news the ridiculous stories of interracial marriages." He continued, "I do feel that the public denouncing of such practices will have a tendency to increase the popularity of other weeklies."[64] In spite of this criticism, the *Afro-American* continued to publish interracial love stories that included, for example, a story of a young black woman in love with a Chinese man. Letters from people such as John Williams countered other readers' warnings that the paper would lose their audience. Williams revealed, "For the past several weeks more than a dozen of my neighbors have started reading your paper. . . . They enjoyed reading your interracial love stories."[65] The *Afro-American*, then, ran the risk of alienating some readers, understanding that they stood to gain even more.

The decision to run the interracial love stories in the *Afro-American*, however, cannot be reduced to a simple desire for higher circulation. The question about the stories helped the paper generate a broader position about intermarriage and other interracial relationships consistent with other black newspapers. The *Afro-American*'s editorials denouncing antimiscegenation law, news and cartoons about black and tans, and related columns reminded readers that fictional accounts of intermarriage could not be reduced to a question of morality or entertainment. Readers' letters about interracial love and sex both figuratively and literally intersected with and expanded other discourses in a black sexual public sphere fostered by the Black Press. More importantly, readers' letters about fictional representations interjected a notion of pleasure that coexisted with political symbolism into discussions about interracial relationships.

The relationship between pleasure and fictive interracial relationships in the Black Press was no more apparent than in the newspaper fiction of George Schuyler. As discussed previously, Schuyler wrote extensively about intermarriage and extolled its benefits in his weekly column in the *Courier*. Throughout the 1930s, Schuyler also wrote newspaper serials and short stories, under at least seven pseudonyms, that focused on love and romantic relationships.[66] Some of the stories that Schuyler wrote involved intimate, interracial encounters that reinforced his belief that intermarriage and white-black sexual relationships were affirming to race relations.[67] Schuyler's story, "Black Mistress," written under the name Samuel I. Brooks, expressed this idea. The opening chapter of "Black Mistress," a twelve-chapter serial, appeared in the November 17, 1934, issue of the *Courier*. The story revolves round Lucy Brown, a nineteen-year-old black woman and recent migrant from the South to Harlem. Lucy agrees to become the mistress of white millionaire Chester H. Porter. Because of this, Harlemites treat Lucy with disdain, as she is simply a mistress and not Porter's wife. In an effort to gain acceptance, Lucy throws a lavish party. She is snubbed by the better class of Harlem but meets Alfred Dancer, a charismatic African American con man. Dancer attempts to blackmail Lucy by threatening to tell Porter that he and she are involved. Porter discovers the plan and promises to have Dancer arrested. The story ends with Porter's offer to marry Lucy and to travel to Paris where they can live free from prejudice.[68]

Like the letters and stories in the *Afro-American*, Schuyler's story combined messages of morality, race pride, and racial liberalism within the context of interracial intimate relationships. The story specifically tapped into a mass black readership's anxieties over relationships between white men and black women through Harlem society's reaction to Lucy's relationship to the white millionaire. The *Courier* did not reference the *Afro-American* issue, published earlier in the same year as "Black Mistress," that asked readers to debate the question of interracial romantic representations in short stories. However, Schuyler more than likely observed the amount of attention readers paid to the *Afro-American's* question. As a long-standing proponent of intermarriage, Schuyler's story amplified the black sexual public sphere on interracial sexual relationships in the *Afro-American* by establishing the idea that white men desired black women within the confines of marriage. Schuyler, aware of the sexually exploitative association between white men and black women, used "Black Mistress" to reconfigure this relationship as racially progressive and one that expressed mutual sexual desirability and pleasure.

A mass black readership had a more difficult time finding pleasure in "Black Mistress" than the stories and question about interracial romantic fiction in the *Afro-American*. The *Courier* began publishing readers' responses to the story one week after the story ended. One of the first letter writers, Felix Neals, a twenty-eight-year-old black male reader from Jacksonville, Florida, wrote, "I think the story, 'Black Mistress' that you are running in your paper, is one of the most out-of-place things I know of." Neals believed that the story encouraged young women to seek out relationships with white men. "Business changes is what we want," remarked Neals, implying that intimate relationships with whites were not high on his list of priorities for racial advancement.[69] Two weeks later, an anonymous reader responded directly to Neals's comments on the story. "Contrary to Felix R. Neals's statement concerning 'Black Mistress,' I think it was very interesting and true to life." "A Reader" from Marietta, Ohio, stated: "I am a woman of 23. I do not see that the printing of your story to be encouragement for our race girls." Indeed, the reader argued that newspapers could not promote interracial relationships since God already ordained them.[70] Even as the *Courier* did not explicitly state its intention to provoke a debate over the appropriateness of "Black Mistress," the paper did so by publishing letters responding to the story and letters that engaged other readers.

The *Courier* continued to publish readers' views on the story over the course of eight weeks after the story ended. Neals and the female reader who responded to his initial letter captured much of the polarization that readers voiced about the story. However, readers who disliked "Black Mistress" expressed more visceral feelings about the tale. Maria Jackson from Lake Providence, Louisiana, claimed, "I was more disgusted with 'Black Mistress' more than any [story]. . . . I thought in the last chapter, the girl would give up the white man and his money." Pittsburgh high school student James E. Fuller also expressed his strong displeasure by describing the story as "nauseating and positively disgusting."[71] The revulsion that Jackson and Fuller expressed spoke to the larger concern that race leaders and the Black Press articulated about sexual relations between white men and black women. However, as discussed in Chapter 3, a mass black readership's conflicted views on African American women's morality certainly influenced some of the strong aversion to "Black Mistress." The idea that the female protagonist was the mistress of a white man, even temporarily, was too much for many readers to bear.

Despite the outrage expressed by some readers, other ones such as E. W. Scott from Buffalo noted their pleasure with the story and assured readers that stories like "Black Mistress" "have a tendency to destroy the artificial barriers set up between white and black races in America." Echoing a similar argument to Schuyler's, Scott viewed interracial relationships with having sufficient power to overhaul the "race problem." Scott closed the letter with a request that the *Courier* continue to publish interracial love and romance stories.[72] Schuyler obliged readers such as Scott. A year after "Black Mistress" ended, Schuyler wrote another serial story titled "A Forbidden Romance: A Story of Strange Love in Deep Dixie," again under the pseudonym "Samuel I. Brooks." Comprising twenty-one chapters, the *Courier* published the novel between February 8, 1936, and July 4, 1936. The story depicted the relationship between African American college student Andrew Richards and Carol Kensington, a young wealthy white woman in an undisclosed town in "Dixie." Andrew and Carol surmount many obstacles over the course of the story and head off to New York where intermarriage is legal.[73]

As they did with "Black Mistress," readers responded to the interracial elements of the story. However, overall, the *Courier* chose to publish less letters expressing approbation with "A Forbidden Romance" than "Black Mistress." A letter from Mrs. Horace Ware is instructive. She stated that the story was "the best of its kind published in a decade" and viewed it as a reflection of real life. Remarking, "it could easily be the autobiography of thousands of mixed couples in this country, who like myself and my husband found romance in a hostile and prejudiced segment of the South—fled the section and are raising a small family in comparative tranquility here in New York City." Mrs. Ware ended her letter with a request that the *Courier* continue to publish stories of interracial marriage that "shed light of truth and knowledge in the vicinity of the ignorant and prejudiced of both races."[74] While Mrs. Ware did not disclose her race, the reference that she made to her and her husband as a mixed couple strongly suggested that she was white. Like the white women who wrote to the *Afro-American* and praised the stories about interracial couples, Mrs. Ware used the black sexual public sphere created by the *Courier* to express her pleasure with fictional accounts that endorsed relationships between white women and black men. Marriage between black men and white women, both real and fictional, while not overtly promoted by race leaders and a Black Press editorial perspective, challenged the antiblack narrative of the violent and sexually degenerate African American man. To this end, the *Courier* and Schuyler fostered a black sexual public sphere that allowed readers to express pleasure about interracial relationships that served a political purpose.

Both stories, "Black Mistress" and "A Forbidden Romance," promoted the idea of interracial relationships as a result of consensual sexual desire between blacks and whites. The tales expanded sexual relations between blacks and whites. Furthermore, readers' letters demonstrated that Schuyler's stories helped a mass black readership to articulate and imagine pleasurable relationships with whites where love and sexuality played a significant role. The style of the stories as "true" or confessional created a realism around interracial sexual relationships that helped readers, ironically white women more than African American men and women, positively identify with the plots and characters. However, the realism of the stories also inspired negative responses from readers who correlated the tales with white exploitation and lack of race pride. Readers' personal feelings aside, the overwhelming response to the stories and the *Courier's* publication of them suggested that newspaper fiction helped readers work out issues related to interracial sexuality and intermarriage.

THE INCORPORATION OF PLEASURE INTO INTERRACIAL SEXUAL RELATIONSHIPS

By the end of the 1930s, black newspapers published short and serial stories less frequently. Much of the space in papers was devoted to the Italo-Ethiopian conflict that preceded the U.S. entrance into World War II. Schuyler began writing a column called "The WORLD This Week" that examined black issues in the context of the beginning stages of America's involvement in World War II. Interracial sexual relationships became secondary in deconstructing racial ideology as black participation and support of U.S. involvement on the world stage became the focus of attention in black newspapers.

Yet, prior to World War II, black papers created a black sexual public sphere that communicated different but overlapping positions on interracial sexual relationships. Du Bois and other race leaders and the Black Press staunchly opposed antimiscegenation and intermarriage laws but maintained a great deal of ambivalence about advocating for intermarriage. Hoping to transcend the barriers that continued to keep African Americans as second-class citizens, black newspapers argued that bans against intermarriage and interracial sexual encounters provided white men with unfettered access to black women's bodies.

Schuyler's columns in the *Courier* were a bold exception to his open promotion of marriage between white and black people. Newspaper editorials and commentaries on black and tans also created another black sexual public sphere that captured the political and judicial factors involved in sexual desire and love between blacks and whites. This view advanced the tentative stance of national race leaders, the NAACP, who were much more reticent in their support of interracial sexual relationships.

The Black Press's coverage of black and tans and stories about interracial romance highlighted its shift from simply protesting antimiscegenation laws to infusing pleasure into interracial social and sexual encounters. Black papers such as the *Afro-American* and the *Courier* went beyond simply imagining that a mass black readership desired images of interracial relationships that pleased them. They provided space for readers to express their views, positive and negative, about interracial romance, marriage, and sexuality. Readers' engagement in a black sexual public sphere predicated on fictional interracial relationships highlighted diverse perspectives on the subject. Still, it is impossible to know what the majority of readers may have thought about sexual and romantic relationships that transgressed racial boundaries. What is more important is that the Black Press's construction of a black sexual public sphere demonstrated that African Americans could see beyond the narrow manner in which race leaders constructed interracial relationships. The Black Press, then, helped expand readers' views by creating a black sexual public sphere where pleasure materialized as an important and political aspect of interracial marriage and sexual relationships. Specifically, the *Afro-American* and the *Courier* advanced a black sexual public sphere that brought attention to the marketplace of ideas about interracial sexuality. The Black Press would provide readers with other opportunities to engage each other about sexuality through the construction of a black sexual public sphere of gender-nonconforming expression and homosexual life among African American men.

Chapter 5

MALE HOMOSEXUALITY AND GENDER-NONCONFORMING EXPRESSION

On February 20, 1926, a news story in the *Defender* titled "Masqueraders Exposed" appeared on the front page. Readers learned from the story that the Chicago police had arrested "Henry Johnson" and "Alonzo Davis" for engaging in sexual activities with two men in a parked car. A photograph accompanied the story, which showed Johnson and Davis in female attire demurely sitting in morals court with their legs crossed and staring sadly into the lens of the camera. The *Defender* article went on to reveal that both individuals had been living as women for over ten years and worked as laundresses. Johnson and Davis recounted, according to the *Defender*, telling a physician that they believed themselves to be of the female sex as evidenced by their early desire to play with feminine toys such as dolls. Although the article's primary purpose was to report the "news" of Johnson and Davis's arrest, the article suggested that the *Defender* believed readers were interested in the inner workings of the two individuals. As will be discussed, black newspapers, particularly the *Afro-American*, regularly featured articles in the 1930s that criminalized black gender-nonconforming and homosexual men. In so doing, the Black Press often attempted to explain the mysteries of gender-nonconforming expression and identity, which was synonymous with homosexual desire and sexual acts in the early twentieth century.

When readers picked up their weekly papers in the early years of the Great Depression, they bore witness to the coverage of female impersonators and homosexual men that coexisted within the broad spectrum of textual and visual representations of sexuality (discussed in previous chapters). George Chauncey argues that a "pansy craze," a public fascination with gay life and female impersonation in American urban life during the late 1920s and early 1930s inspired newspapers, films, novels, and theatrical performances to feature representations of homosexuality and gender-nonconforming expression.[1] While the *Afro-American* intentionally created a debate among readers on the controversial topic of interracial romance and sexual relationships, it and other papers also used news coverage to create opportunities for a black mass readership to discuss the issue of homosexuality and female impersonation.

Scientific ideas about sexuality had a significant impact on the way that men's same-sex sexual desires and female impersonation were discussed in the Black Press. The evolution of medicine and the development of psychiatry in the nineteenth century put "deviant homosexual acts" under a microscope and produced a lexicon that described a range of gender and sexual behaviors and expressions that did not fit within "normal" sexual expression.[2] African American newspaper editors and reporters routinely appropriated the language of the scientific and medical establishment for identifying female impersonators, which was largely synonymous with homosexuality, as an "intermediate sex" or "third sex," a label that remanded them to an abnormal gender status and combined the qualities of both genders.

Black newspapers also used scientific and medical discourses to define, label, and pathologize black male homosexual sexual desire and gender nonconformativity. In like manner, black newspapers drew on popular labels such as "pansy" and "fairy" as well as other homosexual-culturally specific language, derogatory and impartial, in their coverage of female impersonators and homosexual men.[3] Within the coverage, readers, including black female impersonators and gay men, bore witness to their experiences and thoughts on homosexuality, demonstrating, at times, that pleasure was a component of their discourse. Ultimately, Black Press editors and reporters believed that their black mass readership not only sought representations of gender-nonconforming expression and homosexuality but also desired information about the inner workings of female impersonators and gay black men's lives.

When it came to African American women and homosexuality, very few black papers mentioned African American lesbians in the early twentieth century. As argued in Chapter 3, when black lesbians were covered in the Black Press, it was often in the context of criminal or predatory behavior. While black gay men and female impersonators were also criminalized in their treatment by the Black Press, they were assured much more diverse coverage that provided readers with sufficiently complex ways to understand same-sex desire and gender-noncon-forming expression. In one instance, a newspaper might cast same-sex desire among men as the scourge of the black community. Yet, in other cases, the very same newspaper could present a much more benign, if not flattering, approach to female impersonation. In this sense, images of female impersonators appeared along other representations of current events and black accomplishment. While black male impersonation by African American women was not viewed through a lens of criminality due to its association with the entertainment industry, it was not covered with the same frequency as black female impersonation.

This chapter examines how the Black Press, particularly the *Afro-American*, constructed a black sexual public sphere that generated discursive and visual representations of black female impersonators and gay men. Reoccurring coverage in the Black Press rendered female impersonators and men who desired sexual relationships with other men visible and marked them as human and active members of black communities.[4] In order to capture the interests of a mass black readership, African American newspapers fostered and utilized a "politics of ambivalence," contradictory news coverage, that opened up the possibility of pleasure within discourses and representations of female imper-sonators and homosexuality.

HOMOSEXUALITY AND GENDER-NONCONFORMING EXPRESSION IN THE BLACK PRESS

Like the *Defender's* story about Henry Johnson and Alonzo Davis, many of the earliest reports of black male homosexuality and gender-nonconforming ex-pression in black newspapers focused on criminal deeds and public sex acts. A 1925 front-page *Defender* news story reporting on the murder of a male "wife," Mrs. Florence Reed, by "her" husband, Sam Reed, both residents of Ohio, was another case in point. Front-page stories such as these simultaneously placed black male homosexual life and gender nonconformativity in the sphere of crime even as they situated them in the "normal" context of what black papers believed to be newsworthy.[5] Black men's arrests for infractions such as solici-tation, dressing in women's clothing, and socializing at clubs or parties that police deemed degenerate because of male-only attendance represented the majority of crime-related coverage of black male homosexuality and female impersonation in the Black Press. These news reports indicate that regular in-teraction with the police pervaded the lives of female impersonators and men who engaged in sexual relations with other men. The nature of their lives, in every sense, was precarious.

To some degree, female impersonators' transgressive occupancy of public space made them ripe for coverage. News coverage of gay black men's arrests revealed that city parks and streets served as sites for interracial sexual encounters between men. One reporter noted that the beauty of Rittenhouse Park in Philadelphia was "spoiled" as "groups of pansies, white and colored parade proudly along the paved pathways."[6] Many of the reports involving white and black men's sexual interaction in public consisted of black men accepting money from white men for sexual favors. Transactions such as these usually occurred on city street corners, in alleys, and in parked vehicles. One *Afro-American* reporter stated, in reference to Baltimore, "In several streets, including St. Mary's, Madison Avenue, and Biddle Street, 'Pansies' can be found cruising for [white] men."[7] An *Amsterdam News* article observed similar occurrences between white and black men in its report on the arrest of a female impersonator wearing a "stylish silk dress, a pair of high-heeled slippers and black bobbed wig" who solicited "white men only." Another *Amsterdam News* article recounted the brisk capture of a young man running from the police dressed in a fur coat and green slippers. Upon his arrest, he disclosed to police that he also interacted only with white men.[8] Although the Black Press regularly noted illicit interracial homosexual encounters, in most cases they did not function as symbols of racial progress in the ways that heterosexual interracial ones did. Nonetheless, black newspapers, as noted in Chapter 4, defended interracial homosexual spaces such as drag balls when the police scrutinized them for their transgression of racial divisions.

By calling attention to the fact that parks and streets were places where black and white men engaged in sexual liaisons, black papers revealed to readers that white men desiring sex with black men possessed the power and privilege to violate social prescriptions that stigmatized sexual contact between blacks and whites. Yet, papers failed to deem interracial homosexual encounters between white men and black men as exploitive as they did with white male and black female heterosexual relationships (discussed in Chapter 4). Consequently, the reports of white men's trespass into black neighborhoods for homosexual sex did not cast them as sexual abusers. While they certainly were not celebrated, the relative lack of silence from papers and the larger body of black social reformers indicated that the exchange of sex for money between black female impersonators and black gay men and white men, despite its visibility in the Black Press, was unspeakable. Black female impersonators and black gay men were not imagined as victims. Engaging in homosexual sex automatically removed them from the outreach of black progressives and transformed African American female impersonators and homosexual men into sexual pestilence that was considered so bad that they were not spoken of in polite social reform circles.

Articles reporting the arrests of black female impersonators gay men for public sex acts with white men often noted when they had been arrested for similar crimes on previous occasions. The *Afro-American* disclosed the arrest and arraignment of a young black female impersonator and white taxi driver for engaging in sex in a car parked in Druid Hill, a Baltimore city park. When the magistrate asked the young black female impersonator to respond to the fact that the police had discovered him in such a compromising situation, he remarked, flippantly, "Well, this is the first time I've been caught this year." With such an extensive record and experience of being arrested, and upon the magistrate's pronouncement of the fine, he immediately turned to three young "effeminate men" sitting in the audience and stated, "Sisters of the clan, I need money."[9] The three men summarily pooled their money to pay the fine. In contrast, the white taxi driver was imprisoned for his failure to pay his charge. In this instance, a homosexual and gender-nonconforming community operated so effectively that it superseded racial and class differences that might have otherwise caused the young black female impersonator to be imprisoned and the white taxi driver to be released.

The Black Press documented black gay men and female impersonators' appropriation of other public spaces such as cafeterias and nightclubs located throughout Baltimore, New York, Philadelphia, and Chicago. An *Afro-American* article, alerted readers that "Cyril's is the latest café to open which is patronized by perverts, inverts, and abnormalities." Cyril's, along with the "Hobby Horse, Tillie's Kitchen and the Dishpan" were places that allowed female impersonators and gay men to eat and socialize "to the patent gratification of the owner and manager."[10] Despite regular surveillance and raids by police and vice committees in the late 1920s and early 1930s, many of these gathering places were tolerated in an effort to contain the "homosexual threat" to working-class and poorer areas of cities.[11] However, this tolerance peaked and ebbed depending on changing economic and political forces. Officials arbitrarily entered these areas at will, often arresting black female impersonators, men and women socializing at clubs or parties that police deemed degenerate due to their association with homosexual expression. A front-page *Amsterdam News* article revealed in 1928 that "more than thirty men dressed as women" over a period of two weeks were arrested at the Lulu Belle Club in Harlem on Lenox avenue. Citing the police report, the paper informed its readers that the club had been the subject of community complaints for some time. Because of this, undercover police officers staked out the night spot and arrested black female impersonators who invited them to "take an auto ride."[12]

Indiscriminate police scrutiny evolved into an organized attack on cross-dressing men and other forms of homosexual expression in cities such as

Harlem and Chicago during the Great Depression. Floundering for a way to explain the financial crisis that unexpectedly and harshly hit communities, authorities blamed 1920s decadence and liberalism.[13] Male homosexual desire was viewed as an essential part of "new" and "sordid" sexual values. According to a 1931 *Afro-American* article, New York City declared "an open war on pansies in Harlem nightclubs."[14] Female impersonators, male-only clubs, and doors with secret buzzers that alerted club owners and patrons that the police were en route would no longer be tolerated. The article indicated the intersection between race and sexuality, noting that the police summoned and informed mostly Negro, Chinese, and Filipino club operators of these new rules. A little over a year later, the *Afro-American* reported another police war against "pansies," but this time it was against black gay men and female impersonators located on the South Side of Chicago. According to the paper, police were instructed to "arrest any man dressed in woman's clothes found on their beats," in order to check the "alarming" growth of men with same-sex desires.[15]

In some sense, increased policing of homosexuality and gender-nonconforming expression was met with community approval during the Great Depression. Residents in New York called on politicians to rid the city of vice.[16] However, despite the nexus that the Black Press highlighted between crime, female impersonation, and male homosexuality, and the regular appearance of black female impersonators and gay men in African American papers indicated that a black mass readership was conscious of their presence in neighborhoods. Even if some African Americans managed to overlook black female impersonators walking on their neighborhood streets or sitting in cafés, the Black Press reminded them that they were an integral part of the fabric of black families and communities. *Amsterdam News* columnist Romeo L. Dougherty remarked, "from what I read in the local sundown sheets fairies seem to be part of this locale named after the early Dutch [New York City was initially called New Amsterdam]." Dougherty's comments confirmed the existence of black female impersonators and gay men within Harlem.[17]

While Harlem was viewed as the nucleus of black America, news articles that documented men's arrests for sexual encounters with other men or dressing in women's clothing were living proof that cities from the Northeast to the Midwest were sites for a thriving black male homosexual and gender-nonconforming culture. In an attempt to share with its readers the expansiveness of homosexuality in cities outside of New York, one *Afro-American* issue reported, "There are as many pansies in DC as are in Harlem."[18] A disclosure such as this demonstrated how the Black Press served as a clearinghouse of sorts for men with same-sex desires that migrated from rural areas or between urban spaces in the early twentieth century. The identification of cafés, streets, parks, and nightclubs where black gay men could be found meant that other men moving into or through a city might be able to gain vital information on where one might find housing, employment, and food. Even more importantly, advice on how to avoid the police and violence from heterosexual men could be shared among groups of black gay men as well as female impersonators. References to other cities' black gay communities, then, functioned as a narrative network in the Black Press that contained potential nodes of interaction between different communities of African American gay men and female impersonators across northern black urbanscapes.

The attention to black gay life and gender-nonconforming expression in the urban North resulted in regional bias on matters relating to gay life. Papers typically did not cover news that featured black gay men's activities in other parts of the nation, particularly in southern cities where many African Americans continued to reside. Even southern papers such as the *Atlanta Daily World* framed its relatively infrequent references to homosexuality with ANP reports on female impersonators who had been arrested in Harlem or Chicago nightclubs.[19] In other cases, a southern paper might reprint articles on black men's homosexual interactions and female impersonation from the *Afro-American* or the *Tribune*, for example.

By linking black gay life to the urban North, the national and local Black Press simultaneously highlighted sexually liberal communities that were hospitable to male same-sex liaisons, including ones with white men. Notwithstanding being couched in reports about arrests and judicial surveillance, news reports of communities of black men with homosexual desires created opportunities for them to forge connections to other men in different areas of the country. Black Press coverage of black female impersonation and gay men in the context of drag balls developed these bonds, real and imaginary, and extended them further to a black mass readership. Just as importantly, coverage of female impersonation integrated degrees of pleasure into a black sexual public sphere on black gay life and gender-nonconforming expression.

DRAG BALLS IN THE BLACK PRESS

Reports on drag balls between the mid-1920s and late 1930s provided the most opportunities for black newspapers to cover gender-nonconforming and homosexual activity. Drag balls featured a bevy of largely black and white female impersonators who sashayed around dance halls in dazzling and multicolored ball gowns. However, large numbers of African American gay men who did not dress in women's clothing as well as heterosexual men and women, black and white, and lesbians, to a lesser degree, attended these events. Drag balls primarily occurred in northeastern cities in the early twentieth century. Yet, evidence also suggests the presence of drag balls as early as 1907 in St. Louis and possibly other urban areas in the Midwest. The most popular drag ball, the "Masquerade and Civic Ball," hosted annually in February or March by the Grand United Order of Odd Fellows at the Hamilton Lodge took place in Harlem. Black papers commonly referred to it as the "Hamilton Lodge Ball" or "Faggots Ball." Much of the affair revolved around a parade and contest in which female impersonators competed with each other for the honor of wearing the most creative or distinctive gowns. Men usually judged these contests and awarded first, second, and third monetary prizes. Papers noted that these competitions were the highlight of the evening and often published the names and pictures of the winners.[20]

The Black Press's heavy coverage of the Hamilton Lodge Ball was inspired by the large numbers of attendees at the event. Editors, in this sense, did not have to imagine their readers' interest in female impersonators and the balls. Reporters, who also attended the ball, provided firsthand accounts and documented that the Hamilton Lodge Ball was one of the most popular annual events for early-twentieth-century African Americans in and around Harlem. From 1925 to 1937, the numbers of attendees at the ball increased each year and reached an all-time high of 9,000 in 1937. The ball's popularity was such that spectators without tickets congregated around the event, jostling one another to get a better view as female impersonators entered into the event.[21]

The national distribution of the *Afro-American, Courier,* and *Defender* meant that readers residing beyond New York City could vicariously partake in the ball through the papers' regular coverage of the affair. Also, black newspapers from cities such as Indianapolis to Atlanta and beyond featured articles from the ANP as well as direct observations that recounted the gala for readers who were unable to physically attend. For example, The *Norfolk New Journal and Guide* republished a 1932 ANP article that revealed a Mrs. Jones's shock at seeing her husband dressed in women's clothing leaving the ball while she was out with their seven-year-old daughter.[22] The story of a wife's discovery of her wayward mate's attendance at a ball was not isolated. The *Afro-American* treated their readers to the humorous depiction of "a little woman, hatless and with fight in her eyes" who screamed at a man, "What do you want to go in there with those freakish hussies for? Come on home!"[23] Accounts such as this and the one republished by the *New Journal and Guide* were, in part, what made the balls such newsworthy events. Their status as sites of the bizarre and unusual fascinated African Americans across different socioeconomic groups.

Early-twentieth-century coverage of the balls indicated that Harlem's "most prominent lawyers, physicians, teachers, artists, writers and teachers" made up a significant number of the spectators.[24] It was a veritable "who's who" of black society inside the event. Dougherty of the *Amsterdam News* complained, "For weeks before this Hamilton Lodge Affair I am besieged by a number of people who consider themselves the last word in sepia society for tickets."[25] As the ball grew in size and notoriety during the late 1920s and the 1930s, newspapers listed the more prominent attendees by names. Figures such as Countee Cullen and Wallace Thurman, famed Harlem Renaissance writers, and Carl Van Vechten, a white wealthy patron of black artists, made regular appearances on the roster of spectators listed in various articles. Reporting the names of important African American guests made it clear to readers that the Hamilton Lodge Ball was a significant event that even the "crème de la crème" of black society attended. Black papers' specific reference to crowd size and attendees also expanded the black public sexual sphere of gay life and gender-nonconforming expression beyond the immediate black mass readership of African American papers. Readers taking in reports of large crowds of people attending and observing the ball vicariously experienced the pleasure of participating in the event.

Even as the Black Press depicted the Hamilton Lodge Ball and Harlem as the center of black gay life, the *Afro-American* chronicled an active and lively ball culture that also existed in Baltimore. The city was home to the "Annual Masque" or "Elks Lodge" ball held at the local Elks hall. As early as 1924, the *Defender* described the ball as a "Baltimore Jamboree," in which "all of the feminine contingent so gorgeously gowned were men in women's clothing." One year later, the *Afro-American* reported that the annual dance hosted "one hundred and fifty bearded men dressed in female garb."[26] In 1927, the *Afro-American* noted that the Elks Ball hosted their "Fifth Annual Mask Ball" that featured female impersonators from Philadelphia, Atlantic City, New York City, and Washington, DC, suggesting the increasing popularity of the ball for out-of-town female impersonators. The *Afro-American* consistently cited 200 guests at the annual Elks Ball between 1925 and 1935. Still, attendance at the Elks Lodge Ball in Baltimore was considerably less than the Hamilton Lodge Ball in Harlem. The relatively low attendance was obviously due to the smaller number of African Americans residing in Baltimore. On the other hand, one *Afro-American* article noted that invitations to the balls hosted by the Art Club were selectively given and sometimes exclusively distributed among "handsome youths who frequent the Y.M.C.A. and adjacent lunch rooms."[27] The Art Club strictly adhered to a "no spectators rule" that was temporarily lifted in 1931 to "local society folk to view the revels from the balcony." However, the club reinstated the policy in 1932 to the disappointment of hundreds of women, men, and children who "clamored about the entrance in seeking admission" into the event. In spite of the Elks Ball participants' desire for greater privacy than their counterparts in Harlem, the event was just as popular in a proportional sense.[28]

As in Baltimore, drag balls and a culture of female impersonation in nightlife in Philadelphia, Chicago, and Pittsburgh were much smaller in scale than the Hamilton Lodge Ball. During the 1920s, the *Tribune* paid very little attention to local news of female impersonators and gay men in Philadelphia. The *Tribune's* coverage of balls emerged in the early 1930s with a front-page article reporting the occasion of the "Beaux Art" "pansy" ball in Philadelphia. Few reports in the *Tribune* of balls followed. The *Tribune's* conservative reputation and penchant for respectability was consistent with the paper's irregular coverage of the affairs. Similarly, the *Courier* and *Defender* also failed to document many of the female impersonators who performed in nightclubs in Pittsburgh's black Hill District and in Chicago's Bronzeville.[29] Both Robert Vann and Robert Abbott, editors of the *Courier* and *Defender*, respectively, expressed their dislike for sensationalism despite their extensive use of it. According to biographer Andrew Bruni, Vann "disliked stories of interracial sex affairs or sordid crimes which catered to the morbid side of readers' imaginations."[30] All three papers appeared to shield their readers from representations that might offend their sensibilities and imagined a mass black readership with little interest in the subject. Therefore, coverage of female impersonators and black gay men in the *Tribune, Courier,* and *Defender,* and even the *Amsterdam News* to some degree, paled in comparison to the coverage that the *Afro-American* devoted to the subject.

Ironically, if newspapers feared that they would compromise readers' respectability by covering female impersonators, many accounts of balls suggested that they rivaled upstanding women in dress and style. According to *Afro-American* columnist Matthews, "Some of the best dressed 'women' in the night clubs and taverns turn out to be men."[31] Dressed in beautiful ball gowns with perfectly coiffed hair, female impersonators represented the feminine art of refinement. Black Press reports of the balls often contained very detailed descriptions of female impersonators' costumes and clothing. An article in the *New York Amsterdam News* described one impersonator as wearing

> a gown of silver and black brocaded cloth with a diagonal shoulder effect. A thin ermine strap crossed the right shoulder and a ruby clip was used to pin the pointed neck. A silver cape lined with ruby satin, ruby and silver earrings and black and silver slippers completed the outfit. The masquerader wore an iron gray wig.[32]

An issue of the *Amsterdam News* included an article covering the Hamilton Lodge Ball that reported, "Women attending the ball received several hints on style." The *Afro-American* in an article titled "Want to Know What the Well-Dressed Woman Should Wear? . . . Ask the Pansies" advised, "Women who pride themselves on being well-dressed and up to minute on the latest dictates of fashion."[33] Articles such as these not only informed their readers that female impersonators dictated fashion but imagined that their readership was receptive to this notion.

To some extent, articles confirmed Black Press editors and reporters' idea of a mass black female readership that experienced pleasure viewing the clothing that female impersonators wore. An *Amsterdam News* article declared that women often crowded around the procession of "pansies" entering the Lenox Club in Harlem, hoping to get a view of the latest fashionable dresses worn by the female impersonators. The *Afro-American* also reported that "the spectators, mostly women, gasped at the expensive gowns they [female impersonators] wore" at a 1933 Pre-Halloween Ball in Baltimore.[34] However, the coverage of female impersonators' dress and women's reactions to it symbolized more than recognition of female impersonators' good taste in clothing. It also intersected with African American middle-class anxiety about black working-class and migrants' dress that appeared in the Black Press. Fashionable dress not only encompassed efforts to present oneself as respectable and beautiful but included readers' aesthetic pleasure at seeing African Americans, irrespective of sexuality and gender, dressed fashionably.

Even as fashionable images of female impersonators might have highlighted middle-class black social reformers' efforts to police and regulate working-class women's dress and public appearance, they also exposed the misconception that dress would change how poor African Americans were treated.[35] Detailed and flattering descriptions aside, reporters also joked and sneered at female impersonators' bodies. One *Afro-American* reporter stated, "From underneath her dress bunions stood out like mountains between her sandaled feet. The dirt fairly caked around the toes." *Amsterdam News* columnist Rouzeau claimed that some of the contestants looked like "hell." While another *Afro-American* reporter observed, "a few of the 'girls' had big feet." The *Afro-American* went as far as using the newsy comic strip "They Are All in the News of the Week" to decry ball participants with a cartoon image that displayed two men dressed in "drag." In the image, one man smokes a cigar while the other one is shown taking off his wig to reveal his balding pate.[36] Black reporters' ridicule of female impersonators indicated that fashionable dress on its own could not render respectability.

The Black Press's unflattering depictions of black female impersonators, however, did not go unchallenged. The *Afro-American* revealed one female impersonator's disagreement with the paper's mocking representations. Approaching a reporter covering the ball, a female impersonator took issue with the way in which black papers wrote up the previous year's event. According to him, the article had made disparaging comments about "men in evening gowns with hard muscles." "Look at me," commanded the female impersonator, "My arms are as soft as any woman's." The female impersonator's recollection of the preceding year's article and determination to influence future coverage of the ball suggests the significant role that some female impersonators believed black papers played in helping readers imagine and understand gender-nonconforming expression. The female impersonator's comments also demonstrated that female impersonators were a part of a mass black readership that consumed images of gender and sexuality in black papers. In this particular instance, the female impersonator wanted to make sure that the *Afro-American* portrayed the bodies of female impersonators as accurately as possible. Thus, female impersonators actively contributed to a black sexual public sphere, participating in a process of self-cultivation that resisted male reporters use of their images to degrade gender-nonconforming behavior and identity.[37]

Yet, despite negative portrayals, some reporters spoke positively about female impersonators. An *Amsterdam News* reporter observed: "Once a man . . . 'she' spun gracefully on the stand revealing 'her' beautiful calves, 'her' shapely hips, 'her' well portioned breasts, 'her' sensuous lips."[38] While he carefully included quotation marks around the pronoun "her," his comments expressed sexual desire. Roi Ottley, an *Amsterdam News* columnist also expressed his sexual attraction with remarks such as, "Some of the contestants were luscious looking wenches." Another *Amsterdam News* reporter seemed astonished at his sexual attraction to one of the female impersonators, noting, "The amazement of this department reached its height when a dazzlingly beautiful 'girl' made 'her' appearance in a low-cut gown with a silver fox fur yoke."[39] Reporters' comments disclosed to readers that female impersonators were not simply perverts that deserved wholesale rejection. Indeed, their commentary, even ones said in jest, suggested to readers that "normal" men found female impersonators desirable.

In view of the ambiguous approach that black newspapers took in their depiction of female impersonators, it stood to reason that some papers like the *Amsterdam News* and *Afro-American* regularly published pictures of many of the prizewinners, showing off elaborate gowns and feminine physiques, in the sections of the paper dedicated to showcasing the "news of the day" (Figure 5.1).

Hence, a "politics of ambivalence" opened a mass black readership up to differ-ent possibilities and interpretations of desire, gender, and sexuality, which in turn shaped the coverage of female impersonators and gay men.[40] Thus, ridicul-ing female impersonators also helped to construct the "myth of heterosexuality as the morally superior sexuality" and operated as cover against potential attacks on male reporters' sexuality for reporting gender-nonconforming expression and homosexual desire.[41] To some extent, like black womanhood in the Black Press (discussed in Chapter 3), black manhood was heterosexual by default and dependent on the disavowal of homosexuality and female impersonation.[42] Demeaning images of female impersonators meant that heterosexual male readers could use a black sexual public sphere in the Black Press to safely view the images of female impersonators without calling their manhood or sexuality into question.

The ability to maintain a respectable image of manhood was integral to male reporters' ability to explain the ecosystem of drag balls to readers. Reporters often attended balls and provided firsthand accounts and intimate knowledge of the events.[43] Matthews wrote in a front-page article in the *Afro-American*: "Coming out parties among the pansies take two distinct forms. There are the sweet young things . . . and those of spinster age, who . . . cast discretion to the winds and blossom forth in all their glory."[44] A 1932 *Courier* report on that year's Hamilton Lodge Ball struck an anthropological tone, "Dances are their big social events which they look forward to with great anticipation." Similarly, in the same year, an *Afro-American* article on the Elks Ball reported that "steam-ing hot dogs" and "punch" were served to men "dancing together with one of the duo gazing soulfully into the eyes of the other." Making sure to establish that many of the guests engaged in sexual intercourse at the end of the night, Matthews informed readers that black female impersonators and partners went to "various apartments where they paired off" for the evening.[45] In this sense, Matthews' article struck the same tone as the notorious Committee of Four-teen, established by the New York Anti-Saloon League, as well as other anti-vice organizations created to surveil and curb illicit activity in public settings, including homosexuality.[46] However, as much as Black Press coverage of sexual encounters in balls might have sounded like police surveillance, it remained dramatically apart from it. Rather than serving the interests of white social reformers and law enforcement, information about gender-nonconforming expression and homosexuality appeased the imagined curiosity of a mass black readership, which included people with a range of different sexual desires and interests.

Annual "Pansy" Ball Colorful—Larry Gains New British Champ—Prisoner, Given 3rd Degree, Kills Cops

FORD PAYS EARLY MORNING VISIT TO THIS HOUSE.—The dwelling at 1500 Argyle avenue, from which the porch and steps were torn away by this car. The accident was the result of a collision at the corner of Mosher Street and Argyle Avenue between this machine, driven by Earl Harrison, and a Ford roadster, driven by Miss Catherine Brown. Both drivers suffered cuts and bruises.

WILL APPEAR IN EASTER PARADE.—Miss Bernice Kinney, former Douglas Hi graduate, who has held the spotlight in several annual Easter Sunday parades. She will be seen again in a gay colorful spring ensemble this Easter.

THIRD DEGREE METHODS LED PRISONER TO DO THIS.—The shattered cell window in a New Orleans, La., police station, from which Percy Thompson shot and killed two white cops and a fellow trusty after he was beaten severely by cops. The feet of one of the dead men can be seen at the right.

ONE OF BALTIMORE'S SMARTEST DRESSED SOCIAL CLUBS.—The "Tootsie Wootsie" Club as they appeared in a body recently at a basketball game. Left to right, sitting, Misses Sarah Brooks, Mae Henson, Christine Conway, and Cayolyn Riley. Standing, Misses Helen Holland, Vernice Conway, Ruth Mitchell and Mary Butler.

BALTIMORE'S SADDEST FUNERAL.—Pallbearers bearing the casket of Mrs. Anness Creditt Woodford, local teacher, who put up a most desperate but losing fight for her life that she might remain here long enough to rear her two children. She was the wife of Charles Woodford, local high school teacher.

THE NEW CHAMPION OF GREAT BRITAIN AND HIS MANAGER.—Bearing the scars of his victorious battle, Larry Gains, Canadian champion, is shown in his home in London, England, enjoying breakfast with his white wife. Just the night before, Larry won the heavyweight belt from Don McCorkindale.

WIDE AWAKE. — Kate Brooks, the 18-month-old daughter of Mr. and Mrs. A. V. Brooks.

THEY SERVE HARMONY DE LUXE ON THE AIR.—A quintet of musical chefs who are heard weekly over Station WHAS, Louisville, Ky. The principal instrument of the orchestra is a jug, which is played as a wind instrument and gives the sound of a cello.

NO PRINCE?—Milako Bayun, Abyssinian, Howard U. (medical) student, who disclaims royalty. Was sent here by his government.

ODD FIGURES AND GORGEOUS GOWNS FEATURE "PANSY" PROM.—A trio of the "lovely creatures" who attended the annual ball last week at the Elks' Hall. They are, left to right: "Lady Baltimore," H. Neale, D.C., and Madam White. Their ensembles were most complete, including chow gloves, pocket books, jewelry and in some cases, flowers.

TRAINER DROPS DEAD AS HIS CHARGE WINS BOUT.—Photo shows Donald McCorkindale, South African champion, being counted out by the referee after being floored by Larry Gains recently in London. At the ringside, Jack Goodwin, trainer of Gains, fainted and died of heart failure as the decision was announced.' Gains is the new heavyweight champion of the British Empire.

Figure 5.1. "Annual 'Pansy' Ball Colorful," March 26, 1932. Courtesy of *The Afro-American Newspapers*.

The same *Afro-American* article shared with readers "private" conversations between female impersonators attending the event. One conversation disclosed a female impersonator's difficulty purchasing lingerie at a local clothing store and another's trouble working as a housemaid. The same article also revealed that female impersonators worked in "masculine" occupations as elevator operators, handymen, laborers, and dishwashers. The article highlighted the dual identities that men bore as they navigated a "normal" world that barely tolerated open displays of gender nonconformativity and homosexuality. Coverage such as this created a black sexual public sphere that fleshed out female impersonators' lives for a mass black readership. While readers could not literally engage in a debate or discussion with female impersonators, they were afforded an opportunity to learn how individuals with gender-nonconforming identities navigated African American communities.

SEXOLOGY AND FEMALE IMPERSONATORS' SELFHOOD

Black newspapers relied on sexology, the scientific study of human sexuality, to describe black gay men and female impersonators. Reporters' articles, laden with sexology discourse, made homosexual acts and gender-nonconforming expression synonymous with one's selfhood. New developments in psychology indicated that sexuality played a role in personality formation. As a result, the creation of sexual identities and the use of "heterosexual" and "homosexual" as categories became primary ways to identify and classify individuals.[47] Sexologists argued that homosexual behavior reflected mental disorders that characterized people as perverts. Sexual abnormality was pervasive in black and immigrant communities, according to sex experts. In part, sexologists made this assertion in response to the rapidly increasing settlement of immigrants and African Americans into cities in the late nineteenth and early twentieth century. These urban centers contained, as far as they were concerned, large numbers of degenerates and morally defective types that preyed on the "virtuous" and "normal." The Black Press's discussions of homosexuality and gender-nonconforming expression reflected some of these shifts in the meaning of homosexual acts and desire in the medical and science professions. As discussed in Chapter 3, the Black Press, in particular the *Afro-American*, organized their sparse coverage of lesbians around the theme of sexual predation.

Sexology as a means for understanding homosexual desire also shaped the Black Press's coverage of homosexuality and gender-nonconforming expression in the context of the balls. Inspired by the recent occurrence of two balls in Baltimore and New York City, Matthews wrote "Are Pansies People?" for a

1932 issue of the *Afro-American* in an effort to help his readers understand what was responsible for the "neuter gender flooding America." According to Matthews, scientific research "proved" that changes in the activities of certain sex glands could transform a person into the opposite sex. This formed the basis for his explanation to readers of how it was possible for a "man to love a man or a woman to love a woman with a sensuous lustful feeling."[48] Matthew's recitation of scientific facts reflected hormonal research conducted by endocrinologists in the early 1930s that suggested that homosexuality was tied to physiological dysfunction. Medicalizing homosexuality complicated the overarching criminal association that the Black Press created with frequent reports of black gay men and female impersonators' arrest for solicitation and cross-dressing. By calling attention to the biological component of homosexuality, Matthews's article, amid the growing popularity of understanding same-sex sexuality as a byproduct of a physical pathogen, implicitly asked a mass black readership: if female impersonators and men who loved other men were afflicted with a biological malady, how, then, could they be held responsible for actions that were deemed morally reprehensible?

This question troubled prominent AME minister Reverend Charles E. Stewart. Also familiar with theories of sexology, Stewart took "untrained" *Afro-American* readers to task for their inability to scientifically understand homosexuality. Stewart explained in great detail that homosexuality was a deeply rooted psychoanalytical issue that was not necessarily linked to immorality. Spanning two columns in length, Stewart wrote passionately about the "pansy problem." He believed that the real issue resided with people who either ridiculed or criticized "pansies" and concluded, "Biologically, the pansy needs the pity and sympathy of society instead of ostracism and ridicule."[49] Stewart's analysis of same-sex desires mirrored sexologists who described expressions of this sort as if it were a defect of birth as well as increasingly common among African American leaders.[50] Unsurprisingly, then, clergymen as a group generally denounced same-sex acts among men and women and maintained that homosexuality was a scourge that should be wiped out.

The growing presence of black gay men, female impersonators, and lesbians in public space, particularly within the milieu of balls, was cause for ministers' concern. Despite their own participation in sexual scandals that frequently showed up on the front pages of newspapers (see Chapter 1), ministers, as moral leaders, believed that they had a special obligation to warn their congregations of the threat that homosexuality and gender-nonconforming expression posed. Sometimes preachers accused other ministers of homosexual indiscretions. Reverend Adam Clayton Powell, pastor of the Abyssinian Baptist Church in

Harlem, preached that the homosexual menace had infiltrated churches, and the pulpit was the first place in which "moral degenerates" should be expunged. Yet Powell's denunciations appeared less to do with homosexual expression and more to do with a small group of ministers' sexual molestation of young boys and male teenagers. Bothered by the Church's continued support of pastors such as the ones he cited as having been accused by "five boys in sworn affidavits with wrecking them morally," Powell railed at his congregation that homosexuality was one of the most "horrible, debasing, alarming and damning vices of present day civilization."[51] Whether Powell's accusation was correct is unknown. Two significant ideas, however, emerged from it. First, Powell correlated homosexuality with the sexual assault of children. Second, the Black Press propagated the correlation between homosexuality and pedophilia made by Powell. *The New York Age* reported on Powell's sermon in a lengthy article on its front page and the *Afro-American*, in typical fashion, also, though in much shorter form, featured a front-page article on the sermon. Thus, Powell's damning conflation of homosexuality with sexual molestation was strengthened by the attention it received from both papers. Like other news about ministers and sexual scandals, the articles were placed on the newspapers' front pages to attract readers interested in the prominence of Powell and his exposure of other ministers. The papers' decision to run the articles on the front page indicated that they believed homosexuality within the Black Church was a topic of concern and interest for a mass black readership.

The fascination with black female impersonators and homosexuality among everyday African Americans and the threat it posed to morality, in the minds of ministers, motivated Bishop R. C. Lawson, founder and pastor of Refuge Church of Christ in Harlem, to give a "special sermon" titled, "The Fairies' Ball, the Faggots' Ball and What It Means in the Light of the Scriptures." Promoted by display cards and an advertisement in the *New York Age* in the weeks preceding the sermon, Lawson spoke to a standing-room-only "seething mass of humanity" on a Sunday evening on February 23, 1930. It was just two nights after Lawson, along with two of his parishioners, had attended the 62nd Annual Hamilton Lodge Ball so that he might witness for himself the "degeneracy" he had read about, according to him, in the *Afro-American*. However, unable to speak about what he saw, for, as Lawson put it, he was "lost for words," Lawson read verbatim from the paper's coverage of the ball. In using the *Afro-American* to contextualize his condemnation of homosexuality, Lawson reinforced for his parishioners the important role that the Black Press held as a black sexual public sphere of knowledge and discourse on homosexuality.

Black newspapers' publication of ministers' commentary on homosexuality was not an endorsement of their views. Nevertheless, black newspapers' coverage of ministers' use of scientific theories to expound the origins of homosexuality affirmed the Black Church's attempt, as well as that of the Black Press, to serve as an "avenue of truth production" on homoerotic desire.[52] The Black Church, however, fostered a competing but closed black sexual public sphere, which left little room for debate and discussion on how African Americans might understand and experience homosexuality and gender-nonconforming expression. The Black Press, with its diverse representations of female impersonators and its dependence on a mass black readership to sell papers, in contrast, generated dialogue that offered readers the opportunity to weigh in on the meaning of homosexuality and gender nonconformativity.

READERS, HOMOSEXUALITY, AND GENDER NONCONFORMATIVITY

The Black Press's publication of readers' letters to the editor on homosexuality and female impersonators created an opportunity for exchange and dialogue where the Black Church did not. A 1933 front-page *Tribune* article with the headline "Society Looks On as Pansies Frolic" generated the most wide-ranging public debate among everyday early-twentieth-century African Americans on homosexuality and female impersonators. The issue at hand was whether gay men, female impersonators, and drag balls, such as the one held in the Strand Ballroom in Philadelphia, were welcome in black communities. *Tribune* columnist Randy Dixon's comments that "fairies, sissies, faggots, and pansies" were an affront to moral and respectable individuals kicked off the debate. Written in a scathing and derisive tone, Dixon's front-page article on the ball condemned female impersonators, describing them as rising "up from the mists of shame they came to toast their sexual irregularities." Steeped in the language of sexology and religious ideology, Dixon characterized female impersonators as "things" whose souls were born inside out," and closed his commentary by stating, "The whole of it [the ball] inundated the Strand Ballroom with an unnaturalness that was depressing."[53] Dixon's comments were hardly unusual or surprising for that matter. Given that the *Tribune* was relatively conservative compared to its counterparts and featured little coverage of female impersonation and homosexuality, the paper's stance suggested that it believed readers were relatively intolerant of the topic.

Readers' letters challenging Dixon's depiction of black gay men and female impersonators poured into the *Tribune* office for several weeks after the publication of his article. Despite the *Tribune*'s scant coverage of balls, many readers expressed their support not only for the event but for homosexuals generally. The *Tribune*, in an effort to directly address the overwhelming number of responses, devoted a two-column article to discussing the letters. It began: "Many letters have reached us, expressing dissatisfaction with the treatment of the Beaux Art Ball promoted by these inverts." The paper went on to inform readers that twenty-eight choir members at a "well-known uptown church" threatened to stop reading the *Tribune* because their organist was a "pansy." Furthermore, the choir members demanded that the paper retract Dixon's inflammatory statements.[54] Another letter writer recommended that the *Tribune* employ a homosexual man so that they might have someone familiar with the subject. The writer continued by stating that homosexuals were intellectually superior to normal men. One woman chided the *Tribune* for its negative comments, saying that it should have sympathy for the ball participants. Homosexuals, she argued, suffered from "bi-sexuality," though it was unclear what she meant by this term. A different writer also indicated that empathy with homosexuals was in order. Taking a dig at Dixon, the writer went on to state, "These people who are having so much to say should look over some of their own company." A month after the article was published, a father of eight children advised the *Tribune* that some of his children might grow up to be "fairies." "Therefore," he claimed, "we should help . . . and not scorn them. They are human as well as you and I."[55] *Tribune* readers' letters enlarged the black sexual public sphere with viewpoints that countered the pathological and criminal representations produced by a good deal of Black Press coverage.

The paper's publication of readers' letters supporting the ball was an anomaly relative to the meager coverage that female impersonators and gay men typically received in the paper. Letters to the *Tribune* challenged the paper's editorial perspective that a mass black readership pathologized and rejected gender-nonconforming expression and homosexuality. Indeed, *Tribune* readers used the paper to voice diverse positions on gender nonconformativity. Like the debate that the *Afro-American* had fostered over the publication of short stories about interracial sexuality, the *Tribune* imagined that their readership sought opportunities to support, critique, and castigate the topic of homosexuality and female impersonation. In publishing readers' letters supporting homosexuality and gender-nonconforming expression, black newspapers created space for readers to articulate female impersonators' and black gay men's subjectivity.

In spite of the letters criticizing its negative stance on gender and homosexuality, the *Tribune* doubled down on its position: "We still maintain that these inverts, we prefer to call them perverts, should not be permitted to parade their abnormal sex life before the public." One reader supported the *Tribune*'s position so much that he actually took issue with the *Tribune* for publishing the story at all. Recognizing the irony that despite Dixon's negative depiction of the ball, the *Tribune* viewed the ball as newsworthy enough that it featured articles and accompanying pictures that offered readers an opportunity to view it. The reader stated, "Can you imagine any respectable paper of any race featuring such news?"[56] One year after his initial derisive article on the ball, Dixon took a markedly different approach to the balls that he previously excoriated. After he was swept up in a police raid of a ball, his report in a March 29, 1934, issue of the *Tribune* notably lacked the moralistic tone of his earlier report (see Chapter 4).[57]

Readers also used other black papers to discuss homosexuality and gender-nonconforming expression. The *Afro-American* was a particular target of readers' ire. These readers viewed the Black Press as an uplift institution and found it difficult to reconcile the images of homosexuality, vis-à-vis drag balls and crime coverage, that appeared in their papers. At times readers adopted sexology discourse to air their concerns. Edwin B. Henderson of Falls Church, Virginia, called on the *Afro-American*'s editor to "cease to advertise the virtues or vices of . . . the congenitally formed degenerate same-sex lover . . . since in so many ways your paper is stimulating to growth and race pride." Another reader of the paper stated that he did not think it appropriate that the paper publish news on this topic. The *Afro-American* responded: "If pansies figure in the news of the day or week, the *Afro-American* prints that news. It's strictly a business proposition." However, the overwhelming amount of "pansy coverage," in the *Afro-American*, relative to other black papers, suggests that personal interest in female impersonators and homosexual desire among reporters and the editorial staff may have also factored into editorial decisions to publish news on the topic.[58]

Ralph Matthews, one of the most frequent commentators on female impersonation and same-sex sexuality in the Black Press, defended his regular coverage of the balls in the *Afro-American*. In response to readers' letters or what he described as "a furor about pansies," Matthews stated,

> The reading public seems to take the attitude that a newspaper should blush with shame for every article of an unsavory nature that appears in its columns. It is, however, quite all right for these same readers to whisper these same facts across their back fences or discuss them in quiet of their drawing rooms.[59]

Matthews's retort to readers suggested that he believed that the Black Press had an obligation to make public a private black sexual world that existed behind closed doors. The *Afro-American*'s self-imposed authority on homosexuality was not above reproach. One reader challenged the paper's ability to accurately discuss homosexuality. Reader Fred McFlorence, of Atlantic City, New Jersey, remarked to the *Afro-American*, "Only the 'queer' persons themselves can adequately describe such occurrences as you sometimes print and therefore, you have no one who gives the correct interpretation."[60] McFlorence's comments and other readers' letters to the *Afro-American* indicated that, by the 1930s, the paper was well-known for its regular coverage of black gay men and female impersonators. To this end, it was far from simply a black sexual public sphere that included the voices of readers, reporters, and editors. As noted previously, female impersonators and black gay men demonstrated how integral they were to a mass black readership. They also wrote letters and spoke to Black Press reporters about their lives and humanity.

FEMALE IMPERSONATORS' AND BLACK GAY MEN'S VOICES

News coverage of female impersonators in the context of the balls provided female impersonators with occasions to voice their own humanity and incorporate pleasure into their commentary. At times, the *Afro-American* provided its readers with exclusive profiles of female impersonators in their coverage of balls. The paper's report on the 68th Annual Hamilton Lodge Ball included an interview with "Margo, a philosophical pansy" who participated in the affair. Presented as an in-depth conversation between an unnamed reporter and Margo, the objective of the exchange was to divulge the reasons behind female impersonation and men's sexual desire for men.[61] Remarkably, Margo and the reporter's conversation also touched on the legitimacy of men's love, not simply sexual attraction, for other men. Despite the reporter's insistence that same-sex sexual relationships between women were "base debauchery," Margo responded:

> True love is never base. That's where society is so unkind to us. You will eulogize a man's love for his dog, sing the praises of a trusted horse which follows his hero master to his grave on the battle field, but you have only condemnation for the love of man for another.[62]

The interview allowed Margo to center love and desire between men and challenge the pathologization of homosexuality. Citing a couple named Tommy and Bobbie that had been inseparable and faithful to each other for ten years, Margo insisted that gay men loved "deeper than women because society drives us closer together."[63] Margo refashioned the negative medical and scientific discourse on gay men and female impersonators to reveal their sexual subjectivity and humanity.

Other female impersonators speaking to reporters also took the opportunity to reconfigure their relationships into ones that revolved around love and satisfaction. Female impersonator La Belle disclosed her marriage to a twenty-one-year-old man, which was a failure due to the same problems that "normal" people experience. At the 1935 "Annual Masque Ball" held in Baltimore, several female impersonators identified themselves as "respectable married women."[64] La Belle and Margo's stories reenvisioned marriage and rejected heteronormative restrictions that strictly limited the institution to gender-conforming individuals. The *Tribune's* photograph and an announcement that entertainer Ray St. Claire and Sepia Mae West, a female impersonator, presumably of the white film star, had married at the Paradise Grill, a local nightclub, also transformed marriage into a transgressive affair. According to the report, over 200 people were in attendance, and the affair was the "talk of the town."[65] Whether the wedding was a staged event or actual ceremony is unclear. What, perhaps, is more revealing is that the *Tribune* deemed the "wedding" important enough to cover and visually document for its readers. Poignantly, the striking similarity of the photograph to "real" wedding photographs in the paper demonstrated to its audience that the respectability and marital love could be performed by the some of the most marginal figures in the black community.

Not all female impersonators used the Black Press to reclaim gender-nonconforming expression as a site of personal happiness and satisfaction. In 1934, noted Washington, DC, professional female impersonator Louis Diggs wrote a letter responding to *Afro-American* columnist Matthews's article "The Pansy Craze, Is It Entertainment or Just Plain Filth?" which featured Diggs's photograph above the article. The photograph's caption offered a backhanded compliment to Diggs, noting that he and Boots Lavada, another female impersonator in the image, "fall into the higher types of entertainers, in that they possess real talent, which serve them well if they were not masqueraders." Matthews further emphasized his disdain for female impersonators "masquerading" as entertainers, stating, "Many pansies, however, have nothing but the fact that they are freaks," that were "growing to an alarming degree."[66] Matthews bolstered his claims with his authority as the paper's theatrical editor and argued that the sanctity of the theater was at stake if female impersonators continued to be accepted as legitimate forms of entertainment. For Matthews, then, it was not the existence of female impersonators that he objected to but their increased public presence and the acceptance of their bodies as artistic productions.

Writing one week after the publication of Matthews's article, Diggs took issue that his image was used and claimed that he believed it was time to provide readers with "fuller and more authentic criticism" of female impersonators. "The fact remains," argued Diggs, "that those who criticize and condemn the loudest never stop to think what circumstances and conditions produce your so-called pansies and freaks."[67] Nevertheless, Diggs affirmed sexologists' view of female impersonators' diminished mental capacity: "I speak for myself and others when I cite the fact that physically we are as any normal male should be. If there is any of the 'freak' present it must be mental." While Diggs reiterated Matthews's adoption of scientific expert opinion that gay men and female impersonators might suffer from gender and sexual hybridism, he took society to task for its cruel attitude and behavior that branded him into "something I [Diggs] was yet to understand." According to Diggs, his childhood was filled with schoolmates' taunts and asides at his effeminate mannerisms. To his dismay, teachers joined in the mistreatment by giving him a doll and a "verse which expressed effeminacy" upon his graduation from junior high school. Whispers about his feminine character followed him into high school and morphed into open ridicule. Faced with little recourse, Diggs recounted:

> I resolved within myself that I would accept my fate as it was and find consolation in some channel that it offered. So in these few years I have developed into a Louis Diggs that I alone have created—and to a generation that would have me no other way, myself and others.[68]

Diggs ended his letter by disrupting the scientific and medical narrative espoused by Matthews that homosexuality was a social disease which, left unabated, would infiltrate into schools and private spaces of homes and churches. "No normal male-man or boy, would be influenced to become effeminate by viewing female impersonators unless he was already in a stage of developing into an invert. Why then, are we criticized as social menaces?"[69]

Diggs's commentary proved that scientific and medical discourses on homosexuality were flexible enough to allow him to appropriate and challenge them all at once. While Diggs appeared to accept the view that homosexual desire was aberrant, he rejected attempts to make this conception the basis for his dehumanization and that of other black men who were sexually attracted to and loved men.[70] Thus, the challenge of being an effeminate male had less to do with an inverted gender constitution and was due to society's cruel treatment. Diggs's larger message of resilience and pride in transforming himself into a well-known and loved entertainer in Washington, DC, ameliorated the sting of Black Press coverage that characterized him and other female impersonators as perverts and freaks. The satisfaction that Diggs believed he brought audiences through his performances enlarged the black sexual public sphere with pleasure at gender-nonconforming and homosexual expression.

The *Afro-American's* belief that readers either longed for knowledge about female impersonators or took pleasure in castigating their public presence drove the publication of Diggs's letter. Evidence of the contradictory impulses behind the coverage of female impersonators appeared right below Diggs's letter. The *Afro-American* chose to run a letter supporting the views that Matthews espoused in his article. Rather than black gay men, the unnamed letter writer from Cleveland, Ohio, chose to focus his comments on lesbians who, in his opinion, were freaks who sought to debase innocent girls in church circles. As discussed in Chapter 4, homosexual African American women were rarely given opportunities to be viewed as subjects. The writer's reference to roving "women loving" female preachers and Sunday school teachers right below Diggs's letter highlighted the sharp contrast between African American gay men and black lesbians in the Black Press. There was virtually no room for a similar lesbian selfhood in a black sexual public sphere that could complicate the criminal, predatory narrative spun by African American papers.

La Belle also used the *Afro-American* to disclose personal details about her childhood and her understanding of the role it played in her homosexual desire. She attributed her desire for men to the fact that her mother had hoped for a female child, dressed him in girl's clothing, and not allowed him to play with other boys. In some ways, like Diggs, La Belle's story corroborated sexologists who argued that an abnormal childhood redirected normal sexual attraction for the opposite sex toward the same sex. La Belle, however, seemed to suffer little anxiety about her status. She expressed pleasure "that she had a woman's brain and a man's body."[71] In making this claim, readers were presented with a representation of gender that upset the customary male-female gender binary. Yet, La Belle's personal articulation of her subjectivity as acceptable, indeed pleasing, countered pathologizing discourses that maintained a clinical and scientific view of homosexuality. Rather than simply affirming her state as one of perversion, La Belle constructed an alternative narrative that associated homosexual desire and gender-nonconforming expression with pleasure.

The *Afro-American's* publications of female impersonators' personal accounts operated as case histories of gender-nonconforming and homosexual expression for readers it imagined longed for an explanation of such matters. In providing black female impersonators and gay men with a platform to demonstrate their subjectivity, the *Afro-American* remained staunchly ambivalent on male homosexual desire and gender nonconformativity in the interwar period. The fact that the *Afro-American*, one of the most widely circulated national black newspapers of the early twentieth century, steadily covered the subject in such a detailed and nuanced fashion, indicates that it created a black sexual public sphere that linked pleasure to black female impersonators and gay men for a mass black readership.

THE DECLINE OF GENDER-NONCONFORMING
AND HOMOSEXUAL EXPRESSION IN THE BLACK PRESS

Heavy coverage of female impersonators and gay men was relatively short-lived in the Black Press. By the late 1930s, African American newspapers began to cover homosexual expressions and life in the context of balls with less frequency. Articles and news reports also contained less ambiguity and condemned female impersonation and male same-sex sexuality in more strident tones. In so doing, they captured and helped to shape a growing discontent with open discussions of homosexuality. While black newspapers, again mostly the *Afro-American*, continued to report on the balls, articles often highlighted the smaller numbers of attendees.

Reduced coverage also reflected the decreasing popularity of the balls with younger black gay men and female impersonators. The *Afro-American* reported that "mostly spinsters" and female impersonators "well over thirty" attended the Hamilton Lodge Ball held in 1937. Some of the female impersonators in attendance lamented to reporters that the ball was fashionable only among so "few of their own kind." They went on to express their desire for the "good old days when there were more pansies present and less sightseers."[72]

Ironically, the "good old days" would not return for some years, as the Hamilton Lodge Ball ended in 1938. The *Afro-American*'s coverage of the 70th Annual Hamilton Lodge Ball that year recounted a mere 1,500 audience members and a procession of "pansies" that "comprised more whites than color persons." In an obvious effort to revive interest in the ball, event organizers attempted to move it to Brooklyn in November 1938. The *Amsterdam News* reported, "the intriguing gentlemen of the third sex are going to make a Brooklyn debut." No papers, including the *Amsterdam News* provided further coverage of the Hamilton Lodge Ball, once the pinnacle of black gay and gender-nonconforming life, for rest of the 1930s, a sure sign that the ball had reached and passed its zenith in popularity.[73] The ball's declining popularity among spectators and "pansies" stemmed from the culmination of an oppressive judicial and political reaction to homosexuality over the course of the 1930s. The *Amsterdam News* reported the arrests of seventeen female impersonators for homosexual solicitation at the Hamilton Lodge Ball held in 1938. This and other regulation of homosexual life and gender-nonconforming dress was surely one of the reasons that the ball organizers decided not to hold it the following year.

The late 1930s also witnessed newspapers such as the *Afro-American* dramatically shift the tone of their discussions on homosexuality. Front-page *Afro-American* and *Amsterdam* articles in 1939 reported a new discovery in medicine that transformed men with "girlish mannerisms, girlish voices, and girlish physiques—into robust men." Placed next to the *Afro-American* article was a photo of two West Point military cadets that visualized what the medicine could accomplish. These two news items illustrated the shift from black papers' ambivalent coverage of same-sex sexual expression to its disappearance and marginalization by default.[74]

Indeed, by 1941 the *Afro-American*, once the paper that gave the most voice to female impersonators and gay men's personal lives, included malevolent images of homosexuality. An editorial titled "Homosexualism" claimed that communities could not afford to take the homosexual threat lightly. The editorial reminded readers that homosexuality was both an innate and developed condition that contained "ruinous, nervous and physical ailments." An accompanying editorial cartoon featured a gruesome, skeleton face on a curvaceous female form with the name "Miss Homosexualism" listed on her gown. A male is shown standing in the background gazing eagerly at the back of the female figure. The caption read: "1st He: Turn your face, cutie—so I can *see* you. 2nd He: You wouldn't love me, if I did!" This cartoon demonstrated that a significant shift had occurred in the ways that the *Afro-American* covered homosexuality. While sexology continued to provide a language for black newspapers to discuss homosexuality, black papers during World War II suggested that black gay men and female impersonators were synonymous with death of the "race" (Figure 5.2).[75]

Black papers' regular discussion of gender-nonconforming and homosexual identity and expression in the 1920s and 1930s helped to explain to its readers the confounding nature of homosexuality and demonstrated that journalists were experts on male same-sex sexuality for a mass black readership. Reporters' use of modern scientific language and concepts allowed them to operate under the guise of objectivity in their discussions of homosexuality and gender nonconformativity even as they sometimes poked fun at female impersonators who attended "pansy" balls. Yet, even as this "objective" reporting reaffirmed a medical model for homosexuality that deemed female impersonators and men with homosexual interests as abnormal, the regular coverage of black men's same-sex sexual desire fostered a black sexual public sphere on gender-nonconformity

Editorial Cartoon 1 -- No Title
Afro-American (1893-1988); Jul 19, 1941; ProQuest Historical Newspapers: The Baltimore Afro-American
pg. 4

It Can Be Stamped Out

Figure 5.2. "It Can Be Stamped Out," July 19, 1941. Courtesy of *The Afro-American Newspaper.*

and homosexuality. Black papers' coverage between 1925 and 1940, then, proved that black female impersonators and gay men were a visible part of everyday African American life. Editors and reporters delineated the color line in tandem with alienating the abnormal and unusual vis-à-vis news documenting arrests and stories reporting on drag balls. In short, as black newspapers worked to transform black life and uplift it, they held homosexual life up as a spectacle that could not seamlessly fit into the notions of respectability even as regular coverage demonstrated that same-sex desire and gender-nonconforming expression was a vibrant part of black communities in the 1920s and 1930s.

Female impersonator's and black gay men's voices, on the other hand, suggested that they understood that their place in black communities was tenuous at best. Their presence on city streets, in cafeterias, and in nightclubs throughout several cities indicated that black female impersonators and homosexual men had carved out a world within early-twentieth-century African American communities. This world buffered, as much as it could, the sanctions of both black and white moral authorities. Readers, including female impersonators and gay men, drew on these representations and used them to participate in a black sexual public sphere that gave them an opportunity to critique, discuss, debate, and locate pleasure within images of gender-nonconforming and homosexual expression. Readers' responses and engagement, negative and positive, highlighted a mass African American readership's capacity to view their newspapers as a black sexual public sphere that was expansive enough to capture the intricacies of gender-nonconforming expression and homosexuality.

EPILOGUE

Now that the Black Press is just shy of 200 years old, it remains one of the oldest "alternative" print news outlets in the United States. Over the past four decades, much of the discussion around traditional print newspapers is whether they can survive in a technologically based society that receives its news from a wide range of sources that include blogs, online news feeds, websites, and of course television. Many small newspapers have been forced out of the market place as a result of their inability to sustain themselves in the context of the issues facing twenty-first-century journalists. The *Chicago Defender* recently ceased its print edition and presently only publishes an online edition. Thus, vast changes in the way that people access news has forced newspapers to change the ways in which they deliver news.

Yet, despite the tough times for print journalism, the *Philadelphia Tribune, Baltimore Afro-American, New Pittsburgh Courier,* and *New York Amsterdam News,* have managed to defeat the odds and stay in business. Their endurance lies in the fact that black newspapers continue to serve the needs of local communities who view mainstream white publications as not adequately representing their particular concerns. They inform readers about black achievement and raise consciousness about racial injustice. In this sense, today's black newspapers have a great deal in common with black papers published close to ninety years ago during the 1920s and 1930s. Interwar black papers' editors, like their counterparts today, understood that persistent racism required them to spearhead protests and offer up positive representations of African American life to combat the pervasive stereotypes that plagued most blacks.

Still, today's black papers are diametrically different than the ones that Chandler Owen felt compelled to justify in 1925. Early-twentieth-century newspapers attracted a diverse set of readers that comprised different and emerging socioeconomic classes. Much of the class diversity stemmed from large numbers of African Americans moving into the urban North and Midwest in the years preceding World War I and World War II. Yet, newspapers' greater attention to gender and sexual orientation in their coverage also demonstrated that papers recognized that African Americans were not limited to class divisions. Still, perceptions of class differences shaped a great deal of coverage and ultimately led newspapers to focus a fair share of their news on topics they believed would target their largest and fastest growing audience of readers, a new middle- and working-class segment of black communities. News stories with a heavy dose of crime, sexually provocative images, and scandal mixed in, argued black editors and journalists, attracted readers to newspapers. Thus, black papers of the 1920s and 1930s looked strikingly similar to tabloid publications. However, their mission to uplift and transform public images of African American life kept black papers from being tabloids, although they shared a great deal in common with them. Newspapers' campaigns to end racist activities such as lynching, to increase employment and housing opportunities, and to further African Americans' participation in politics made black newspapers one of the most powerful black institutions of the twentieth century.

Nonetheless, the Black Press's fight against racial injustice has tended to overshadow the coverage that helped make black newspapers popular and powerful instruments for public dialogue and exchange for everyday African Americans. News of divorce trials, images of bathing beauties, crime reports that involved gay men and lesbians, coverage of drag balls, and real and fictional stories about interracial relationships generated widespread interest from black readers. On the surface, these topics seemed to lack significance for understanding the history of black communities. Closer examination, however, reveals the ways this coverage disclosed a set of black sexual public spheres that reflected African Americans' positions on sexuality and its intersection with race, class, and gender.

Opportunities for readers to respond to coverage through letters to the editor and sometimes through news reports highlighted newspapers' function as a black sexual public sphere were particularly important in the 1920s and 1930s, at the height of a shift in sexual values where liberalism supplanted traditional and Victorian mores that emphasized restraint and passionlessness, especially for middle-class Americans. Since pervasive stereotypes used to demean African Americans revolved around the idea that they were sexually immoral and promiscuous, new representations of black sexuality in this era took on even more significance in this context. Black newspapers along with other print publications regularly challenged the associations made between blackness and sexuality and restructured public images of African Americans to promote the idea that blacks were civilized and respectable. Yet, when modern sexual values called for the incorporation of sexual liberalism into everyday encounters and interactions, African American newspapers were faced with the dilemma of how to retain a respectable public image but at the same time make their coverage relevant within an evolving moral and sexual system.

In truth, black newspapers never truly resolved what appeared to be contradictory representations of sexuality. Some papers, however, maintained a much more conservative approach. This stance produced differences between newspapers that make it difficult to use the moniker, the "Black Press" to suggest that all black newspapers shared a uniform ideology. Some readers recognized these differences and praised papers that were more conservative while excoriating papers that expressed greater sexual liberalism in their coverage. Nonetheless, other readers sought out certain sexual representations and encouraged their papers to produce more.

Regular front-page coverage of divorces among some of the most prominent members (ministers and physicians) of the African American community seemed to be out of place for many readers when they were plagued with pressing concerns about low wages and high unemployment rates. Perceived by editors as generating readers' interest, however, news reports on divorce trials also shed greater insight into class stratification among African Americans in the early twentieth century as a small segment of the community seemed to hold themselves apart from and above the masses. Newspapers' disclosure of the private lives of elite and middle-class blacks, however, demonstrated the fallacy of representations that deemed some blacks as more moral or respectable.

Respectability, though, as papers illustrated in their coverage of bathing beauty pageants, was never a stable or static notion. The overt display and sexualization of black women's bodies in the context of bathing beauty contests and recreational sunbathing on public beaches and at pools was placed in the realm of respectability by newspapers. These images worked to transform pernicious notions of black women as ugly, mannish, and uncivilized. Juxtaposed to scant images of lesbians that were generally situated in violence and predatory behavior, photographs of ostensibly heterosexual women in swim attire rose to the surface to serve as a symbol of race advancement and pride.

In both cases—the divorce trials and images of bathing beauties—newspaper editors chose not to publish readers' responses or readers did not respond to the coverage. The lack of readers' voices on these matters almost surely had to do with the fact that the images of divorce and bathing beauties could be seamlessly integrated into a public image of African American life that was consistent with the communal face that black newspapers desired to promote. Divorce was increasingly more common among American citizens and was viewed as a hallmark of modern society. Too, the commodification and sexual objectification of women's bodies through bathing beauty pageants was naturalized in the backdrop of a growing consumer society.

Other well-covered topics, namely intermarriage between blacks and whites and male homosexuality and female impersonation, nonetheless were much more contentious issues that prompted African Americans to publicly voice their views about race, gender and sexuality. Readers grappled with issues related to interracial sexuality and its potential to transform race relations between whites and blacks. Viewed by newspapers, and in most cases by readers, as the most racially and sexually charged topic of the 1920s and 1930s, newspapers wondered how much coverage, particularly fictional stories, readers could handle. Readers responded with a variety of positions that both countered and supported the views of traditional black leaders. An ongoing debate between readers on this issue appeared in papers through much of the 1930s.

Black papers gendered and racialized homosexuality and made intelligible to its readers what it perceived to be black male sexual aberrations. Readers and African American homosexual men responded to this coverage by imbuing their own meanings of homosexuality onto the bodies of African American men. Letters to editors divulged instances of contest and negotiation between reporters and their readers as they struggled to understand the intersections between race, gender, and homosexuality.

On the eve of the U.S. entrance into World War II, African Americans were once again faced, as they were during World War I, with whether they would fully support America's military position on the world stage. The U.S. commitment to fighting fascism abroad when many African Americans were treated poorly at home struck many blacks as hypocritical. Black newspaper coverage reflected the issues surrounding this dilemma. The front pages of newspapers were dominated with news of the war throughout the first half of the 1940s. Many African Americans coalesced their identity around their position as African Americans living in wartime America. The full manner in which sexuality played a role in Black Press coverage in this period is unclear and has yet to be explored.

What is clear, however, is that new images of sexuality emerged in other black print publications in post–World War II America. Black newspapers' circulation declined in the years following the war; it would rise briefly again during the Civil Rights Movement. An increasing racially integrated society and the emergence of black magazines were largely responsible for the waning of black papers. By the 1950s, readers could view and respond to representations of sexuality in magazines such as *Ebony Magazine, Jet Magazine,* and *Tan Confessions,* all publications founded by publisher John H. Johnson in the aftermath of World War II. In the 1980s and 1990s, the female-oriented African American magazine *Essence* presented sexual topics and images to African Americans, largely women.

In recent years, lifestyle magazines such as *Black Men* and *King Magazine* have targeted African American men with sexually explicit photographs of black women that arguably rival 1920s images of bathing beauties. In the latter half of the twentieth century and the early twenty-first century, these publications' images have functioned to some degree in the same ways that representations of sexuality in black papers did over fifty years earlier. They attracted and engaged readers with sexual images that were both relevant and intriguing to many African American men. What these publications lacked, however, is the diversity of images and the forum for readers to debate and dialogue about their meaning. Whether contemporary magazines and their readers use the images in these publications as a means to discuss intersecting factors such as race, gender, class, and sexuality in other settings is difficult to ascertain.

Online black news platforms, such as TheRoot.com and Blavity.com, as well as digital surrogates of print black newspapers now dominate the black news cycle. With selective coverage of the most popular and pressing topics and African American celebrity news, a sense of black people's everyday concerns, sexual and otherwise, have been put to the side. Although black readers and viewers are provided with the space to respond to representations and news coverage in a much more democratic fashion than the readers of the earlier form of the Black Press, it often occurs around spectacular events. This results in fewer occasions for dialogue and discussions of how sexuality informs everyday African American life.

Ironically, the emergence of social media platforms in the twenty-first century has captured the essence, to some degree, of the early-twentieth-century Black Press. Exposed to a plethora of sexual images and discourses, African Americans have unprecedented opportunities to respond and discuss them via blogs and social media platforms such as Facebook, Twitter, and Instagram. Furthermore, they can now do this to a large degree without the regulating and intervening filter of editorial control and selection. Like their equivalents in the 1920s and 1930s, black people continue to debate the meaning of African American women's bodies, homosexuality, gender-nonconforming expression, marriage, and interracial relationships. A different racial landscape, however, has changed the way that African Americans view interracial relationships and marriage. Moreover, it is startling to realize that to some degree particular views—for example, on black homosexuality—were more progressive in the first decades of the early twentieth century than they are today. Yet, even as it is relatively easy to document evolving African American sexual attitudes in social media on a range of sexual topics, the necessary preoccupation with black sexual stereotypes continues to form a great deal of the underlying basis for discussions around sexuality. What has ultimately changed, however, is that the relative safety of a black space to discuss sexual matters outside the purview of whiteness is mitigated by the openness of the internet. To be sure, the Black Press was always accessible to white readers. Yet, racial segregation and rigid racist systems made it unlikely that a critical number of whites would purchase black newspapers. Conversely, twenty-first-century African Americans are now confronted with the increased likelihood of nonblack voices weighing in on hyper-public online discussions about black sexuality. As a result, African Americans' efforts to find pleasure in viewing and discussing sexual representation and how they highlight broader gender, class, and racial issues within black communities are hampered by their efforts to ward off racist interlopers eager to marginalize and oppress black people anew in a digital format.

Early-twentieth-century black newspapers and their readers engaged in the constitutive process of developing black sexual public spheres that, at their core, were predicated on the pleasure of engagement with sexuality. The history of black sexuality and the Black Press offers a useful lesson from the past for today's African Americans confronted with the persistent hypersexualization of black humanity in social and traditional media. It suggests that images that appear, at least on the surface, to be anathema to progress for African Americans can actually yield cathartic discussions that disclose deeper ideas about relationships within the black community. Finally, as today's black print and digital newspapers endure under the various changes wrought by a virtual world of online news, they can look at their interwar counterparts for examples of how to foster black sexual public spheres that provide African Americans opportunities to experience and connect pleasure to sexuality.

NOTES

Introduction

1. Chandler Owen, "Why the Press Prints Crime and Scandal News," *Chicago Defender*, April 18, 1925, 1.

2. Edward G. Martin, "Front Page News," *New York Amsterdam News*, August 12, 1931, 8.

3. Owen, "Why the Press Prints Crime and Scandal News," 1.

4. Floyd J. Calvin, "The Digest: Owen's Theory," *Pittsburgh Courier*, April 25, 1925, 16.

5. Owen, "Why the Press Prints Crime and Scandal News," 3.

6. Catherine R. Squires, "Rethinking the Black Public Sphere: An Alternative Vocabulary for Multiple Public Spheres," *Communication Theory* 12, no. 4 (2002): 448.

7. Michael Dawson, "The Black Public Sphere and Black Civil Society," in *The Oxford Handbook of African American Citizenship, 1865–Present*, ed. Lawrence D. Bobo, Lisa Crooms-Robinson, Linda Darling-Hammond, Michael C. Dawson, Henry Louis Gates Jr., Gerald Jaynes, and Claude Steele (Oxford: Oxford University Press, 2012), 375–76; Michael G. Lacy and Kent A. Ono, *Counterpublics and the State* (Albany: State University of New York Press, 2001), 4–5.

8. Nancy Fraser, "Rethinking the Public Sphere: A Contribution to the Critique of Actually Existing Democracy," *Social Text* no. 25/26 (1990): 56.

9. Michael Huspek, "Transgressive Rhetoric in Deliberative Democracy: The Black Press," in *Critical Rhetorics of Race*, ed. Michael G. Lacy and Kent A. Ono (New York: New York University Press, 2011), 161, 162.

10. Fraser, "Rethinking the Public Sphere, 67.

11. Ibid., 70.

12. Squires, "Rethinking the Black Public Sphere," 452–53.

13. See Jeremiah Moses Wilson, *Creative Conflict in African American Thought: Frederick Douglass, Alexander Crummell, Booker T. Washington, W. E. B Du Bois, and Marcus Garvey* (Cambridge: Cambridge University Press, 2004); Manthis Diawara, "Malcolm X and the Black Public Sphere: Conversionist versus Culturalists," in *The Black Public Sphere: A Public Culture Book*, ed. The Black Public Sphere Collective (Chicago: University of Chicago Press, 1995), 39–40; James H. Cone, "Martin and Malcolm on Nonviolence and Violence," *Phylon* 49, no. 3/4 (2001): 173–83; Brittney C. Cooper, *Beyond Respectability: The Intellectual Thought of Race Women* (Urbana: University of Illinois Press, 2017).

14. Catherine Squires, "The Black Press and the State: Attracting Unwanted (?) Attention," in *Counterpublics and the State*, ed. Robert Asen and Daniel C. Brouwer (Albany: State University of New York Press, 2001), 113.

15. Kendra H. Barber, "Whither Shall We Go? The Past and Present of Black Churches and the Public Sphere," *Religions* no. 6, 1 (2015): 247.

16. LaKisha Michelle Simmons, "'To Lay Aside All Morals': Respectability, Sexuality and Black College Students in the United States in the 1930s," *Gender & History* 24, no. 2 (2012): 432.

17. Martin Summers, *Manliness & Its Discontents: The Black Middle Class & the Transformation of Masculinity, 1900–1930* (Chapel Hill: University of North Carolina Press, 2004), 277–78.

18. "Appreciating the Newspaper," *Pittsburgh Courier*, April 12, 1930, 12.

19. Betty Lou Kilbert Rathbun, "The Rise of the Modern American Negro Press: 1880–1914" (PhD diss., State University of New York at Buffalo, 1979), 262–63; Julia L. Sandy-Bailey, "The 'Negro Market' and the Black Freedom Movement in New York City, 1930–1965" (PhD diss., University of Massachusetts, 2006), 30–35.

20. Benedict R. Anderson, *Imagined Communities: Reflections on the Origin and Spread of Nationalism* (London: Verso, 2016), 35.

21. Julia Guarneri, *Newsprint Metropolis: City Papers and the Making of Modern Americans* (Chicago: University of Chicago Press, 2017), 4.

22. Kevin J. Mumford, *Interzones: Black/White Sex Districts in Chicago and New York in the Early Twentieth Century* (New York: Columbia University Press, 1997), xii–xiii.

23. Michele Mitchell, "Silences Broken, Silences Kept: Gender and Sexuality in African-American History," *Gender & History* 11, no. 3 (November 1999): 440.

24. Tera Hunter, *To Joy My Freedom: Southern Black Women's Lives and Labors after the Civil War* (Cambridge, Mass.: Harvard University Press, 1997), 168; Davarian L. Baldwin, *Chicago's New Negroes: Modernity, The Great Migration, and Black Urban Life* (Chapel Hill: University of North Carolina Press, 2007), 165; Victoria W. Wolcott, *Remaking Respectability: African American Women in Interwar Detroit* (Chapel Hill: University of North Carolina Press, 2001), 116.

25. Kimberly Springer, "Policing Black Women's Sexual Expression: The Cases of Sarah Jones and Renee Cox," *Genders* no. 54 (2011); Opposing Viewpoints in Context, http://link.galegroup.com/apps/doc/A269689991/OVIC?u=purdue_main&xid=af07d979.

26. Victor Nell, *Lost in a Book: The Psychology of Reading for Pleasure* (New Haven, Conn.: Yale University Press, 1988), 3.

27. Elizabeth McHenry, *Forgotten Readers: Recovering the Lost History of African American Literary Associations* (Durham, N.C.: Duke University, 2002), 12, 17; Ellen Gruber Garvey, *Writing with Scissors: American Scrapbooks from the Civil War to the Harlem Renaissance* (New York: Oxford University Press, 2013), 133; Nazera Sadiq Wright, *Black Girlhood in the Nineteenth Century* (Urbana: University of Illinois Press, 2016), 94.

28. Frances Smith Foster, ed., *Love & Marriage in Early African America* (Lebanon, N.H.: University Press of New England, 2008), xviii.

29. Nell, *Lost in a Book*, 3.

30. Albert Lee Kreiling, *The Making of Racial Identities in the Black Press: A Cultural Analysis of Race Journalism in Chicago, 1878–1929* (Chicago: University of Illinois at Chicago, 1979), 382.

31. For this debate, see Langston Hughes, "The Negro Artist and the Racial Mountain," *The Nation* 122, no. 3181 (June 23, 1926): 692–94; W. E. B. Du Bois, "Criteria of Negro Art," *The Crisis* 32 (October 1926): 290–97. George Schuyler, "The Negro-Art Hokum," *The Nation* 122 (June 16, 1926): 662–63. Alain Locke, "Art or Propaganda?" *Harlem*, 1, no. 1 (November 1928): 12–13.

32. Baldwin, *Chicago's New Negroes*, 9.

33. Ibid.

34. Michele Mitchell, *African Americans and the Politics of Racial Destiny* (Chapel Hill: University of North Carolina Press, 2004), 13.

35. Mumford, *Interzones*, xii; Chad Heap, *Slumming: Sexual and Racial Encounters in American Nightlife, 1885–1940* (Chicago: University of Chicago Press, 2009), 70–71.

36. Roderick A. Ferguson, *Aberrations in Black: A Toward a Queer of Color Critique* (Minneapolis: University of Minneapolis Press, 2004), 78.

37. Alford A. Young and Donald R. Deskins, "Early Traditions of African American Sociological Thought," *Annual Review of Sociology* 27 (2001): 463–64.

38. Melani McAlister, *Epic Encounters: Culture, Media, and U.S. Interests in the Middle East, 1945–2000* (Berkeley: University of California Press, 2001), 5. Todd Vogel, *The Black Press: New Literary and Historical Essays* (New Brunswick, N.J.: Rutgers University Press, 2001), 1–2.

39. Squires, "Rethinking the Black Public Sphere," 456.

40. Barbara Dianne Savage, *Your Spirits Walk beside Us: The Politics of Black Religion* (Cambridge, Mass.: Harvard University Press, 2008), 9.

41. John Burma, "An Analysis of the Present Negro Press," *Social Forces* 26, no. 2 (December 1947): 175.

42. Terry Smith, *Thinking Contemporary Curating* (New York: Independent Curators International, 2012), 29.

Chapter 1. The Black Press and a Mass Black Readership

1. "Mad Love Kills Wife," *Pittsburgh Courier*, August 12, 1933, 1; "Scottsboro Fund," *Pittsburgh Courier*, August 12, 1933, 1; Ralph Matthews, "Watching the Big Parade: A Furor about Pansies," *Baltimore Afro-American*, March 28, 1931, 1; "You Can't Fool the Voters, They Want a 'New Deal,'" *Pittsburgh Courier*, August 12, 1933, 1.

2. Samuel E. Cornish and John B. Russwurm, "To Our Patrons," *Freedom's Journal*, March 16, 1827.

3. Jannette L. Dates and William Barlow, *Split Image: African Americans in the Mass Media* (Washington, DC: Howard University Press, 1990), 347.

4. Frankie Hutton, "Social Morality in the Antebellum Press," *Journal of Popular Culture* 26, no. 2 (Fall 1992): 71.

5. Ibid., 73.

6. Benjamin P. Fagan, *The Black Newspaper and the Chosen Nation* (Athens: University of Georgia Press, 2016), 23; Wolcott, *Remaking Respectability*, 6–7.

7. For more on the concept of "the politics of respectability," see Evelyn Brooks Higginbotham, *Righteous Discontent: The Women's Movement in the Black Baptist Church, 1880–1920* (Cambridge, Mass: Harvard University Press, 1993); Kwando Kinshasa, *Emigration vs. Assimilation: The Debate in the African American Press, 1827–1861* (Jefferson, N.C.: McFarland, 1988), 2–3, 111; Bernell Tripp, *Origins of the Black Press: New York, 1827–1847* (Northport, Ala: Vision Press, 1992), 14, 82–91; Frankie Hutton, *The Early Black Press in America, 1827–1860* (Westport, Conn.: Greenwood Press, 1993), x, xii.

8. Fagan, *The Black Newspaper and the Chosen Nation*, 6.

9. Wright, *Black Girlhood in the Nineteenth Century*, 19–20; Fagan, *The Black Newspaper and the Chosen Nation*, 22.

10. Dates and Barlow, *Split Image*, 349.

11. Charles A. Simmons, *The African American Press: A History of News Coverage during National Crises, with Special Reference to Four Black Newspapers, 1827–1965* (Jefferson, N.C.:McFarland & Co., 1998), 15; S. Armistead and Clint C. Wilson II Pride, *A History of the Black Press* (Washington, DC: Howard University Press, 1997), 76; Henry Lewis Suggs, "Introduction: Origins of the Black Press in the South," in *The Black Press in the South, 1865–1979*, ed. Henry Lewis Suggs (Westport, Conn.: Greenwood Press, 1983), 3.

12. Vishnu V. Oak, *The Negro Newspaper* (Westport, Conn.: Negro University Press, 1948), 44–45.

13. *Negro Yearbook*, ed. Monroe N. Work (Tuskegee Institute, Ala: Negro Year Book Publishing Co., 1937–1938), 254–55.

14. Rathbun, "The Rise of the Modern American Negro Press," 262–63; Henry Vance Davis, "The Black Press: From Mission to Commercialism, 1827–1927" (PhD diss., University of Michigan, 1990), 129.

15. Gordon also included the *Norfolk Journal and Guide*. Eugene Gordon, "The Negro Press," *American Mercury* 8, no. 30 (May 1926): 208.

16. Lewis H. Fenderson, *Development of the Negro Press: 1827–1948* (Pittsburgh: University of Pittsburgh, 1948), 51.

17. Melissa Mae Elliott, "News in the Negro Press," (unpublished thesis, University of Chicago, 1931), 9.

18. Kreiling, *The Making of Racial Identities in the Black Press*, 355.

19. Gordon, "The Negro Press," 214.

20. Maxwell Brooks, "A Sociological Interpretation of the Negro Newspaper" (PhD diss., Columbus: Ohio State University, 1937), 82.

21. "Negroes in the United States, 1920–1932," ed. U. S. Department of Commerce (Washington, DC: United States Government Printing Office, 1935), 55.

22. Alford A. Young and Donald R. Deskins, "Early Traditions of African American Sociological Thought," *Annual Review of Sociology* 27 (2001): 463–64.

23. Gunnar Myrdal, *An American Dilemma: The Negro Problem and Modern Democracy* (New York: Harper and Bros, 1944), 114; James R. R. Grossman, *Land of Hope: Chicago, Black Southerners, and the Great Migration* (Chicago: University of Chicago Press, 1991), 75.

24. Grossman, *Land of Hope*, 13, 79; Lawrence R. Rodgers, *Canaan Bound: The African-American Great Migration Novel* (Urbana: University of Illinois Press, 1997), 15.

25. Lawrence D. Hogan, *A Black National News Service: The Associated Negro Press and Claude Barnett, 1919–1945* (Cranbury, N.J.: Associated University Presses, 1984), 23.

26. Paul K. Edwards, *The Southern Negro as a Consumer* (New York: Prentice Hall), 175.

27. Grossman, *Land of Hope*, 35.

28. Ibid.; "Some Don'ts," *Chicago Defender*, May 17, 1919, 20.

29. "Bronzeville Finds Its Voice," *Associated Negro Press*, 1940? (unpub.), 9.

30. Elliott, "News in the Negro Press," 9; Armistead and Pride, *A History of the Black Press*, 137.

31. Kreiling, *The Making of Racial Identities in the Black Press*, 356.

32. Accurate circulation data for black newspapers in the early twentieth century is difficult to obtain. Many papers inflated their numbers to accommodate the well-known tendency of readers borrowing single issues up to twelve times. Catherine Squires states that scholars of the Black Press have recommended Black Press circulation should be multiplied upward to five times to gain a better sense of actual circulation numbers. Squires, "The Black Press and the State," 118. This study relies on circulation data from N. W. Ayer and Son's American Newspaper Annual Directory, Philadelphia, Penn.: 1920–1945.

33. D'Weston Haywood, *Let Us Make Men* (Chapel Hill: University of North Carolina Press, 2018), 123.

34. Roi Ottley, *The Lonely Warrior: The Life and Times of Robert S. Abbott* (Chicago: H. Regnery, 1955), 298–301.

35. Andrew Buni, *Robert L. Vann of the* Pittsburgh Courier (Pittsburgh: University of Pittsburgh Press, 1974), 42–44.

36. N. W. Ayer and Son's American Newspaper Annual Directory, Philadelphia, Penn.: 1920–1945.

37. H. C. Reid, "Editor's Mail," *Pittsburgh Courier*, October 4, 1924, 16.

38. Buni, *Robert L. Vann of the* Pittsburgh Courier, 42; "Negroes in the United States, 1920–1932," 55; Abraham Epstein, *The Negro Migrant in Pittsburgh* (Pittsburgh: University of Pittsburgh, 1918), 21.

39. Ibid., 187–88, 90–94, 228–30, 34, 36–39, 48–49, 56–57.

40. Ibid., 52–53, 131–32, 45–46.

41. Ibid., 145, 257.

42. Hayward Farrar, *The Baltimore Afro-American, 1892–1950* (Westport, Conn. .: Greenwood Press, 1998), 2.

43. Ibid., 9.

44. Edward Lewis, "Baltimore," *Journal of Educational Sociology* 17, no. 5 (1944): 288; Rathbun, "The Rise of the Modern American Negro Press: 1880–1914," 227.

45. Lewis, "Baltimore," 288; "Negroes in the United States, 1920–1932," 745; Ira De A Reid, *The Negro Community of Baltimore: A Summary Report of Social Study Conducted for the Baltimore Urban League* (Baltimore: Baltimore Urban League, 1935), 9, 15; Sherry H. Olson, *Baltimore: The Building of an American City*, Bicentennial ed. (Baltimore: Johns Hopkins University Press, 1997); 325, Farrar, *The Baltimore Afro-American, 1892–1950*, 103.

46. Reid, *The Negro Community of Baltimore*, 27, 29, 40.

47. Brooks, "A Sociological Interpretation of the Negro Newspaper," 17.

48. Farrar, *The Baltimore Afro-American, 1892–1950*, xiv, 103–7. For further information concerning racial uplift, see Kevin Gaines, *Uplifting the Race: Black Leadership, Politics, and Culture in the Twentieth Century* (Chapel Hill: University of North Carolina Press, 1996), 1–7, 100–127, 52–78.

49. Farrar, *The Baltimore Afro-American, 1892–1950*, 7–8, 10, 13–14; John D. Stevens, "The Black Press Looks at 1920's Journalism," *Journalism History* 7, no. 3–4 (1980): 110.

50. Farrar, *The Baltimore Afro-American, 1892–1950*, 14.

51. Thelma Berlack-Boozer, "The Story of the Amsterdam News," *New York Amsterdam News*, June 29, 1940, 10.

52. Aubrey Bowser, "A Brief History of the Amsterdam News," *New York Amsterdam News*, December 18, 1929, A1-A2; Berlack-Boozer, "The Story of the Amsterdam News," 10.

53. "Negroes in the United States, 1920–1932," 779; Irma Watkins-Owens, *Blood Relations: Caribbean Immigrants and the Harlem Community, 1900–1930* (Bloomington: Indiana University Press, 1996).

54. Rathbun, "The Rise of the Modern American Negro Press: 1880–1914," 205, 208; Elliott, "News in the Negro Press," 12–13.

55. Eugene Gordon, "The Negro Press," *Annals of the American Academy of Political and Social Sciences* 140 (1928): 254.

56. Thelma Berlack-Boozer, "Amsterdam News: Harlem's Largest Weekly," *Crisis* 45 (1938): 106; Berlack-Boozer, "The Story of the Amsterdam News," 10; Armistead and Pride, *A History of the Black Press*, 142; Bowser, "A Brief History of the Amsterdam News," 13; "Discrimination Practiced by Julius Rosenwald's Concern," *New York Amsterdam News*, May 1, 1929, 1.

57. "Drs. Powell, Savory Take Over Weekly," *New York Amsterdam News*, January 11, 1936, 1; Claude McKay, *Harlem: Negro Metropolis* (New York: E. P. Dutton and Company, 1940), 94–95.

58. "Thank You, Harlem," *New York Amsterdam News*, May 16, 1936, 1.

59. McKay, *Harlem: Negro Metropolis*, 95–96.

60. Dorothy Pauline Anderson, *The History of the* Tribune (Philadelphia: *The Tribune*, 1959), 4–14.

61. Charles Pete T. Banner-Haley, "The *Philadelphia Tribune* and Persistence of Black Republicanism during the Great Depression," *Pennsylvania History* 65, no. 2 (1998): 194; Anderson, *The History of the* Tribune, 19.

62. Mossell was a doctoral student at the University of Pennsylvania and later the first African American woman to receive a PhD in the United States. Sadie Tanner Mossell, "The Standard of Living among One Hundred Negro Migrant Families in Philadelphia," *Annals of the American Academy of Political and Social Science, Child Welfare* 98 (1921): 177.

63. Ibid., 174; "Negroes in the United States, 1920–1932," 802.

64. V. P. Franklin, "Voice of the Black Community": The *Philadelphia Tribune*, 1912–41. *Pennsylvania History: A Journal of Mid-Atlantic Studies* 51, no. 4 (1984): 277–278. http://www.jstor.org/stable/27773002.

65. Kathryn F. (Kitty) Woodard, interview by Charles Hardy, March 26, 1984, "Goin' North: Tales of the Great Migration Oral History Project," Louie B. Nunn Center for Oral History, University of Kentucky Libraries.

66. Annette John-Hall, "Local Treasure Starting Tomorrow, Philadelphia's First Woman Publisher—Kathryn Fambro Woodard—Will Be Filling People in on Her Life and Legacy," *Philadelphia Inquirer*, November 19, 1997, D01.

67. Emmett J. Scott, "Letters of Negro Migrants of 1916–1918." *Journal of Negro History* 4, no. 3 (1919): 290–340. doi:10.2307/2713780; Emmett J. Scott. "More Letters of Negro Migrants of 1916–1918," *Journal of Negro History* 4, no. 4 (1919): 412–65. doi:10.2307/2713449.

68. Squires, "The Black Press and the State," 113.

69. "Bronzeville Finds Its Voice," Claude A Barnett Papers, 1940?, 5.

70. Rathbun, "The Rise of the Modern American Negro Press," 167, 228; Rodgers, *Canaan Bound*, 24; "Negroes in the United States, 1920–1932," 162–63; Scott, "More Letters of Negro Migrants of 1916–1918," 337.

71. "Letter to the Editor," *Pittsburgh Courier*, November 24, 1923, 16.

72. "Bringing It with Them," *Pittsburgh Courier*, July 26, 1924, 16.

73. Rodgers, *Canaan Bound*, 22; Rathbun, "The Rise of the Modern American Negro Press: 1880–1914," 223, 38; "Negroes in the United States, 1920–1932," 287.

74. Buni, *Robert L. Vann of the* Pittsburgh Courier, 44.

75. "The Loyalty of Our Readers to Our Newspapers," *Chicago Defender*, September 17, 1938, 16.

76. Elliott, "News in the Negro Press," 33; "Education," *Opportunity: Journal of Negro Life* 9–10 (October 1931): 319.

77. Floyd Calvin, "The New Day in Negro Journalism," *Pittsburgh Courier*, May 26, 1928, 20.

78. Edwards, *The Southern Negro as a Consumer*, 170.

79. "Merit Is Often Recognized," *Norfolk New Journal and Guide*, January 20, 1940, 8.

80. Lucius C. Harper, "Dusting Off the News," *Chicago Defender*, April 6, 1940, 1.

81. Floyd J. Calvin, "Tells of Stories He Was Sent to Cover and Why; Had Many Friends." *Pittsburgh Courier*, March 21, 1931, 11.

82. McKay, *Harlem: Negro Metropolis*, 96.

83. "Tabloid," *Afro-American*, April 20, 1929, 9; "Back to Normal," *Afro-American*, May 11, 1929, 6.

84. Harper, "Dusting Off the News," 2.

85. Alain Locke, "Enter the New Negro," *Survey Graphic: Harlem Mecca of the New Negro*, March 1925.

86. Nannie H. Burroughs, "Do Not Read Negro Papers," *Philadelphia Tribune*, April 3, 1930, 16.

87. Baldwin, *Chicago's New Negroes*, 78.

88. Frederick G. Detweiler, *The Negro Press in the United States* (College Park, Md.: McGrath Publishing Company, 1968 [c1922].), 113, 24–25; Edwards, *The Southern Negro as a Consumer*, 194; Buni, *Robert L. Vann of the* Pittsburgh Courier, 49–50; "Troubles Aired as Wifie No. 1 Is Exposed," *Pittsburgh Courier (1911–1950)* 1926, 16; Davis, "The Black Press," 264.

89. Detweiler, *The Negro Press in the United States*, 113–15; Edwards, *The Southern Negro as a Consumer*, 173–76; Rathbun, "The Rise of the Modern American Negro Press: 1880–1914," 173–76; Floyd Calvin, "Spivey's Records Biggest Seller," *Pittsburgh Courier*, February 25, 1928, A1.

90. "Questionable Advertising Must Go," *Philadelphia Tribune*, April 11, 1929, 16; Wolcott, *Remaking Respectability*, 101; T. H. S., "On Bleaching Skins," *Chicago Defender*, April 11, 1936, 16; George S. Schuyler, "Views and Reviews," *Pittsburgh Courier*, June 8, 1929, 11.

91. Buni, *Robert L. Vann of the* Pittsburgh Courier, 134; Sandy-Bailey, "The 'Negro Market' and the Black Freedom Movement," 39.

92. Buni, *Robert L. Vann of the* Pittsburgh Courier, 223.

93. Myrdal, *An American Dilemma*, 922.

94. Fenderson, *Development of the Negro Press: 1827–1948*, 47.

95. Sandy-Bailey, "The 'Negro Market' and the Black Freedom Movement," 41, 55–57; Hogan, *A Black National News Service*, 68; Ottley, *The Lonely Warrior*; Grossman, *Land of Hope*, 131; "Appreciating the Newspaper," *Pittsburgh Courier*, April 12, 1930, 12; St. Clair Drake and Horace A. Cayton, *Black Metropolis: A Study of Negro Life in a Northern City*, (Chicago: University of Chicago Press, 1945), 411.

96. John Louis Clarke, "Chapman's Reasoning Is Fallacious, Opinion: Varied Clientele of Press Makes Variety of News Essential," *Pittsburgh Courier*, September 19, 1931, A10.

97. Rathbun, "The Rise of the Modern American Negro Press: 1880–1914," 185, 250; Sandy-Bailey, "The 'Negro Market' and the Black Freedom Movement," 30–35; "Appreciating the Newspaper," 12.

98. W. E. B. Du Bois (William Edward Burghardt), 1868–1963, "The American Negro Press," ca. February 1943, W. E. B. Du Bois Papers (MS 312), Special Collections and University Archives, University of Massachusetts Amherst Libraries.

99. Michael Simon Bessie, *Jazz Journalism: The Story of the Tabloid Newspapers* (New York: E. P. Dutton and Co., Inc., 1938), 24–25; Aurora Wallace, *Newspapers and the Making of Modern America: A History* (Westport, Conn.: Greenwood Press, 2005), 27; Buni, *Robert L. Vann of the* Pittsburgh Courier, 225–26.

100. Elliott, "News in the Negro Press," 48.

101. Ibid., 50; Richard M. Perloff, "The Press and Lynchings of African Americans," *Journal of Black Studies* 30, no. 3 (2000): 328.

102. Gordon, "The Negro Press, 209.

103. Elliott, "News in the Negro Press," 39.

104. Ibid., 37.

105. Dr. A. Wilberforce Williams, "Fever and the Ten Commandments," *Chicago Defender*, February 14, 1925, 12; "Dr. Charles Lewis Agrees to Conduct Health Column," *Philadelphia Tribune*, October 18, 1924, 9.

106. Drake and Cayton, *Black Metropolis*, 202, 204–5; Myrdal, *An American Dilemma*, 142–43.

107. Jacqueline Najuma Stewart, *Migrating to the Movies: Cinema and Black Modernity* (Berkeley: Berkeley University Press, 2005), 7.

108. Myrdal, *An American Dilemma*, 919.

109. E. Franklin Frazier, *Black Bourgeoisie: The Rise of a New Middle Class in the United States*, ed. Collier Books (New York: Macmillan, [1957] 1962), 170.

110. Kreiling, *The Making of Racial Identities in the Black Press*, 382.

111. David Horace Murdock, *Some Business Aspects of Leading Negro Newspapers* (Lawrence: University of Kansas, 1935), 43.

112. Elliott, "News in the Negro Press," 59–60; "Churches Do Not Appreciate Value of Newspaper Advertising," *Philadelphia Tribune*, April 9, 1927, 14.

113. Elliott, "News in the Negro Press," 59.

114. Floyd J. Calvin, "Press Holds Dominant Place in Negro Life," *Pittsburgh Courier*, November 13, 1926, A1; "The Negro Ministers and the Negro Newspapers," *New York Amsterdam News*, November 18, 1925, 8.

115. Edwin Emery et al., *The Press and America: An Interpretive History of the Mass Media*, 8th ed. (Boston: Allyn and Bacon, 1996), 269, 84; Wallace, *Newspapers and the Making of Modern America*, 22; Bessie, *Jazz Journalism*, 114.

116. Elliott, "News in the Negro Press," 59; Savage, *Your Spirits Walk beside Us*, 39.

117. Kelly Miller, "Black 'Yellow' Journalism," *New York Amsterdam News*, July 18, 1928, 16.

118. "Appreciating the Newspaper," 12.

119. T. Ella Strother, "The Race-Advocacy Function of the Black Press," *Black American Literature Forum* 12, no. 3 (Autumn 1978): 94, 98–99.

120. Claude Barnett, "History of the Black Press in Chicago," (Claude Barnett Papers, 1940).

121. Clarke, "Chapman's Reasoning Is Fallacious," Opinion, A10.

122. Langston Hughes, *The Collected Works of Langston Hughes: Essays on Art, Race, Politics and World Affairs*, ed. Christopher C. de Santis (Columbia: University of Missouri Press, 2002), 44.

123. Henry F. Arnold, "Impossible to Print News and Leave Scandal Out," *Baltimore Afro-American*, August 8, 1925, 20.

124. Consuelo C. Young, "A Study of Reader Attitudes toward the Negro Press," *Journalism Quarterly* 21, no. 2 (June 1944): 150.

125. Arnold, "Impossible to Print News and Leave Scandal Out," 20.

126. "'Y' Executive Wants Scandal Suppressed," *Philadelphia Tribune*, March 9, 1933, 3.

127. Carnes McKinney, "Duties of a Newspaper," *New York Age*, April 15, 1933, 4.

128. "Crime and Scandal News," *New Norfolk Journal and Guide*, October 13, 1928, 16.

Chapter 2. Divorce Trials and Sex Scandals

1. "Bare Scandal in Divorce Case: Clergyman and Wife in Hot Tilt," *Chicago Defender*, July 18, 1925, 1.

2. Alain Locke, "Enter the New Negro," *Survey Graphic: Harlem Mecca of the New Negro* (March 1925): 631; Anne Elizabeth Carroll, *Word, Image, and the New Negro: Representation and Identity in the Harlem Renaissance* (Bloomington: Indiana University Press, 2005), 2.

3. Baldwin, *Chicago's New Negroes*, 5.

4. Lewis H. Fenderson, "The Negro Press as a Social Instrument," *Journal of Negro Education* 20, no. 2 (1951): 181; Marjorie McKenzie Lawson, "The Adult Education Aspects of the Negro Press," *Journal of Negro Education* 14, no. 3 (1945): 432.

5. E. Franklin Frazier, *The Negro Family in Chicago* (Chicago: University of Chicago), 108–9.

6. See definitions of *upper class* in Myrdal, *An American Dilemma*, 702, 1387–88; Drake and Cayton, *Black Metropolis*, 543; E. Franklin Frazier, *The Negro Family in the United States* (Notre Dame: University of Notre Dame Press, 1939 reprint, 2001), 394–95, 423–25; Baldwin, *Chicago's New Negroes*, 28.

7. Frazier, *The Negro Family in Chicago*, 82.

8. Grossman, *Land of Hope*, 152–53.

9. Ibid., 146–51; Wolcott. *Remaking Respectability*, 57–58.

10. A. L. Jackson, "The Onlooker: Public Manners," *Chicago Defender*, December 3, 1921, 16; "Where We Are Lacking," *Chicago Defender*, May 17, 1919, 20; "Some Don'ts," *Chicago Defender*, May 17, 1919, 20.

11. This book relies on the class system that Drake and Cayton outlined in their study about Chicago in *Black Metropolis*, 522, and in Myrdal's work, *An American Dilemma*, 700–701.

12. Myrdal, An American Dilemma, 703.

13. Ibid., 702.

14. Eugene Gordon, "Negro Society," *Scribner's Magazine* 88, no. 2 (August 1939): 135.

15. "Old Settlers Club Famous Chicago Fire of '71," *Chicago Defender*, October 17, 1931, 3.

16. William H. Jones, *Recreation and Amusement among Negroes in Washington, DC*, (Washington, D.C.: Howard University Press, 1927) 50.

17. St. Clair Drake, *Churches and Voluntary Associations in the Chicago Negro Community*, Mimeograph. Report of Official Project 465-54-3, 386, Works Progress Administration, 219.

18. Drake and Cayton, *Black Metropolis*, 688–89.

19. Myrdal, *An American Dilemma*, 919.

20. Barnett, "History of the Black Press in Chicago."

21. Drake and Cayton, *Black Metropolis*, 720.

22. Ibid., 526; John K. Galm, "Hot Versus Sweet," in *Encyclopedia of the Harlem Renaissance*, ed. Cary D. Wintz and Paul Finkelman (New York: Routledge, 2004), 615.

23. Hughes, "The Negro Artist and the Racial Mountain, 692–94.

24. Rudolph Fisher, "Blades of Steel," *The Atlantic Monthly* 140 (1927): 183.

25. Kelly Miller, "Negro Delights in Seeing Someone Roasted, So the Press Pleases Him," *Philadelphia Tribune*, June 4, 1931, 9.

26. Drake and Cayton, *Black Metropolis*, 519.

27. Anastasia Curwood, *Stormy Weather: Middle Class African American Marriage between the Two World Wars* (Chapel Hill: University of North Carolina Press, 2010), 15.

28. Christina Simmons, "Companionate Marriage and the Lesbian Threat," *Frontiers: A Journal of Women Studies* 4, no. 3 (1979): 55. doi:10.2307/3346150; Christina Simmons, "Modern Marriage for African Americans, 1920–1940," *Canadian Review of American Studies* 30, no. 3 (2000): 280.

29. Mumford, *Interzones*, 152–53.

30. Frazier, *The Negro Family in the United States*, 325.

31. Curwood, *Stormy Weather*, 31–32.

32. Elaine Tyler May, *Great Expectations: Marriage and Divorce in Post-Victorian America* (Chicago: University of Chicago Press, 1980), 90–91.

33. Kristin Celello, *Making Marriage Work: A History of Marriage and Divorce in the Twentieth- Century United States* (Chapel Hill: University of North Carolina Press, 2009), 25.

34. May, *Great Expectations*, 2–3.

35. Zora Neale Hurston, "Monkey Junk: A Satire on Modern Divorce," *Pittsburgh Courier*, March 5, 1927, SM1.

36. T. Ella Strother, "The Race-Advocacy Function of the Black Press," *Black American Literature Forum* 12, no. 3 (Autumn 1978): 94, 98–99.

37. Charles De Leon L. Ponce, *Self-Exposure: Human Interest Journalism and the Emergence of Celebrity in America, 1890–1940* (Chapel Hill: University of North Carolina Press, 2002), 44–48, 52, 65.

38. Ibid., 50–53.

39. Elliott, "News in the Negro Press," 9; Armistead and Pride, *A History of the Black Press*, 68.

40. Gordon, "Negro Society," 136.

41. William Pickens, "Preachers Now Raising Hell instead of Talking about It: People Tiring of Scandals," *Philadelphia Tribune,* August 21, 1930, 15.

42. "Has the American Negro Grown Up?" *Philadelphia Tribune,* June 20, 1929, 9.

43. Reverend Councill M. Harris, "Are Preachers Raising Hell?" *Pittsburgh Courier,* September 6, 1930, A3.

44. Drake and Cayton, *Black Metropolis,* 419.

45. Myrdal, "The Negro Press," in *An American Dilemma,* 861, 75–76; Carter G. Woodson, *The Negro Professional Man and the Community: With Special Emphasis on the Physician and the Lawyer* (New York: Negro Universities Press, 1934), 77–80; Drake and Cayton, *Black Metropolis,* 418–20.

46. Drake and Cayton indicated that less than one-third of members of storefront churches in Chicago were women. Drake and Cayton, *Black Metropolis,* 612–13, 70–72, 86; Wolcott, *Remaking Respectability,* 113–19, 89–92; Eustace Gay, "Facts & Fancies: Store Front Churches," *Philadelphia Tribune,* March 26, 1936, 5; "Urge Churches to Select Qualified Men as Leaders," *Chicago Defender,* May 23, 1936, 1.

47. Peter Gottlieb, *Making Their Own Way: Southern Blacks' Migration Pittsburgh, 1916–1930* (Urbana: University of Illinois Press, 1987), 198.

48. "Damaging Charges Hurled at Wife by W. Augustus Jones," *Pittsburgh Courier,* January 24, 1925, 1.

49. "Mrs. Jones Hits Back in Tirade," *Pittsburgh Courier,* February 14, 1925, 1–2.

50. Drake and Cayton cited the presence of 300 "lower-class churches" in Chicago in the 1930s. Drake and Cayton, *Black Metropolis,* 611–13; "Local Pastor Exposes Wife as 'Woman of Many Loves,'" *Pittsburgh Courier,* January 24, 1925, 1, 3; "Rev. Jones Files Divorce Suit," *Pittsburgh Courier,* January 31, 1925, 1; "Mrs. Jones Hits Back in Tirade"; "Preacher's Wife Pleads for Mercy," *New York Amsterdam News,* February 11, 1925, 3.

51. Ira De Augustine, Social Conditions of the Negro in the Hill District of Pittsburgh; survey conducted under the direction of the Ira De Augustine, director, Department of research the National Urban League, Pittsburgh: General Committee on the Hill Survey, 1930, 99.

52. Cheryl D. Hicks, *Talk with You like a Woman: African American Women, Justice and Reform In New York, 1890–1935* (Chapel Hill: University of North Carolina Press, 2010), 183.

53. "Rev. Jones Vindicated by Council," *Pittsburgh Courier,* March 14, 1925, 1; "Pittsburgh Minister Granted Divorce," *New York Amsterdam News,* March 10, 1926, 1.

54. "Flipper vs. Flipper," *Pittsburgh Courier,* October 29, 1927, 11.

55. "Scandal Rocks Sandy Springs M. E. Church," *Baltimore Afro-American,* November 17, 1928, 1.

56. "Mrs. Bishop Asks Pastor's Wife to Retract Remarks," *Baltimore Afro-American,* December 8, 1928, 11.

57. Eugene Gordon, "Racial Consciousness Takes New Turn, Says Journalist," *Chicago Defender,* June 29, 1929, A1; Harris, "Are Preachers Raising Hell?" 3.

58. Drake and Cayton, *Black Metropolis,* 663, 716.

59. Athes, "Jewelry Gone, Asks Divorce: Mrs. Ruth Osborne Blames 'In-Laws for Strife and Unhappiness,'" *Baltimore Afro-American,* November 7, 1925, 2; "Sensational Charges

in Divorce Suit: Says Husband Is Extremely Cruel to Her," *Chicago Defender*, November 7, 1925, 3.

60. Ibid.; Frazier, *The Negro Family in the United States*, 422, 38. Drake and Cayton's categories of the Negro middle class would have also included the Osbornes; see Drake and Cayton, *Black Metropolis*, 524.

61. "Eve Lynn Chats 'About Society and Folks,'" *Pittsburgh Courier*, July 5, 1924, 14.

62. "Sensational Charges Stir D.C. Society," *Chicago Defender*, January 22, 1927, 1.

63. "Real Estate Dealer Name Correspondent," *Baltimore Afro-American*, November 14, 1925, 2.

64. Dylan C. Penningroth, "African American Divorce in Virginia and Washington, D.C. 1865–1920," *Journal of Family History* 33, no. 1 (January 2008): 24.

65. "Five Neighbors Aid Osborne Divorce," *Baltimore Afro-American*, November 28, 1925, 2.

66. "Mrs. Osborne Gets Control of Gloria," *Baltimore Afro-American*, December 5, 1925, 2.

67. "Washington Woman Gains Legal Point," *Chicago Defender*, December 19, 1925, 2.

68. "Sensational Charges Stir D.C. Society."

69. Allan Brandt, *No Magic Bullet: A Social History of Venereal Disease in the United States since 1880* (New York: Oxford, 1985; reprint, 1987), 135; Elizabeth Fee, "Venereal Diseases: The Wages of Sin," in *Passion & Power: Sexuality in History*, ed. Kathy Peiss and Christina Simmons (Philadelphia: Temple University Press, 1989), 179; W. Little Dr Geo, "Frank Talk about Social Diseases," *Pittsburgh Courier*, December 8, 1928, B9; Curwood, *Stormy Weather*, 35–36.

70. Dr. Carson seems to be Dr. Simeon L. Carson, founder and director of Carson Hospital, a private hospital for African Americans in Washington, DC, in the early twentieth century. For more information, see "Simeon Lewis Carson" (Association for the Study of African-American Life and History, Inc., 1955); Christina Simmons, "African Americans and Sexual Victorianism in the Social Hygiene Movement, 1910–40," *Journal of the History of Sexuality* 4, no. 1 (1993): 58–59. http://www.jstor.org/stable/3704179.

71. Drake and Cayton, *Black Metropolis*, 202, 10, 559–60; Simmons, "African Americans and Sexual Victorianism," 59; Michele Mitchell, *Righteous Propagation: African Americans and the Politics of Racial Destiny after Reconstruction* (Chapel Hill: University of North Carolina Press, 2005), 101–4.

72. Brandt, *No Magic Bullet*, 131; Fee, "Venereal Diseases," 180.

73. "'My Dearest' Pinn-Osborne Love Letter Read," *Baltimore Afro-American*, January 29, 1927, 3.

74. "Air Scandal in Divorce Suit," *Chicago Defender*, January 29, 1927, 1; "'My Dearest' Pinn-Osborne Love Letter Read," 3; Drake and Cayton, *Black Metropolis*, 248.

75. Christophe Regina, "Private Sphere and Public Sphere: Economic Issues and the Judicial Arena: Women and Adultery in Marseilles during the Eighteenth Century," *Western Society for French History* 37 (2009): 121.

76. "Sensational Osborne Divorce Trial Is Ended," Pittsburgh Courier, January 29, 1927, 10; "Forecast End of Osborne Divorce Case," *Baltimore Afro-American*, March 26, 1927, 3.

77. "Decision in Osborne Case Given," *Pittsburgh Courier*, April 2, 1927, 8; "Pinn-Osborne Love Nest Had Y. M. C. A. Okey," *Baltimore Afro-American*, April 2, 1927, 3.

78. "Osborne Case to Be Appealed," *Baltimore Afro-American*, September 24, 1927, 3; Frazier, *The Negro Family in the United States*, 389.

79. "Ex-Cop Testifies as to Tea Room Girl's Torn Dress," *Baltimore Afro-American*, February 1, 1930, 3.

80. "Sensations Continue to Pile Up in the Curtis Case," *Baltimore Afro-American*, February 1, 1930, 2.

81. "Tea Room's Girl's $20,000 Love Suit in D.C. Court," *Baltimore Afro-American*, January 25, 1930, 1.

82. Arthur Bunyan Caldwell, "Arthur Leo Curtis," in *History of the American Negro* (Atlanta: A. B. Caldwell Pub. Co., 1922), 55–56; Louis T. Wright, "The Negro Physician," *Crisis* 9 (1929): 305–6.

83. "Hubby Must Pay $5,300," *Philadelphia Tribune*, February 1, 1930. 3.

84. "Tea Room's Girl's $20,000 Love Suit," 1; C. Williams Henry, "True in Some Cases," *Chicago Defender*, 1930, 18.

85. "Eva Fitzhugh Awarded $5,000 from Curtis," *Chicago Defender*, February 8, 1930, A1.

86. E. W. Baker, "Dr. A. L. Curtis and Wife Must Pay $5,350," *Baltimore Afro-American*, February 8, 1930, 1.

87. "Ex-Cop Testifies," 2; William N Jones, "Gallery of Colorful Group at Curtis-Fitzhugh Finale," *Baltimore Afro-American*, February 8, 1930, 1.

88. Viña Delmar, "Bad Girl," *Pittsburgh Courier*, November 15, 1930, A1.

89. Leslie J. Reagan, *When Abortion Was a Crime: Women, Medicine and the Law in the United States, 1867–1973* (Berkeley: University of California Press, 1997), 114–15.

90. Ibid.

91. Ibid., 114; "Sensations Continue to Pile Up," 2; Henry, "True in Some Cases," 1.

92. George Baba, M.D., "The Use of Tampax [Tampons] in Menstrual Protection and in the Treatment of Vaginal Discharge," Presented before the Obstetrical and Gynecological conference on February 21, 1946, in Chicago (Chicago: Loyola University, 1946), 3; "Hubby Must Pay $5,300."

93. "The Curtis Case, "*Baltimore Afro-American*, February 8, 1930, 6.

94. "Calls Curtis Defense Display of Muddy Hands," *Baltimore Afro-American*, February 8, 1930, 3.

95. Rachel P. Maines, *The Technology of Orgasm: "Hysteria," the Vibrator, and Women's Sexual Satisfaction* (Baltimore: Johns Hopkins University Press, 1999).

96. "Calls Curtis Defense Display of Muddy Hands," 3.

97. "'Tea Room Girl' Wins Suit against Curtises," *Pittsburgh Courier*, February 8, 1930, 17.

98. "Psychiatrist Is Star Witness in Startling Case," *Baltimore Afro-American*, February 3, 1930, 3.

99. "Hubby Must Pay $5,300," 3.

100. "'Tea Room Girl' Wins Suit," 1; Paul W. Moore, "A Word to J. Wilson," *Chicago Defender*, June 28, 1930, 1; "Tea Room Girl Wins $5,300 Verdict," *New York Amsterdam News*, February 12, 1930, 1; "Eva Fitzhugh Awarded $5,000 from Curtis," A-1.

101. William N Jones, "The Every-Day Life Tragedies," *Baltimore Afro-American*, February 8, 1930, 6.

102. Ross, *Manning the Race*, 186, Stewart, *Migrating to the Movies*, 123–24.

Chapter 3. Bathing Beauties and Predatory Lesbians

1. J. Wilson, "Are Our Women as Bad as This?" *Chicago Defender*, May 24, 1930, 14.

2. For an excerpt of letters responding to Wilson, see M. W. Simpson, "And Still They Come," *Chicago Defender*, July 26, 1930, 14. P. Jasper Wilkins, "There's a Difference, 'White-Minded,'" *Chicago Defender*, July 12, 1930, 14. Dumas J. Sanford, "Agrees with Wilson," *Chicago Defender*, July 5, 1930, A2. C. E. Robinson, "Through Smoke-Colored Glasses," *Chicago Defender*, July 5, 1930, A2. Henry C. Wilson, "True in Some Cases," *Chicago Defender*, June 28, 1930, 14. Moses S. Ballard, "They're O.K. with This War," *Chicago Defender*, June 14, 1930, 14. Ethel McGraw Moran, "This Ought to Make Wilson's Ears Burn," *Chicago Defender*, June 14, 1930, 14. E. L. Riley, "A Reason," *Chicago Defender*, June 14, 1930, 14. Miss Minnie Brown, "A Woman Speaks," *Chicago Defender*, June 14, 1930, 14. Mrs. J. H. Graham, "Why, Indeed!" *Chicago Defender*, June 7, 1930, 14. Sgt. Walter D. Mayes, "In Defense of Women," *Chicago Defender*, June 7, 1930, 14.

3. June Waytes, "Here's a New Angle," *Chicago Defender*, June 28, 1930, 14. William Kegg Fisher, "Not So Good," *Chicago Defender*, June 14, 1930, 14. Paul W. Moore, "A Word to J. Wilson," *Chicago Defender*, June 28, 1930, 14.

4. Darlene Clark Hine, "Rape and the Inner Lives of Black Women in the Middle Women: Preliminary Thoughts on the Culture of Dissemblance," *Signs* 14, no. 4 (Summer, 1989): 912–20.

5. Higginbotham, *Righteous Discontent*.

6. Nancy Cott, "Passionlessness: An Interpretation of Victorian Sexual Ideology, 1790–1850," *Signs* 4, no. 2 (Winter 1978): 220.

7. John D' Emilio and Estelle B. Freedman, *Intimate Matters: A History of Sexuality in America*, 3rd ed. (Chicago: University of Chicago Press, 2012), 172–73.

8. Summers, *Manliness & Its Discontents*, 242.

9. D'Emilio and Freedman, *Intimate Matters*, 258.

10. Julia Jerome, "Do Decent Girls Flirt?" *Afro-American*, February 15, 1930, 11.

11. "Cupid's Corner," *Baltimore Afro-American*, December 29, 1928, 4.

12. Mary Strong, "Friendly Advice to Young Girls," *Pittsburgh Courier*, April 30, 1927, 1.

13. Summers, *Manliness & Its Discontents*, 244.

14. Julia Jerome, "Art of Love: Women Prefer Bold Men," *Afro-American*, December 15, 1928, Illustrated Feature Section, 8; Julia Jerome, "Art of Love: Mrs. Jerome Warns the 'Fast Worker,'" *Pittsburgh Courier*, November 17, 1928, Illustrated Feature Section, 4.

15. Deborah Willis, *The Black Female Body: A Photographic History* (Philadelphia: Temple University Press, 2002), 241.

16. bell hooks, "In Our Glory: Photography and Black Life," in *Picturing Us: African American Identity in Photography*, ed. Deborah Willis (New York: New Press, 1994), 45–46.

17. Willis, *The Black Female Body*, 1–2, 4, 145–47.

18. John W. Baddy, "Negro Womanhood's Greatest Needs," *The Messenger* (1928): 45.

19. Ibid.

20. Maxine Leeds Craig, *Ain't I a Beauty Queen: Black Women, Beauty, and the Politics of Race* (Oxford: Oxford University Press, 2002), 14; Noliwe Rooks, *Ladies Pages: African American Women's Magazines* (New Brunswick, N.J.: Rutgers University Press, 2004), 52–53.

21. Carolyn Kitch, *The Girl on the Magazine Cover: The Origins of Visual Stereotypes in American Mass Media* (Chapel Hill: University of North Carolina Press, 2009), 95.

22. Roscoe Holloway, "The Color Line within the Race!" *Chicago Defender*, May 5, 1934, 11.

23. Rooks, *Ladies Pages*, 70, 79.

24. "Beautiful Women—From Colleges, Social Circles and the Home," *Chicago Defender*, December 12, 1936, 1.

25. Rooks, *Ladies Pages*, 70, 79; Letter to E. Washington Rhodes, Claude A. Barnett Papers, October 16, 1929; Letter to Theus Photo Service, Claude A. Barnett Papers, October 19, 1929.

26. Buni, *Robert L. Vann of the* Pittsburgh Courier, 145.

27. Wolcott, *Remaking Respectability*, 101.

28. Susan A. Glenn, *Female Spectacle: The Theatrical Roots of Modern Feminism* (Cambridge, Mass: Harvard University, 2000), 189.

29. Jayna Brown, *Babylon Girls: Black Women Performers and the Shaping of the Modern* (Durham, N.C.: Duke University Press, 2008), 164.

30. Glenn, *Female Spectacle*, 189–90.

31. Brown, *Babylon Girls*, 164.

32. "Ooh! My, My, My!" *Pittsburgh Courier*, March 23, 1929, A6.

33. Orrin C. Evans, "Confessions of an Ex–Chorus Girl," *Philadelphia Tribune*, April 25, 1929, 9.

34. Eva Jessye, "Chorus Girl Has Helped Glorify Modern Woman," *Pittsburgh Courier*, August 25, 1928, A1.

35. Ibid.

36. Brown, *Babylon Girls*, 191; Jessye, "Chorus Girl Has Helped Glorify Modern Woman," A1.

37. Maurice Dancer, "Chorus Girl Not as Scarlet as Men Think, Says Writer," *Chicago Defender*, November 30, 1929, 6.

38. Ralph Matthews, "Has the World Given the Chorus Girl an Even Break?" *Baltimore Afro-American*, October 4, 1930, 8.

39. Joanne Meyerowitz, "Women, Cheesecake and Borderline Material: Responses to Girlie Pictures in the Mid-Twentieth-Century U. S.," *Journal of Women's History* 8, no. 3 (1996): 10.

40. Willis, *The Black Female Body*, 103. For examples of the debate over nudity, see Floyd J. Calvin, "What of Nudity on the Stage?" *Pittsburgh Courier*, November 6, 1926, Second Section, 1; "Pretty Stage Star, Arrested Recently for Being in Immoral Play, Comes to Support of Nudity on Stage," *Pittsburgh Courier*, November 27, 1926, A1; "Pretty Chorine Defends 'Nudity,'" *Pittsburgh Courier*, December 18, 1926, A1.

41. Calvin, "What of Nudity on the Stage?"

42. "Pretty Chorine Defends 'Nudity.'"

43. Elwood Watson, ed., *There She Is, Miss America: The Politics of Sex, Beauty, and Race in America's Most Famous Pageant* (New York: Palgrave Macmillan, 2004), 3.

44. Lois Banner, *American Beauty* (New York: Knopf, 1983), 256–57. Craig, *Ain't I a Beauty Queen*, 48–49.

45. Craig, *Ain't I a Beauty Queen*, 50. Angela J Latham, "Packaging Woman: The Concurrent Rise of Beauty Pageants, Public Bathing, and Other Performances for Female 'Nudity,'" *Journal of Popular Culture* 29, no. 3 (1995): 6.

46. Susan K. Cahn, *Coming on Strong: Gender and Sexuality in Twentieth Century Women's Sport* (New York: Macmillan, 1994), 19–23, 35–36. "Health and Beauty Hints: To Retain Your Beauty," *Philadelphia Tribune*, February 26, 1916, 2.

47. Cahn, *Coming on Strong*, 37, 39.

48. Shane White and Graham J. White, *Stylin: African-American Expressive Culture from Its Beginnings to the Zoot Suit* (Ithaca: Cornell University Press, 1999).

49. "Women Condemn Beauty Parades," *New York Times*, May 9, 1924, 16. Hazel Carby, "Policing the Black Woman's Body in an Urban Context," *Critical Inquiry* 18, no. 4 (1992): 747.

50. Craig, *Ain't I a Beauty Queen*, 53. "Bathing Beauty Contest Planned," *Pittsburgh Courier*, November 2, 1929, 7. "Prizewinner," *Pittsburgh Courier*, July 13, 1929, 3.

51. "Directs Bathing Beauty Contest," *Pittsburgh Courier*, June 30, 1928, A12. "All Roads Lead to Falcon Park," *Pittsburgh Courier*, May 18, 1929, A7.

52. Wolcott, *Remaking Respectability*, 56.

53. "American Club Women Meet at Washington," *Chicago Defender*, August 4, 1928, 12. "The Misses 'Appomattox,'" *Chicago Defender*, August 4, 1928, 12. "Bathing Beauty," *Chicago Defender*, May 7, 1932, 24.

54. "Interesting News of the Week in Pictures," *Chicago Defender*, May 7, 1932, 24.

55. Wolcott, *Remaking Respectability*, 97–98. For more on definition of "respectability," see Higginbotham, *Righteous Discontent*, 14–15.

56. "Death Stills Pen of Julia B. Jones," *Pittsburgh Courier*, March 10, 1945, 1. White, *Stylin'*, 212–13.

57. LaKisha Michelle Simmons, *Crescent City Girls: The Lives of Young Black Women in Segregated New Orleans* (Chapel Hill: University of North Carolina Press, 2015), 185.

58. "See World's Dazzling Cuties in the Flesh." *New York Amsterdam News*, August 5, 1931, 7. "Get in the Swim: Let the Universe Know You're Good!" *New York Amsterdam News*, July 27, 1927, 6.

59. Sarah Banet-Weiser, *The Most Beautiful Girl in the World: Beauty Pageants and National Identity* (Berkeley: University of California, 1999), 147, 49.

60. White, *Stylin'*, 41. Craig, *Ain't I a Beauty Queen*, 47, 52–53.

61. "Sensational Osborne Divorce Trial Is Ended," A11. "First Prize in Bathing Beauty Contest," *Pittsburgh Courier*, May 18, 1929, A8. "Bathing Beauty Contest July 31," *Pittsburgh Courier*, July 7, 1928, 4.

62. LaShawn Harris, *Sex Workers, Psychics, and Numbers Runners: Black Women in New York City's Underground Economy* (Urbana: University of Illinois Press, 2016).

63. "They Couldn't Be Cuter," *Chicago Defender*, August 27, 1938, 10. "Pittsburgh Pulchritude Pictured Here May Lead the Nation in 'Miss Bronze America' Contest," *Pittsburgh Courier*, August 3, 1940, 13.

64. "Pretty, but Not Pretty Enough," *Chicago Defender*, September 17, 1938, 4.

65. Harris, *Sex Workers, Psychics, and Number Runners*, 162.

66. "Chicago Beaches Offer More than Relief from Heat," *Chicago Defender*, August 20, 1938, 7.

67. "What Happens at Druid Hill Park," *Baltimore Afro-American*, July 6, 1929, 13.

68. Sarah Banet-Weiser, "Miss America, National Identity, and the Identity Politics of Whiteness," in *The Politics of Sex, Beauty, and Race in America's Most Famous Pageant*, ed. Elwood Watson and Darcy Martin (New York: Palgrave Macmillan, 2004), 71–72.

69. Hicks, *Talk with You like a Woman*, 220–21.

70. Charles A. Ford, "Homosexual Practices of Institutionalized Females," *Journal of Abnormal and Social Psychiatry* 23 (1929): 446.

71. "'Unusual' Type, Say Cop of Women Caught in Raid," *Chicago Defender*, December 9, 1922, 1. "Women Rivals for Affection of Another Woman Battles with Knives, and One Has Head Almost Severed from Body," *New York Age*, November 27, 1926, 1.

72. Cookie Woolner, "'Woman Slain in Queer Love Brawl': African American Women, Same-Sex Desire, and Violence in the Urban North, 1920–1929," *Journal of African American History* 100, no. 3 (2015): 408–9. doi:10.5323/jafriamerhist.100.3.0406.

73. Jennifer Terry, *An American Obsession: Science, Medicine, and Homosexuality in Modern Society* (Chicago: University of Chicago Press), 37.

74. George Chauncey, "From Sexual Inversion to Homosexuality: The Changing Medical Conceptualization of 'Female Deviance,'" in *Passion Power: Sexuality in History*, ed. Kathy Peiss and Christina Simmons (Philadelphia: Temple University Press, 1989), 89–90. Terry, *An American Obsession*, 64–65.

75. Lisa Duggan, *Sapphic Slashers: Sex, Violence, and American History* (Durham, N.C.: Duke University Press, 2000), 43. Sherrie A. Inness, "Who's Afraid of Stephen Gordon? The Lesbian in the United States Popular Imagination," *NWSA Journal* 4, no. 3 (1992). Simmons, "Companionate Marriage and the Lesbian Threat."

76. "Girls Eat with Their Hands at Melvale," *Baltimore Afro-American*, March 30, 1930, 1.

77. Ibid.

78. Hicks, *Talk with You like a Woman*, 183.

79. "P. S. Girls Figure in Sex Circuses," *New York Amsterdam News*, March 27, 1929, 1.

80. Ibid.

81. Ralph Matthews, "Love Laughs at Life in Harlem," *Baltimore Afro-American*, March 11, 1933, 19.

82. James F. Wilson, *Bulldaggers, Pansies and Chocolate Babies* (Ann Arbor: University of Michigan Press, 2011), 32.

83. Ralph Matthews, "She Wolf: But She Preyed on Her Own Sex," *Baltimore Afro-American*, November 17 and November 24, 1934, 24.

84. Ibid.

85. Ibid.

86. Ibid.; Grossman, *Land of Hope*, 80–86.

87. See text and discussion of Ma' Rainey's "Prove It on Me Blues," in Angela Davis, *Blues Legacies and Black Feminism: Gertrude "Ma" Rainey, Bessie Smith and Billie Holliday* (New York: Vintage Books, 1998), 39–40, 45, 238.

88. Davis, *Blues Legacies and Black Feminism*, 40; Eric Garber, "A Spectacle in Color: The Lesbian and Gay Subculture of Jazz Age Harlem," in *Hidden from History: Reclaiming the Gay and Lesbian Past*, ed. Martha Vicinus, George Chauncey Jr., and Martin Bauml Duberman (New York: NAL Books, 1989), 320.

89. "Prove It on Me Blues," 928, 7.

Chapter 4. The Question of Interracial Sexual Relationships and Intermarriage

1. "Lawmakers Legislate, Lynchers Lynch, but Interracial Love Affairs Go On," *Baltimore Afro-American*, July 1, 1933, 13.

2. Jeffrey B. Ferguson, *The Sage of Sugar Hill: George S. Schuyler and the Harlem Renaissance* (New Haven: Yale University Press, 2005), 103.

3. Myrdal, *An American Dilemma*, 62.

4. Amanda Frisken, "A Song without Words: Anti-lynching Imagery in the African American Press, 1889–1898," *Journal of African American History* 97, no. 3 (2012): 241.

5. Ida B. Wells-Barnett, *The Red Record: Tabulated Statistics and Alleged Causes of Lynching in the United States* (Cirencester, England: Echo Library/Paperbackshop Ltd, 2005).

6. "Georgia Mob Beats Preacher," *Chicago Defender*, September 14, 1912, 1.

7. "Southern White Gentlemen Burn Race Boy at Stake," *Chicago Defender*, May 20, 1916, 1; Grossman, *Land of Hope*, 75; "Virginia Mob of 1000," *Baltimore Afro-American*, April 25, 1925, A1.

8. "Need Chivalry for Colored Women Also, Says Md. Mother," *Baltimore Afro-American*, January 6, 1932, 3.

9. W. E. B. Du Bois, "The Social Equality of Whites and Blacks," *The Crisis* 21, no .1 (November 1920): 18.

10. Jan Doering, "A Battleground of Identity: Racial Formation and the African American Discourse on Interracial Marriage," *Social Problems* 61, no. 4 (November 2014): 563.

11. Christina Simmons, *Making Marriage Modern: Women's Sexuality from the Progressive Era to World War II* (New York: Oxford University Press, 2012), 88.

12. Du Bois, "The Social Equality of Whites and Blacks," 18.

13. Ibid.

14. Alex Lubin, *Romance and Rights: The Politics of Interracial Intimacy, 1945–1954* (Jackson: University of Mississippi Press, 2004), 74.

15. Peggy Pascoe, *What Comes Naturally: Miscegenation Law and the Making of Race in America* (Oxford: Oxford University Press, 2011), 185–86.

16. "Intermarriage," *Crisis* 5, no. 4 (February 1913): 181.

17. "Intermarriage Bill Is Placed before Congress," *Chicago Defender*, January 27, 1923, 1; "Social Equality 'Bunk' Desire to Protect Women," *Philadelphia Tribune*, June 13, 1925, 9; "What Do You Say about It?" *Chicago Defender*, March 25, 1933, 15.

18. Pascoe, *What Comes Naturally* 118–19, 73–85; "Uniform Marriage Bill Is Introduced," *Pittsburgh Courier*, February 8, 1930, 18; Kelly Miller, "The Marriage Bar," *New York Amsterdam News*, January 22, 1930, 20.

19. George S. Schuyler, *Racial Intermarriage in the United States: One of the Most Interesting Phenomena in Our National Life*, ed. E. Haldeman-Julius (Girard, Kansas: Haldeman-Julius Publications, 1929), 30; Pascoe, *What Comes Naturally*, 187–88.

20. George S Schuyler, "A Negro Looks Ahead," *American Mercury* XIX, no. 74 (1930): 217.

21. Ibid., 218; Saks, "Representing Miscegenation Law," 69; Pascoe, *What Comes Naturally*, 190.

22. George Schuyler, "Views and Reviews," *Pittsburgh Courier*, March 23, 1935, 10.

23. Andrew Larson, "Says Schuyler Apologizes for Being a Negro," *Pittsburgh Courier*, August 19, 1933, A2; Frank St. Claire, "Inter-Marriage," *Pittsburgh Courier*, August 5, 1933, A2.

24. Theophilus Lewis, "The Harlem Sketch Book: Comment and Gossip of the Uptown White Way," *New York Amsterdam News*, January 22, 1930, 9.

25. Mumford, *Interzones*, xii; Heap, *Slumming*, 70–71; Cary D. Wintz and Paul Finkelman, *Encyclopedia of Harlem Renaissance*, Vol. 2 (New York: Routledge, 2004), 909–12.

26. Heap. *Slumming*, 34.

27. Mumford, *Interzones*, 30–33; Heap, *Slumming*, 143–44, 206–10; "Protests Storm on District Attorney Who Orders No Black-Tan Nite Clubs," *Philadelphia Tribune*, January 7, 1932, 9.

28. Cary D. Wintz and Paul Finkelman, *Encyclopedia of Harlem Renaissance*, Vol. 1 (New York: Routledge, 2004), 909–12.

29. Heap, *Slumming*, 206.

30. "Brundage Puts Law on Sunset; Skips Tearney," *Chicago Defender*, May 6, 1922, 3.

31. "Editorial Cartoon," *Chicago Defender*, August 26, 1922, 12.

32. Heap, *Slumming*, 209–10.

33. "What the People Say: Against Intermarriage," *Chicago Defender*, January 30, 1936, A8.

34. Heap, *Slumming*, 222; "Brundage Puts Law on Sunset," 3; "'My Dearest' Pinn-Osborne Love Letter Read," A5; Sally O'Brien, "Petting Orgy Sweeps 'Sunset Club,' Jazz and Gin Rule over All," *Pittsburgh Courier*, April 23, 1927, B1.

35. Heap, *Slumming*, 207.

36. Mumford, *Interzones*, 139.

37. Ibid., 31.

38. Pascoe, *What Comes Naturally*, 185–86; Moore, "A Word to J. Wilson," 7.

39. Terry, *An American Obsession*, 96–97.

40. Randy Dixon, "Police Tyrant Faces Ousting after Raid upon 'Pansy' Dance," *Philadelphia Tribune*, March 29, 1934, 1.

41. "The 'Fairies' Ball," *Philadelphia Tribune*, March 29, 1934, 4.

42. Harry Webber, "The Voice of Philadelphia," *Philadelphia Tribune*, May 7, 1932, 5.

43. Dixon, "Police Tyrant Faces Ousting," 1.

44. Fred McFlorence, "What Do You Know about It?" *Baltimore Afro-American*, March 1934, 1–2.

45. Ibid.

46. Floyd G. Snelson, "Strange 'Third' Sex Flooding Nation, Writer Reveals," *Pittsburgh Courier*, March 19, 1932, 6; "Oddfellows Harlem Ball Seen as Bizarre Affair," *Chicago Defender*, March 7, 1936, 3.

47. "3,000 Attend Ball of Hamilton Lodge: Bonnie Clark, Last Year's Prize Winter, Disgruntled as Another 'Sweet Young Thing' Is Chosen for First Place," *New York Amsterdam News*, March 1, 1933, 2.

48. George Chauncey, *Gay New York: Gender, Urban Culture, and the Making of the Gay Male World, 1890–1940*, 263; "3,000 Attend Ball of Hamilton Lodge," 2.

49. Earl Lewis and Heidi Ardizzone, *Love on Trial: An American Scandal in Black and White* (New York: W. W. Norton), 76.

50. "Where Is Your Boiling Point on the Race Question?" *Baltimore Afro-American*, April 7 and 14, 1934, 1.

51. Ibid.

52. Ibid.

53. Ruth St. John, "Her Father Was Colored," *Baltimore Afro-American*, July 16, 1932, 24.

54. "What Do You Say about It?" 15.

55. Joseph Lourie, "Interracial Fiction a Chapter Too Long Closed to the Reading Public," *Washington Afro-American*, April 21, 1934, 4; Leroy Pullum, "Atlanta Says Yes," *Washington Afro-American*, April 21, 1934, 4; Nelson O. Johnson, "He's for Black and White Love," *Baltimore Afro-American*, April 21, 1934, 4.

56. Karin Wahl-Jorgensen, "Letters to the Editor as Forum for Public Deliberation: Modes of Publicity and Democratic Debate," *Critical Studies in Media Communication* 18, no. 3 (September 2001): 314–15.

57. Mrs. Clara Collins, "She Loves to Read Interracial Love Stories," *Baltimore Afro-American*, April 28, 1934, 4; Mrs. Sarah Livingstone, "Interracial Love Stories? Yes! Yes! Yes!" *Baltimore Afro-American*, May 5, 1934, 4; Mrs. Jason Phelps, "The Lady Gets Practical," *Baltimore Afro-American*, May 12, 1934, 4.

58. H. G. Burton, "The Newspaper Is a Mirror Which Reflects What It Sees," *Baltimore Afro-American*, July 14, 1934, 4; President Stratford, "They're Not Real Here, but I Like Them," *Baltimore Afro-American*, May 12, 1934, 4.

59. "He Never Said a Mumbling Word," *Baltimore Afro-American*, July 21, 1934, 1.

60. A. Jeffers, "We Will Read It," *Baltimore Afro-American*, May 12, 1934, 4: Mae Odum, "Let 'Em Spread," *Baltimore Afro-American*, May 26, 1934, 4: Adrian Wells, "By All Means, Yes," *Baltimore Afro-American*, April 28, 1934, 4: James T Thomas, "On with the Interracial Love Stories I Can Stand Them," *Baltimore Afro-American*, May 12, 1934, 4.

61. Lou Ella McNorton, "Objects Most Strenuously," *Washington Afro-American*, April 21, 1934, 4; Edward Dirickson, "It Does Not Help," *Baltimore Afro-American*, May 5, 1934, 4.

62. E. Thornton Talbot, "Interracial Love Affairs Point to the 'Social Equality' Known to Slave Mothers," *Baltimore Afro-American*, May 12, 1934, 4; "Millions of Other Colored Husbands Feel the Same Way," *Baltimore Afro-American*, June 9, 1934, 4; Georgia Hawkins, "She Doesn't Like Interracial Love Stories," *Baltimore Afro-American*, June 23, 1934, 4.

63. Robert Anderson, "Empress: A True Love Story of the Love of an Ofay Lad for a Brown Girl," *Baltimore Afro-American*, April 28, 1934, 4; "Thinks Empress Story Was Disgraceful and Insulting," *Baltimore Afro-American*, May 19, 1934, 4; Floyd G. Snelson Jr., "Harlem Limited Broadway Bound," *Pittsburgh Courier*, January 23, 1931, A8, 1; A. Philanderer, "Paradise Lost: An Interracial Love Story," *Baltimore Afro-American*, May 26, 1934, 1.

64. Anderson, "Empress," 24; "Thinks Empress Story Was Disgraceful and Insulting," 4; Rev. W. J. Rogers, "So the Afro's a Sexy Tabloid, Hey? Tain't So!" *Baltimore Afro-American*, June 16, 1934, 4; Rev. D. D. Turpeau Jr., "Our Policy? To Publish Whatever the Public Wishes to Read Let the Chips Fall Where They May," *Baltimore Afro-American*, June 16, 1934, 4.

65. Robert Anderson, "Chinese Love: The Story of an Interracial Love that Was Slightly Hampered by an Old Chinese Custom," *Baltimore Afro-American*, June 2, 1934, 24; John Williams, "We'll Try to Satisfy You," *Baltimore Afro-American*, July 14, 1934, 4.

66. Robert A. Hill and R. Kent Rasmussen Hill, "Bibliography: George S. Schuyler's Pittsburgh Courier Fiction, 1933–1939," in *Black Empire*, ed. Robert A. Hill and R. Kent Rasmussen (Boston: Northeastern University Press, 1991), 337–44.

67. Ibid.

68. Samuel I. Brooks, "Black Mistress—a Thrilling Novel of the Strange Life of Harlem's Half World," *Pittsburgh Courier*, November 17, 1934, A1.

69. Felix R. Neals, "He's out of Place," *Pittsburgh Courier*, February 9, 1935, 10.

70. A Reader, "Defends Story," *Pittsburgh Courier*, February 23, 1935, A2; "On Black Mistress," *Pittsburgh Courier*, March 16, 1935, 10.

71. Marie Jackson, "I Was Disgusted!" *Pittsburgh Courier*, March 16, 1935, A2; James E. Fuller, "On 'Black Mistress,'" *Pittsburgh Courier*, April 20, 1935, A2.

72. E. W. Scott, "Black Mistress," *Pittsburgh Courier*, March 16, 1935, A2.

73. Samuel I. Brooks, "A Forbidden Romance: A Story of Strange Love in Deep Dixie," *Pittsburgh Courier*, February 8, 1936, A1.

74. Mrs. Horace Ware, "Praises 'Forbidden Romance' as One of the Finest Stories in a Decade," *Pittsburgh Courier*, April 18, 1936, A2.

Chapter 5. Male Homosexuality and Gender-Nonconforming Expression

1. Chauncey, *Gay New York*, 301.

2. Terry, *An American Obsession*, 77.

3. Chauncey, *Gay New York*, 14–16.

4. Michael Warner, *Publics and Counterpublics* (New York: Zone Books, 2010), 203.

5. "Slayer of Man 'Wife' Held for Murder," *Chicago Defender*, February 7, 1925, 1.

6. Harry R Webber, "The Voice of Philadelphia: Snapshots about Town," *Baltimore Afro-American*, May 7, 1932, 8.

7. Will B. Little, "Baltimore's Red Lights," *Baltimore Afro-American*, November 21, 1931, 19.

8. "Bass Voiced 'Girlfriend' Sentenced-Alas! And Only Because 'She' Turned Out to Be He," *New York Amsterdam News*, August 28, 1929, 2; "She Turns Out to Be a 'He' In Court: Fur-Coated 'Woman' Gives Cop Liveliest Chase of His Life," *New York Amsterdam News*, February 8, 1928, 16.

9. "Men Made Love in Park; Both Draw Fines," *Baltimore Afro-American*, July 23, 1932, 11.

10. Levi Hubert, "On Seventh Avenue," *Baltimore Afro-American*, December 27, 1930, 9; Chauncey, *Gay New York*, 131–49.

11. Chauncey, *Gay New York*, 247.

12. "Citizens Claim that Lulu Belle Club on Lenox Avenue Is Notorious Dive," *New York Amsterdam News*, February 15, 1928, 1. James Wilson has documented the popularity of the Lulu Belle Club for both black and white gay men, female impersonators, and lesbians during the 1920s and 1930s in his book. For more on this subject, see Wilson, *Bulldaggers, Pansies, and Chocolate Babies*, 81, 109–10.

13. Chauncey, *Gay New York*, 332, 334; Terry, *An American Obsession*, 268–69.

14. "N. Y. Police Ban 'Pansies' in Nite Clubs," *Baltimore Afro-American*, July 25, 1931, 17; "New York Cops Hit Vulgar Dance in Cafes," *Chicago Defender*, March 17, 1934, 5.

15. "Southside Wars on 'Pansies' in Vice Cleanup," *Baltimore Afro-American*, December 24, 1932, 18.

16. Terry, *An American Obsession*, 271.

17. Romeo Dougherty, "People of the Half-World and Other Things," *New York Amsterdam News*, April 14, 1934, 6.

18. Malcolm B. Fulcher, "Believe Me," *Baltimore Afro-American*, March 9, 1935, 12.

19. "Police Arrest Impersonator," *Atlanta Daily World*, March 3, 1937, 6; "Things Theatrical: Café Ordered Closed as Chicago Bans Impersonators," *Atlanta Daily World*, December 16, 1935, 2.

20. Chauncey, *Gay New York*, 257–58.

21. "Gracious Me! Dear, 'Twas To-oo Divine," *New York Amsterdam News*, March 7, 1936, 8.

22. Associated Negro Press, "Lovely Ball," *Norfolk New Journal and Guide*, March 12, 1932, 10.

23. "Depression Chief Guest at Pansy Ball," *Baltimore Afro-American*, March 26, 1932, 23.

24. Chauncey, *Gay New York*, 257–58.

25. Dougherty, "People of the Half-World and Other Things," 6.

26. "'Girls' Had Beards and Heavy Voices at Baltimore Jamboree," *Chicago Defender*, March 15, 1924, 1; "Men Dance at Vagabonds Ball: Women Are Barred," *Baltimore Afro-American*, March 7, 1925, 20; "'Pansies' Stage Colorful Ball . . .," *Baltimore Afro-American*, March 21, 1931, 10.

27. Ralph Matthews, "Male Dance with Male 'Flappers' at Artists' Ball," *Baltimore Afro-American*, March 19, 1927, 20; Ralph Matthews, "31 Debutantes Bow at Local 'Pansy' Ball," *Baltimore Afro-American*, March 21, 1931, 1.

28. "Depression Chief Guest at Pansy Ball," 23.

29. Laura Grantmyre, "'They Lived Their Life and They Didn't Bother Anybody': African American Female Impersonators and Pittsburgh's Hill District, 1920–1960," *American Quarterly* 63, no. 4 (2011): 993; "Men Step Out in Gorgeous Finery of Other Sex to Vie for Beauty Prizes," *New York Amsterdam News*, March 2, 1932, 2.

30. Bruni, *Robert L. Vann of the* Pittsburgh Courier, 52.

31. Ralph Matthews. "Clothes Make the Woman as Well as the Man but the Modistes Play Queer Pranks Sometimes, Pansies Prove," *Baltimore Afro-American*, March 3, 1934, 7.

32. "Men Step Out in Gorgeous Finery of Other Sex to Vie for Beauty Prizes," *New York Amsterdam News*, March 2, 1932, 2.

33. "When 'Odd Fellows' Cavorted," *New York Amsterdam News*, March 5, 1938, 2; Lawrence Levey, "Want to Know What the Well-Dressed Woman Should Wear? . . . Ask the Pansies," *Baltimore Afro-American*, March 6, 1937, 24.

34. "Pansies Ramble in 'Drag' at Pre-Halloween Ball," *Baltimore Afro-American*, November 11, 1933, 1.

35. Rooks, *Ladies Pages*, 66.

36. "Gracious Me! Dear," 8; Edgar T. Rouzeau, "Snow and Ice Cover Streets as Pansies Blossom Out at Hamilton Lodge's Dance," *New York Amsterdam News*, February 28, 1934, 1; "Men Dance at Vagabonds Ball," 20; Fred B. Watson, "They Are All in the News of the Week," *Baltimore Afro-American*, April 23, 1927, 11.

37. Matthews, "31 Debutantes Bow at Local 'Pansy' Ball," 1–2.

38. Rouzeau, "Snow and Ice Cover Streets, 1.

39. Roi Ottley, "Hectic Harlem," *New York Amsterdam News*, March 7, 1936, 13; "Gracious Me!" Dear, 8.

40. Sarah Banet-Weiser, *Authentic^{TM}: The Politics of Ambivalence in a Brand Culture* (New York: New York University Press, 2012), 219.

41. E. Patrick Johnson, "The Specter of the Black Fag: Parody, Blackness and Hetero/Homosexual B(r)others," *Journal of Homosexuality* 45, no. 2–4 (2003): 221.

42. Summers, *Manliness & Its* Discontents, 197.

43. Kim Gallon, "'No Tears for Alden': Black Female Impersonators as 'Outsiders Within' in the *Baltimore Afro-American*," *Journal of the History of Sexuality* 27, no. 3 (2018): 382–83.

44. Matthews, "31 Debutantes Bow at Local 'Pansy' Ball," 1–2.

45. Snelson, "Strange 'Third' Sex Flooding Nation," 6; "Depression Chief Guest at Pansy Ball," 23.

46. Chauncey, *Gay New York*, 138.

47. Chauncey, "From Sexual Inversion to Homosexuality, 93–98.

48. Ralph Matthews, "Are Pansies People?" *Baltimore Afro-American*, April 2, 1932, 3; Snelson, "Strange 'Third' Sex Flooding Nation," 6.

49. Rev. Charles Stewart, "Debunking Pansy Talk," *Baltimore Afro-American*, October 27, 1934, 19; "Stewart, Charles E.," in *The Encyclopaedia of the African Methodist Episcopal Church*, ed. R. R. Wright Jr. (Philadelphia: Book Concern of the A. M. E. Church, 1947), 264.

50. Terry, *An American Obsession*, 43.

51. "Absyssian Pastor Fires a Broadside into Ranks of Fellow Ministers, Churches," *New York Age*, November 16, 1929, 1.

52. Terry, *An American Obsession*, 14.

53. "Randy Dixon, "Society Looks On As Pansies Frolic," *Philadelphia Tribune*, April 6, 1933, 1.

54. Ray O. Light, "Organist 'Pansy' Choir Members Say," *Philadelphia Tribune*, April 13, 1933, 1.

55. Ibid.; "Another Criticism of Pansy Ball Story," *Philadelphia Tribune*, April 27, 1933, 16; "We Shouldn't Condemn 'Other Fellows,'" *Philadelphia Tribune*, May 18, 1933, 4.

56. Jesse R. Davis, "Story of Pansies' Frolic, 'Disgusting,'" *Philadelphia Tribune*, April 27, 1933, 16.

57. Randy Dixon, "Police Tyrant Faces Ousting after Raid upon 'Pansy' Dance," *Philadelphia Tribune*, March 29, 1934, 1, 15.

58. "Writer Deplores AFRO's Homo-sexual Articles," *Baltimore Afro-American*, December 18, 1937, 4; McFlorence, "What Do You Know about It?" 4; John Louis Clarke, "J. L. Moore of Chester, Pa, Says that the Afro Should Not Publish News of Pansies," *Baltimore Afro-American*, March 10, 1934, 7.

59. Matthews, "Watching the Big Parade," 6.

60. McFlorence, "What Do You Know about It?" 4.

61. "Mere Male Blossoms Out in Garb of Milady at Big Hamilton Lodge Ball," *New York Amsterdam News*, February 19, 1930, 3.

62. "Margo a Philosophical Pansy Tells of Loves, Woes, and Jealousies of Third Sex," *Baltimore Afro-American*, March 1936, 10.

63. Ibid.

64. Levey, "Want to Know," 24; "Other Fellows Frolic at Annual Masque Ball," 1–2.

65. "Sepia Mae West in 'Marriage' Fete," *Philadelphia Tribune*, February 20, 1936, 14.

66. Ralph Matthews, "The Pansy Craze, Is It Entertainment or Just Plain Filth? *Baltimore Afro-American*, October 8, 1934, 7.

67. "A Defense of Pansies by One of Them," *Baltimore Afro-American*, October 13, 1934, 7.

68. Ibid.

69. Ibid.

70. Terry, *An American Obsession*, 263.

71. Levey, "Want to Know?" 24.

72. Ibid.

73. "'Odd Fellows" Ball Is Set for Brooklyn," *New York Amsterdam News*, November 12, 1938, 14.

74. Chauncey, *Gay New York*, 332–33; "Sexes: Hormones Used to Change Effeminate Men," *Baltimore Afro-American*, November 11, 1939, 1; "New Tablets Make Effeminate Men Normal," *New York Amsterdam News*, November 11, 1939, 1; "Two Cadets at West Point Now," *Baltimore Afro-American*, November 11, 1939, 1.

75. "Homosexualism," *Baltimore Afro-American*, June 19, 1941, 4.

INDEX

KIM GALLON is an assistant professor in the Department of History at Purdue University.

THE NEW BLACK STUDIES SERIES

The University of Illinois Press
is a founding member of the
Association of University Presses.

———————————————————

Composed in 10.75/13 Arno Pro
with Berthold Akzidenz Grotesk display
by Lisa Connery
at the University of Illinois Press
Cover designed by Jennifer S. Fisher
Cover illustration: Cover page of April 20, 1935,
issue of *The Afro American* newspaper, Baltimore.
Courtesy of the AFRO American Newspapers Archives.
Manufactured by Sheridan Books, Inc.

University of Illinois Press
1325 South Oak Street
Champaign, IL 61820-6903
www.press.uillinois.edu